# FILM
# PRODUCTION

## THE CREATIVE PROCESS

by Ron Newcomer

KENDALL/HUNT PUBLISHING COMPANY
4050 Westmark Drive    Dubuque, Iowa  52002

Copyright © 2007 by Ron Newcomer

ISBN 978-0-7575-4533-7

Kendall/Hunt Publishing Company has the exclusive rights to reproduce this work,
to prepare derivative works from this work, to publicly distribute this work,
to publicly perform this work and to publicly display this work.

Printed in the United States of America
10 9 8 7 6 5 4 3 2 1

Dedicated to

Diane

My Creative Producer

and

Miles and Meghann

My favorite Independent Producers

# CONTENTS

# CHAPTER 7/THE DIRECTOR

# ACKNOWLEDGMENTS

This is the book I wish I had when I first started in film, television, and theater. There are a great number of people that I have known over the years that taught me the little things that add quality to a script or production. They include Robert Wise, Edward Anhalt, John Houseman, Philip Dunne, Sterling Silliphant, Max Youngstein, Pat Kehoe, Lillian Gish, Ray Walston, Richard Edlund, Marcia Nasatir, Burgess Meredith, and James Newcomer.

The material in this book is from personal experiences over my years in this constantly changing industry. Quotations are pulled from interviews conducted for this book and the Internet Movie Database. I gratefully acknowledge the following individuals and companies for their time and generous efforts: Stephen Wade Nebgen, Esq.; Terence Donnelly; Gus Edward; Gordon Jesse; Marybeth Abodeely; and Kathy Buster for her blood, sweat, and excellent editing advice.

# Foreword

> "The stuff dreams are made of."
>
> —Humphrey Bogart as Sam Spade
> in *The Maltese Falcon*

After World War II, cameras became lighter, had faster lenses, and were affordable to a new generation of filmmakers. This opened the doors for the French New Wave in the 1950s and led to the New Hollywood of the late 1960s and 1970s.

With high-definition camcorders selling for less than five thousand dollars, a new movement is afoot, this time with millions of ambitious young directors who blindly subscribed to the auteur theory. Included with the purchase of a high-definition (HD) camera is a lengthy, dry, and sometimes exceedingly confusing operational manual that unlocks the mysteries of how the lightweight piece of machinery works. Everything is there: speed control, zoom lens, filters, playback, color correction, wide screen recording, and other special features that were unimaginable to earlier filmmakers who shot on the streets of Paris and New York with clumsy sixteen-millimeter cameras.

The instructional handbooks that come with modern cameras give all the details about how to aim and shoot—but not how to make a good movie. With the French New Wave, the young critics who later became directors praised moviemakers like Alfred Hitchcock and Howard Hawks but also rebelled against the standard Hollywood Studio glossy look of this era. The film students that created the New Hollywood grew up watching movies and were heavily influenced by the legendary directors of the Studio System and innovative foreign directors with names like Godard, Truffaut, Bergman, De Sica, Fellini, Antonioni, and Kurosawa.

The groundbreaking directors like Hitchcock, John Ford, David Lean, and Stanley Kubrick—who literally created the visual language of movies—had a style that was unmistakable. The directors that followed these men reflected the influence of their styles, which they absorbed by watching favorite movies and breaking them apart scene by scene. The next wave of filmmakers began to imitate the directors that preceded them until, gradually, through this process, styles became mixed and reinvented; and today most movies look like they were shot by the same unidentifiable director. There are notable exceptions. There is no mistaking a Martin Scorsese film or movies by Joel and Ethan Coen, Alegandro Gonzalez Inarritu, Yimou Zhang, and Quentin Tarantino.

Through the 1930s and 1940s, there were probably no more than a hundred directors who had access to cameras. The toys of moviemaking were owned by the studios, and only the directors under contract had the privilege of using them. Every decade thereafter, through advancements in technology, saw a larger number of people around the world making films. Now, with inexpensive cameras and equipment, millions of people have the resources to shoot a spectacular motion picture.

Mathematically, this should result in hundreds of thousands of great movies, future classics that will endure the test of time. But it does not. A look at the motion pictures of 1939 and then at the ones from last year shows that exceptional films are a rarity. Over the years, the advances in technology have received widespread attention but many of the traditional steps involved in good moviemaking have not been taught. Almost from the beginning, movies told a story that engaged mass audiences. Many of these old films still endure—because the stories, not the technology, have endured for twenty-five, fifty, a hundred years.

This book is written because of my concern that many of the valuable lessons from our film heritage about visual storytelling are being lost. *Film Production: The Creative Process* is not about how to operate a camera but how to create something exciting, entertaining, and perhaps significant for the camera to capture. The creative process in filmmaking goes beyond understanding the technology, which is information that can be found in abundance. It is the process of bringing to life characters on the screen that audiences will relate to as real people.

The book also focuses on the business of motion pictures and the role of a creative producer. Too often, basic business fundamentals are left out of a fine arts education, but in film this knowledge is essential. More than ever before, the filmmaker needs to make his or her own opportunities, but during this sometimes difficult journey not lose sight of what makes a good movie work.

*Film Production: The Creative Process* covers the business of film, developing a project, the steps of production, and interpreting visual language. Much of the information comes from years of talking with some of the outstanding individuals in this art form and hearing their personal experiences in filmmaking. Sometimes these lessons were hard learned, but, without exception, the aim of each individual was to make a movie that would entertain present and future audiences. Hopefully, these lessons will prove valuable to you on your next project.

Ron Newcomer

# Introduction

> " This is the biggest electric train
> set a boy ever had!
>
> —Orson Wells

In 1894, the Edison Company registered the first motion picture with the U.S. Copyright Office, a silent short, less than five seconds long, titled *Fred Ott's Sneeze*. Fast forward 110 years, and film has gone from magical images that mesmerized early audiences, to something so commonplace that feature-length movies are being shot on cell phones. During this blink in world history, filmmaking has become the central art form in every country around the world. In many countries, people watch some form of filmmaking on an average of 4.5 hours per day, or almost one-third of their waking hours. This would be the equivalent of watching each year 1,642.5 hours of opera or reading 98,550 pages of fiction.

The forms of filmmaking include first-run motion pictures in theaters, DVDs on home media centers, interactive computer games, personal greetings on cell phones, music videos on iPods, digital shorts downloaded off the Internet, and television programs ranging from news to sitcoms to hour-long dramas to reality shows to classic movies. It also includes tens of thousands of films, from three-minute shorts to features, made by promising independent directors or students; and this figure is almost doubling each year because of the access to inexpensive digital cameras and editing software.

Technically, anyone with a camera or some revolutionary new device that captures a moving image (which includes toys from Fisher-Price for three-year-old children) is a director—or, to be

**Fred Ott's Sneeze,** copyrighted by the Edison Studio on January 7, 1894, is the five-second film that launched the motion picture industry.

more exact, an *auteur,* because this grassroots directing process includes adjustments for light (cinematography), audio recording (sound engineering), the length of the shot (editing), and the personal interpretation of an individual moment in time. With film, no matter if it is Super 8 or seventy-millimeter, light meters and test footage are used to get the right f-stops for a single shot. With the Digital Revolution, anyone can switch on a camera; aim; shoot; and get a clear, well-defined image. And if the time is taken to watch the tutorial about the camera and read the hundred-some pages of directions, a first-time director can produce something that looks like a David Lean epic.

It is almost impossible to imagine in the future that sixteen-millimeter or thirty-five-millimeter film will not be used in some way for making motion pictures. But since the early 1990s, the word *film* has gone from being a noun that describes a celluloid substance to a verb that represents the process of an image being captured by any form of technology. Currently, there is speculation that film, the celluloid substance used since Edison's first flicker, will be completely replaced because of the innovations in digital technology.

The breach between these two forms of motion capture is represented by Steven Spielberg and George Lucas. Spielberg, arguably the most influential director thus far in film history, refuses to change over to digital cameras and editing; whereas Lucas, his close friend from the early days of the New Hollywood, is the wizard behind the curtain of digital filmmaking and the advancements in computer-generated imagery (CGI).

However, as directors, they share a common ground with all directors, from D. W. Griffith forward: a comprehensive understanding of the basic filmmaking process and an intuitive knowledge of the visual language of motion pictures. Spielberg, Lucas, and their contemporaries grew up in a time when baby boomers were surrounded by television and film, an era the critic Pauline Kael dubbed "the movie generation." There were no film schools or behind-the-scene books in the 1950s and 1960s. During the formative time period, these young moviegoers became students simply by watching films and discussing them. This self-imposed mission led to many run-down revival houses to catch as many movies as possible by certain directors.

Through this passionate process, these young directors, who later would establish the New Hollywood of the 1970s, absorbed the style and techniques of the old masters that literally created the movies. Admittedly, this process was easier and more effectively learned during the pivotal years of the mid-twentieth century. Most motion pictures were comprised of less than six hundred edits, approximately five each minute, whereas today films have at least ten times this number.

The moguls of the Studio System advocated a look that became known as "seamless filmmaking," meaning that the audience should not be aware of camera movement and editing.

These limitations seem highly restricting to modern filmmakers, but this system produced Alfred Hitchcock, John Ford, Michael Curtiz, Billy Wilder, Orson Welles, John Huston, Howard Hawks, David Lean, and foreign directors like Federico Fellini, Ingmar Bergman, and Akira Kurosawa, all of whom had individualistic styles that were easy to study. What becomes fascinating to observe is the complexity of the films by these directors. Almost every shot is filled with information that pertains to character and story development. This is brought about through the subtle use of camera placement, blocking of actors, lighting, costumes, and scenic design and complemented by sound and music.

Spielberg, Lucas, and the many other graduates of this self-taught film program grew up watching hundreds of movies by legendary directors and vicariously learned the art of the motion pictures. Through sheer observation, they cultivated a visual encyclopedia that they would tap into countless times later while directing their own movies. By watching and memorizing the great moments from classic films, they developed an intuitive sense of storytelling that is unique to motion pictures. And, most important, they learned what made a good film work.

## Technology Revolution

> Color television! Bah, I won't believe it until I see it in black and white.
> —Samuel Goldwyn

The major studios turned out a film each week, a balance of star features and B movies, like westerns, mysteries, horror films, and fast-paced comedies. Each motion picture had a story structure with a clearly designed beginning, middle, and end and dialogue that was crafted by a small army of studio writers. These films were the end result of months of development and planning. There was undeniably some deadwood among the classics to the Studio System's assembly-line approach to filmmaking; but overall, these movies represent a consistently high level of accomplishment in all areas.

The arrival of television changed the mass audience expectations of quality production. Like radio, television was free to anyone with rabbit ears or an outdoor antenna. The horizontal image would roll, and the screens were tiny. The early television cameras needed lots of bright, even light; and the resulting images had no depth of field or dynamic contrasts. The sound was muffled on the live shows, and the performances had a slight tinge of desperation due to lack of rehearsals. Each day, the three networks had to crank out over fifteen hours of shows, including morning children programs, soap operas, game shows, news, sitcoms, variety shows, and dramatic prime-time specials. If an episode of a favorite program disappointed, oh well, maybe it would be better next week. There was no reason to complain, because there were no high expectations placed on free entertainment.

With this flood of television shows without refined production values, the studios had to fight for the hearts of the moviegoers with technological advancements. Giant screens, stereophonic sound, faster lenses, improved light-sensitive film stock—all added up to event moviemaking. The old Studio System philosophy was to keep the camera invisible to the audience; but with this new wave of technology, the camera became the star. And somewhere during this revolutionary process, the toys of filmmaking began to overshadow the basic elements of cinematic storytelling. The creative process of putting a film together is a comprehensive understanding of all the art form and how each individual piece fits into a massively complex puzzle.

With the lightning-fast advancements in technology turning anyone with five hundred dollars into a filmmaker, there are problems—giant ones. Film is an art form for the masses; and because of this popularity, film is often not taken seriously as a subject to study in many academic circles, unlike theater, dance, or music, which have always been given great attention. Almost every high school or college has a theater, dance studio, or concert hall, but very few have a sound stage. Yet each frame of film represents these art forms, with acting, sets, costumes, musical underscoring, choreography of movement, and a script.

There are also photography, design, drawing, and sculpture, which in film equate to cinematography; production design; storyboards for previsionalization; and the highly skilled craftsmanship put into miniatures, props, and realistic sets that create imaginary worlds. Independently, each of these art forms is appreciated as a solo achievement. For example, in theater the audience enjoys how a good play was performed by the ensemble of actors; and a great painting, like Renoir's *Boating Party,* can be studied for hours upon end. In film, no single artistic discipline should stand out alone but, instead, each is designed to be perfectly assimilated into a singular emotional effect one frame at a time, twenty-four times a second.

## The Visual Language of Film

> In every technique, visually there is a language far more complex than words.
> —Conrad Hall

The blending of these art forms into a unified experience creates the visual language of film. The success of this language to produce a single frame depends upon cameras, lighting equipment, miles of cable, trucks, sound stages, editing and sound

Stanley Kubrick's widescreen visual masterpiece *2001: A Space Odyssey* (1968) was made less than seventy-five years after *Fred Ott's Sneeze,* an incredible leap in art and technology.

mixing consoles, dozens and sometimes hundreds of actors, and piles of legal paperwork. As director Vincente Minnelli observed, a memorable moment of film is the result of a hundred unnoticed things; whereas, with Samuel Beckett's *Waiting for Godot,* all that is required to entertain an audience for two hours is five actors, a bare tree, and general stage lighting. Backstage, there might be a stage manager, a light operator, a prop person, and one or two wardrobe personnel.

In comparison, film has often been considered a technical art form, closer to magic trickery than true art, because of the small army of highly skilled people necessary to achieve two hours of screen time, each person working with the objective of having his or her contribution blend seamlessly into each single shot. Because of the technical circus of filmmaking, which gathers for three months (after a year or more of preproduction) to make a feature on locations and sound stages against historic landmarks and green screens, what is inevitably overlooked is the power of a single frame. Cut one frame from David Lean's *Lawrence of Arabia,* Stanley Kubrick's *2001: A Space Odyssey,* Terrence Malick's *Days of Heaven,* or Francis Ford Coppola's *Apocalypse Now,* blow it up into a large image, put a frame around it, hang it in the Museum of Modern Art, and patrons will observe the artistry. But an average feature film is 86,400 individual frames, each different by a fraction of motion.

Today, any book that focuses on the use of current technology to teach filmmaking takes the risk of being out of date before it is published. Visual language is the key to successful filmmaking, and the understanding of visual language is what separates average films from great ones. The same can be said for any art form. Without practicing musical scales for years, it is absurd to believe that an individual can suddenly walk on stage and perform Beethoven's Piano Concerto no. 5 in E-flat Major with the Berlin Philharmonic Orchestra. Pablo Picasso, the father of abstract art, drew hundreds of realistic life-forms to gain an understanding of perspective. And J. R. R. Tolkien spent almost twenty-five years writing *The Lord of the Rings,* inventing a new language in the process.

However, because of the numerous offshoots from film that bombard people every day, including television shows, commercials, news clips, and video games on cell phones, there is the misinformed belief, born perhaps from a conditioned arrogance from seeing so many movies, that filmmaking is the simple process of pointing a camera and depressing the "on" button. This was true for the early motion pictures, in which seeing a train coming toward the camera was exciting for audiences. But then D. W. Griffith took all the little discoveries that evolved during that era of film pioneering and through experiments in hundreds of shorts gradually formed what actress Lillian Gish referred to as "visual grammar," which is now commonly known as visual language.

The basic alphabet of visual storytelling has not changed since Griffith's days. In its infant form, this alphabet consists of three elements: long shot, medium shot, and close shot. Cutting between these three camera setups can create tension, suspense, or humor—and reveal how a character feels internally. Perhaps Griffith's greatest contribution to motion pictures was crosscutting, also known as intercutting, in which two or more stories are in motion at one time, all headed toward a dramatic showdown. In 1915, there were actually complaints from moviegoers that Griffith's rapid editing gave them headaches. These adverse physical reactions were triggered by a half-dozen cuts per minute. Today a beer commercial can have thirty or more edits in thirty seconds.

## Borrowing from the Masters: Everyone Needs to Make a Short Film

> " I never appreci-
> ated a bad film—until
> I made my own. "
>
> —Anonymous

In general, the study of film is approached from two different camps, each debating the essential understanding of film. There are the critics and the scholars, who have increased in almost endless numbers because of the Internet. And there is the constantly expanding group of people that know (or think they know) the techniques of film and see it as the art of the common person to pursue. Everyone has a voice in what they like or dislike about films, but very few know firsthand how a film is put together and all the little tricks that can only be discovered through the process of shooting a motion picture.

It is one thing to study great motion pictures, but it is something completely different to make a short film. It is only in the physical filmmaking process that the difficulty of making a good movie becomes clear. Because Orson Welles was just twenty-five when he made *Citizen Kane,* the popular assumption is that creating a cinematic masterpiece is a piece of cake. To truly appreciate the art of film, everyone needs to make a short movie, no more than five minutes long. This seemingly simple exercise will give a new respect for *any* film that finds its way to the screen. Suddenly, the worst B horror movie will seem like a worthy directorial effort.

With a first-time short, most likely there will be sound problems, actors that do not show up, actors that show up not knowing their lines, a dramatic lighting mood that is nonexistent, and mismatched editing because not enough coverage of a key scene was shot. After this humbling experience, the next step is to go back and closely examine what makes a great film work. Turn off the sound and just watch the editing patterns, the lighting effects, the choice of camera angles, and the influence of the set and costumes. At this point, both the complexity and the overall simplicity of visual language become readily apparent. A hundred little details will become obvious, and the ease with which a director like Stanley Kubrick orchestrates these details will give the illusion of being remarkably simple. First, what is noticed is the director's style; but, upon further examination of other classic films, what then becomes obvious is that this style is borrowed from different directors—and then personalized.

*Film Production: The Creative Process* is broken into chapters that demonstrate the various steps of putting together a film. One of the primary objectives is to reveal the dynamics of visual language so it becomes a common knowledge to not only directors but anyone involved in the filmmaking process. There is an abundance of books about the technical side of filmmaking, but what is often overlooked is the creative process involved in shaping a good film—perhaps even a great film—that will endure the test of time. Each chapter presents a brief history or overview of a particular step in film production. At times, the book endeavors to illustrate the similarities and differences between film, television, and theater. Film is the greatest of all art forms, because it encompasses all the arts. And only a comprehensive understanding of each phase of filmmaking, from business to production to marketing, will result in the mastering of this lively art form.

# PART ONE

# THE BUSINESS OF FILM

> "I was always an independent producer, even when I had partners."

—Samuel Goldwyn

# CHAPTER ONE

# A BRIEF HISTORY OF THE MOVIE BUSINESS

> " Those of us who became film producers hailed from all sorts of occupations—furriers, magicians, butchers, boilermakers—and for this reason highbrows have often poked fun at us. Yet one thing is certain: every man who succeeded was a born showman. And once in show business he was never happy out of it. "
>
> —Adolph Zuckor

## How It All Began

"This is the greatest business in the world, because people pay money before they get the goods." This was advice given to young Barney Balaban by his mother while visiting his first nickelodeon. This financial insight, as reported by his daughter Judith, obviously made an impression, because Barney became president of Paramount Pictures, a position he held from 1936 to 1966.

At the beginning of the silent film era, this practical insight summarized the overwhelming interest in the "flickers." The fascination of early motion pictures

Greta Garbo and John Barrymore romance in *Grand Hotel*, an example of the MGM Star System that claimed to have "more stars than there are in the heavens."

was an international phenomenon. People bought tickets to see anything that moved, from westerns to prize fights to Rin Tin Tin, the Wonder Dog. But this period of childlike wonderment wore off, and soon audiences had to be persuaded to be departed from their hard-earned dimes and quarters before they entered a theater.

Movie palaces replaced the old storefront nickelodeons, and mass marketing began with elaborate one-sheet posters and hard-sell previews of coming attractions. By the time *The Jazz Singer* introduced sound in 1927, studios were turning out a film a week in different genres to fill a wide range of demographic interests. There were westerns, musicals, gangster films, period romances, screwball comedies, "weepers," and action serials. Some studios specialized in musicals, like MGM, and others gangster films, like Warner Bros. As the competition grew, studios went to greater lengths to catch the attention of the reluctant ticket buyer.

The Star System became the most bankable commodity of the major studios. The early stars were well rewarded but treated like commodities with long-term contracts and usually had no say in what films they selected or what directors they worked with. All studios had stars. MGM had "more stars than there are in the heavens," including Clark Gable, Greta Garbo, and Joan Crawford. Warner Bros. had Bette Davis, James Cagney, and Humphrey Bogart. Paramount claimed Gary Cooper and Claudette Colbert. RKO was the home to Fred Astaire and Ginger Rogers and, for awhile, Katharine Hepburn. Republic had John Wayne and Gene Autry. The studio moguls' greatest fear—and what they tried fruitlessly to control—was that stars would keep demanding higher salaries and eventually ask for a percentage of the profits. Today, Tom Cruise or Tom Hanks makes more money on one film than the combined salaries of all these legendary movie stars.

But the basic philosophy of Barney Balaban's mother is still relevant about motion pictures: Audiences by the millions on any given weekend have been primed by television, magazines, previews, the Internet, and an increasing variety of hidden persuaders to gamble money on something they have not seen. Imagine if movies were like trying on clothes: The buyer tries on many garments but only purchases what fits well and looks best. If people paid *after* they "tried on" a feature, then the motion picture industry would have potentially disappeared after D. W. Griffith's 1916 box office disaster *Intolerance.*

## International Commerce

> The public is
> always right.
> —Cecil B. DeMille

Photography became the first art form that could be exhibited simultaneously in multiple locations. The Civil War photographer, Mathew Brady, had several galleries displaying his dramatic photographs from the aftermath of battles. But these touring exhibitions were not widespread.

Gilbert and Sullivan opened their operettas in London and New York within weeks of each other to prevent pirated versions from cropping up before a major tour could begin. These popular musical productions had similar costumes and scenery but different casts and, occasionally, alternate verses. With film, dozens of prints could be made and used in as many different theaters. By the mid-1920s, this number grew to hundreds; and after blockbusters like *Jaws* and *Star Wars,* the number escalated into thousands of prints, all released on the same day.

As an emerging art form, this demanded a completely different way of thinking. If a successful Broadway production ran for a year, the producers might form two or three touring companies. The Ringling Bros. and Barnum & Bailey Circus and Buffalo Bill's Wild West Show toured from one city to the next, and people came from hundreds of miles around to see the spectacular events. A few ballet troupes toured, but most large cities had opera houses, concert halls, and art museums built for the local citizens. The management concept of operating hundreds of shows in different cities—and eventually different countries—had never been considered before the arrival of film.

The closest thing that approached this scale of interstate touring was vaudeville. After the Civil War, minstrel shows became highly popular and toured from city to city. These shows were typically comedy routines mixed with lively folk songs. Showboats became floating circuses, taking these black-face musical revues up and down the Mississippi River. By the turn of the twentieth century, vaudeville began replacing minstrel shows, and promoters like the Shubert brothers and Abe Erlander and Mark Klaw of the Theatrical Syndicate had a highly competitive circuit of theaters.

At first, motion pictures did not seem like a rival to these "legitimate" art forms. A short film ran for less than a minute and had to be viewed in crowded, often rundown storefront parlors, which became known as nickelodeons. But by 1907 in the United States more than two million people attended continuously running shows daily in over eight thousand nickelodeons. Because these shorts were shot like full-figured stage plays, a film could be made one day and shown the next. And because these moving pictures were silent, often accompanied by an organ or piano, immigrants from around the world could enjoy them without a language barrier. The movies were the art form of the common people.

The wholesale nature of film attracted individuals who had made successful businesses from transporting goods to a network of cities. The founders and moguls of studios came from various backgrounds, most of them Jewish immigrants. Louis B. Mayer (MGM) grew up in the scrap metal business; Samuel Goldwyn (Goldwyn Studios) made his success in the garment industry; Carl Laemmle (Universal Studios) was a manager and bookkeeper in a large clothing store; Adolph Zukor was a furrier; and Harry Cohn was a promoter for a sheet music printer. The Warner brothers and Marcus Loew, founder of the Loews Theaters and MGM, started out investing in small movie arcades. All of these men made their fortunes by exhibiting D. W. Griffith's *The Birth of a Nation* (1915) and quickly realized from this experience that to expand they needed to produce their own motion pictures.

## The Studio System: Vertical Integration

> " I want to make beautiful pictures about beautiful people. "
> —Louis B. Mayer

With the arrival of sound, studios became known as "dream factories." Each of the major studios turned out a film per week, like an assembly line at Ford Motor Company. The "Big Five" studios were MGM, Warner Bros., Paramount, RKO, and 20th Century-Fox, all of which owned their own movie theaters. The other studios included Columbia (now Sony), Universal, United Artists, Republic, and Monogram. The independents were Samuel Goldwyn, David O. Selznick, Walt Disney, and Walter Wagner.

Because early sound technology required a noise-proof staging environment, studios built giant sound stages and then created back lots for exterior shooting. Everything needed to make a motion picture was found in these sprawling studios. There were costume and scene shops, film development lab's, recording rooms, bungalows for stars, a large commissary, and offices for writers and directors. If an establishing shot from Boston, Paris, or the jungles of Africa was needed, a small second unit crew would be sent to the location. Otherwise, throughout the 1930s and 1940s, most actors rarely left the studio grounds.

Adolph Zukor is credited with revolutionizing the motion picture industry by organizing production, distribution, and exhibition within a single company, a process known as *forward vertical integration.* This process allowed the majors to produce movies, cartoons, serials, short subjects, and travelogues, market them in-house, and then show them in theaters and movie palaces owned by the studios—a complete soup-to-nuts operation. A studio could monitor the run of each film and test the appeal of new starlets. If a movie was a hit in Chicago but struggling in San Francisco, it could be held over in one theater and replaced in another.

Each city had an exclusive run of a film, and no other theater within approximately one hundred miles could show the same feature. This is a practice that did not change until 1972 with *The Godfather,* which was the first A-list film to open wide. The distribution of movies up until this landmark event still reflected the days of vaudeville and traveling shows. The marketing of films was like the circus coming to town. Colorful posters would appear weeks before an opening, followed by local premieres, advanced previews or "teasers," and radio broadcasts with streamlined scenes performed live by stars, plus a parade down Main Street with stars or character actors from the movie waving to the crowds.

The financial roots established over these highly eventful years are still evident in motion picture production today. The biggest thing that vertical integration did was to make the movies a secure business investment for banks. The most notable example of this is Bank of America, which owes much of its enormous growth to studio loans. The studios owned vast amounts of property in the rapidly growing city of Los Angeles. They also kept detailed records regarding the marketing of successful film genres; had movie stars under long-term contracts; used in-house distribution; and, in the case of the Big Five, operated an international chain of theaters with a perpetual cash flow. With the possible exception of the radio, there was no competition.

The most remarkable statistic is, from the early Depression years to 1946, approximately every American went to the movies at least once a week. Most people went twice, because many theaters changed features midweek. A typical billing would be two cartoons, a newsreel (where for the first time people saw live-action footage with news reports), a short of some kind (either a comedy, like The Three Stooges, a minidrama to promote the war effort, or a backstage tour of Hollywood), three or four previews of coming attractions followed by a B movie such as a western or murder mystery, and then a star-filled feature. This public appetite for entertainment has not changed much. Today people will sit down and watch cable news, a sitcom, an hour long drama, and then a new release on DVD with three or four previews of coming attractions. The big difference is that now the average person only goes to a movie theater once a month, a statistic that has been declining each year.

# The Decline of the Studio System: Five Events That Changed Hollywood

> "We are in the business primarily to provide entertainment, but in doing so we do not dodge the issue if we can provide enlightenment.
> —Darryl F. Zanuck

The most successful year for the studios was 1946, the year after World War II ended. By 1949, every studio was on the verge of bankruptcy. The turmoil that followed over the next twenty-five years would create a new business model for motion pictures. What would become known as the New Hollywood is a mix of the old Studio System and modern conglomerates that have a wide range of diversified businesses. There are five events that shaped this new studio model. Ironically, each of these events was bitterly resisted but ultimately over time provided strength to the modern studio. They are the formation of the guilds, the antitrust action, foreign films, television, and independent producers and directors.

## 1. Formation of Motion Picture Guilds

> "You can't go around the theaters handing out cards saying, "It isn't my fault." You go on to the next one.
> —Preston Sturges

Screen Actors Guild activities in 1938, including James Cagney, Henry Fonda, and Lionel Barrymore.

the studios provided apprenticeships for technicians and young directors and constant training for actors. When the Studio System began to collapse in the early 1950s, the guilds were there to continue these training programs. This allowed the studios to cut back on full-time contracts and be able to hire experienced personnel on a film-by-film agreement.

## 2. Antitrust Lawsuits

> Pictures are for entertainment, messages should be delivered by Western Union.
> —Samuel Goldwyn

Like with every large business, the studios' desire to keep costs down was finally met with resistance from overworked employees. In the early sound era, actors and crews would work sixteen hours per day, six days a week, under a flat-rate contract. The studios had been hit hard by the Depression and needed to maximize income. Starting in 1928, after the success of *The Jazz Singer,* all theaters had to be equipped for sound at an approximate cost of ten thousand dollars per screen. For the first few years of the Depression, theater attendance dropped significantly, forcing studios to lower box office prices. At the same time, the Catholic Church and other religious organizations threatened a boycott if the shocking subject matter of movies was not changed. This resulted in the strict enforcement of the Hollywood Production Code in 1934 by the Hays Office.

Despite the fact that everyone at first was delighted to be employed during the Depression, working and safety conditions continued to deteriorate. These issues led to a series of walkouts and strikes, resulting in the eventual formation of major trade guilds, including the Screen Actors Guild (SAG) and the Writers Guild of America (WGA) in 1933 and the Directors Guild of America (DGA) in 1936. The studio moguls felt betrayed by the formation of these guilds, believing employees should be happy with long-term contracts and secure income. During the 1930s,

In 1938, Paramount was involved in an antitrust suit filed by the Society of Independent Motion Picture Producers (SIMPP). Because of the need for morale-boosting movies during World War II, this suit was delayed several times. Finally, in 1948, with the *United States v. Paramount,* the Supreme Court handed down a decision that divested the studios of their theater chains and abolished the practice of block bookings. Theater owners had been forced by the studios to rent a block of films, mostly B features without stars, in order to guarantee the next Clark Gable movie, Technicolor musical, or popular franchise like the Andy Hardy or Thin Man series.

This Supreme Court ruling almost proved to be the death toll for the Studio System. It certainly ended what is known as the Golden Age of Hollywood, a run that effectively lasted twenty years. Now theater owners could bid for films after they previewed them. There were still package deals and exclusives, but it resulted in a cutback in the number of films a studio would produce each year. In effect, all movies became A features with popular stars in order to compete in this changing world.

However, it quickly became evident to the smaller theaters that there was no democracy in being independent. In order to survive, they resorted to door prizes, magic acts, kiddie shows, guest appearances by cowboy stars, and eventually the showing of films not approved by the Hollywood Production Code. The older theaters, especially ones near college campuses, took on a new identity; they became "art houses" or "revival theaters." These theaters ran festivals of old movies and became the home of foreign films that poured out of Italy, France, England, Sweden, and Japan after the war.

## 3. The Influence of Foreign Films

> When I was a kid, movies from Hollywood seemed very glamorous, but when you look back at them as a young man, you can see out of the thousands of films that came out of Hollywood there were really very few good ones statistically, and those few that were good were made in spite of the studios. I saw European films as a young man and they were very much better. There's no comparison.
>
> —Woody Allen

Sadly, today it is almost impossible to imagine the enormous popularity of films from foreign countries made by unknown directors and with hard-to-read subtitles. These low-budget movies attracted younger audience members who were bored with the predictable glossy Hollywood melodramas and musicals that were completely out of touch with the growing appeal of country-western and rock 'n' roll music. This was the age of the Beat poets and teenage rebels who vigorously protested against wholesome prepackaged American values.

After the war, movie stars like Gable, James Stewart, and others returned from service and picked up where they had left off. There were no young stars in Hollywood. This changed with the rise of the Method Actors like Montgomery Clift, Marlon Brando, and James Dean. But by the mid-1950s, Clift's career was effectively over, Brando's was declining, and Dean had been killed in a car accident. Hollywood was completely out of touch with this growing baby-boomer audience. The foreign films attracted thousands of young adults looking for something new and shocking— something to rebel about.

Quickly these unknown directors became legendary—Vittorio De Sica, Federico Fellini, Michelangelo Antonioni, Francois Truffaut, Jean-Luc Godard, Tony Richardson, Ingmar Bergman, and Akira Kurosawa. With these raw, thought-provoking films, new, provocative, and very sexy stars emerged. Overnight, Brigitte Bardot, Jeanne Moreau, Sophia Loren, Marcello Mastroianni, Dirk Bogarde, and Bibi Andersson became the screen gods and goddesses for the boomer generation.

The biggest effect these filmmakers had was to revolutionize the look of movies. The leaders of the Italian Neorealism movement and the French New Wave shot films on the street with existing lighting, using handheld cameras, not caring if there were jump cuts, improvising dialogue with nonprofessional actors, and filling their films with a universe of strange, wonderful faces. These films were personal and autobiographical; and they fearlessly approached the themes of religion, violence,

The Grim Reaper arrives for a game of chess in Ingmar Bergman's art house classic *The Seventh Seal* (1957).

and sex, which were taboo in Hollywood movies because of the Production Code. These directors were crowned with the title of *auteur*, and there was a sense of immediacy about their films, like they were documentaries of a forbidden world.

Immediately, the arrival of these movies influenced American directors. First there was the realization that great, meaningful movies could be made outside the walls of the studios for a tenth of the cost. This meant that the films could have a personal point of view, like a book by Ernest Hemingway or a play by Tennessee Williams, and this concept veered sharply away from the mass entertainment philosophy of Old Hollywood.

This new wave of American filmmakers began to take chances with social themes. They made directing choices that broke free of the seamless style of studio era directors. The real influence of these films began in the late 1960s and lasted through the 1970s in what has become known as the New Hollywood. Arthur Penn, Dennis Hopper, Martin Scorsese, Brian De Palma, Hal Ashby, Robert Altman, William Friedkin, Peter Bogdanovich, Francis Ford Coppola, Sydney Pollack, Steven Spielberg, Woody Allen, John Cassavetes, and George Lucas all talk about the impact these films had on their thinking and careers.

## 4. Television: The Little Giant

> " Tonight, we have a real big show...
> —Ed Sullivan "

Television had been given a major promotion at the New York's World Fair in 1939; but during the war years, there was not the time or resources to expand this new medium into a profitable enterprise. The opportunity presented itself when soldiers returned home and the baby boom began. Couples were able to afford new tract houses in the suburbs of cities, and for many men and women who had been traveling nonstop for almost four years, the idea of staying in one place was appealing. In 1947, there were seven million television sets in America. By 1949, there were over twenty-five million. The three networks evolved from radio; the Columbia Broadcasting System (CBS), the National Broadcasting Company (NBC), and the American Broadcasting Company (ABC).

Early television shows were called the rebirth of vaudeville. Comics from the old days of vaudeville and burlesque brushed off their routines and headlined variety shows—like Jimmy Durante, Sid Caesar, Red Skelton, George Burns and Gracie Allen, and Milton ("Mr. Television") Berle. Ed Sullivan's *Toast of the Town* ran from 1948 to 1971. Performers that were always on the fringe of stardom in movies overnight became household names in successful half-hour *situation comedies*, a term that was quickly abbreviated to *sitcoms*. The stars of the airwaves included Phil Silvers, Spring Byington, Jack Benny, Eve Arden, and a redhead named Lucille Ball with her husband Desi Arnaz.

*I Love Lucy*, seen weekly with Lucille and Desi, set a standard that is followed to this day: The show was done before a live audience, like one-act plays, and filmed by three cameras, a sys-

Millions tuned in each week to see Lucy and Ricky, along with Fred and Ethel, in *I Love Lucy,* the landmark sitcom that ruled the television airwaves from 1951 to 1957.

tem created by Karl Kreund, an Academy Award-winning cinematographer whose work goes back to Fritz Lang's *Metropolis* (1927). Lucille Ball swung open doors that were closed to her in the movies. She became the co-owner and eventually president of Desilu Studios, which produced such landmark shows as *The Untouchables, The Andy Griffith Show, Mission Impossible,* and *Star Trek.* The prejudice that met the early flickers from the legitimate theater actors forty years before went full circle, with motion picture stars looking down on television in its early years. With the success of Lucille Ball and the fact that she controlled her own company, this snobbery about the small tube slowly vanished.

Television was originally based in New York, and shows were done live, from afternoon soap operas to the evening news to prestige evening dramas. After the war, New York was the center of the artistic world, and this was a golden age for American theater. A new generation of directors, writers, and actors was emerging, sharpening its skills on live episodic television programs like *Playhouse 90, The Philco Television Playhouse,* and *The Kraft Television Theater.*

At no other time has theater been so much at the center point of American life. Audiences were able to see such dynamic Broadway stars as Lee J.

Cobb and E. G. Marshall and new faces like James Dean and others. Writers such as Paddy Chayefsky, Reginald Rose, Dale Wasserman, and Rod Sterling and directors like Sidney Lumet, John Frankenheimer, Arthur Penn, and Norman Jewison all got their starts in this fast-paced new medium.

As the studios were making deep cutbacks, television quickly became the new training ground for designers, cinematographers and technicians. Short-format television programs like westerns, *The Twilight Zone,* and *Alfred Hitchcock Presents* became a continuation of the B movies that the studios used to churn out. Deserted sound stages and studio back lots were now being rented by television companies. Many of the directors and producers that learned to master this free-wheeling, rapid-paced format helped usher in the New Hollywood, including Norman Jewison, Sidney Lumet, and John Frankenheimer. Eventually television, which was originally perceived and feared as the little monster that would eat Hollywood, became the medium that saved the motion picture studios on three different occasions.

***Film Libraries*** Thousands of vintage studio features, shorts, and cartoons were literally rotting in studio warehouses, usually in stifling heat. Network television programs came on around 7 a.m. with children programs, followed by soap operas and games shows, then the evening news, all leading up to the prime-time shows that went to 10 p.m. After this, local stations would sign off with the traditional "Star-Spangled Banner." RKO became the first major studio to sell its film library in 1955, including the Fred Astaire and Ginger Rogers musicals, John Wayne Westerns, *King Kong, Citizen Kane,* and *Gunga Din.* Other studios quickly followed, and old movies became a traditional late-night affair on television, with horror "fright nights" every Friday. While the studios were producing fewer and fewer movies, their old films became a bankable commodity. And because the studios had been under the thumb of the Hollywood Production Code, all these movies were wholesome entertainment for the entire family.

***Television Production***   Television began with Philo Farnsworth's Image Dissector in 1927. John Logie Baird demonstrated the world's first color transmission one year later. In 1939, Paramount invested in television and even opened experimental stations in Los Angeles and Chicago. But television's potential was cut short when in 1942 the War Production Board halted the manufacture of television and radio equipment for civilians, which lasted until 1945. With the Supreme Court antitrust rulings starting with Paramount, the studios never had an opportunity to merge or buy into television, thus allowing Hollywood's future biggest rival to boom without opposition.

This leaves a mystery about what the studios might have done if they could have bought into television during its infancy. Obviously, the primary intention would have been to control a potential competitor before it exploded on the American scene. But the question remains whether the studios would have changed gears and downscaled to a short-film format. Because early television was directly connected to live theater based in New York, it is doubtful the studios would have done this, especially after record-breaking years during the war. Ultimately, it was this stubborn viewpoint that almost destroyed the studios, a kind of macho artistic attitude of big screen versus small screen.

Like sound, television rapidly took over the popular public attention. While CBS, NBC, and finally ABC were renting space on studio sound stages and back lots, the remaining moguls oddly did not try to produce low-budget television programs themselves. Instead, the studios put all their dollars into Technicolor, 3-D, CinemaScope, VitaScope, and Cinerama, and epics like *The Robe*, *Around the World in 80 Days*, and *Ben-Hur*. When power agent Lew Wasserman purchased Universal Studios from Decca Records in 1958, he immediately set up deals for his A-list clients such as Bette Davis, Ronald Reagan, and James Stewart. Three years earlier, he had brought Alfred Hitchcock to Universal from Warner Bros. to host *Alfred Hitchcock Presents*, which ran for ten years. Seeing the future, Wasserman shifted Universal's primary focus from film to television production; and by the late 1960s, almost half of the television programs were being produced by the studio. Today, studios like Fox, Warner Bros., Disney, and Sony are secure because of television revenue, which allows them the opportunity to produce big-budget motion pictures.

***Marketing and Merchandising***   Cowboy stars like Hopalong Cassidy, Gene Autry, and Roy Rogers first started the highly lucrative merchandising phenomenon, with cap guns, lunch boxes, comic books, records, bedspreads, and breakfast foods. This was something that George Lucas remembered very clearly as a child, which is why he negotiated the licensing rights to *Star Wars*.

Walt Disney was the only studio head in the early years to understand the impact of television as a marketing tool. His show, *Disneyland*, when it was first aired in 1954 was in reality a weekly, hour-long promotion for his new theme park. This was so successful, the show continued over the years with different names to promote his feature films. Merchandising for Davy Crockett made three times the money of box office revenues. However, with the exception of Robby the Robot from *Forbidden Planet*, studios did not use television as a way to promote spin-off items for a movie. And, with the exception of Disney, the studios were not making the kinds of films that inspired toys and games.

Actor William Boyd spent years getting complete rights to Western hero Hopalong Cassidy; the widespread merchandising attracted young fans like George Lucas.

Perhaps the great irony is that the studios did not use television to advertise new motion picture releases for almost twenty years. During these years, a thirty-second spot on television was no more expensive than print advertisement in major cities, plus television during prime time reached tens of millions of viewers instead of ten thousand newspaper readers. In 1975, the producers of *Breakout,* a low-budget action movie with Charles Bronson, thought they had a real box office dog on their hands and bought limited television advertising in selected locations. The film went into profits by the third week. That summer, Lew Wasserman put approximately three million dollars into television promotion for *Jaws* and opened it in 675 theaters. The rest is blockbuster history.

## 5. Independent Producers and Directors

> As an artist I feel we must try many things—but above all we must dare to fail.
> —John Cassavetes

The final thing that changed Hollywood was the rise of the independent producer and the producer-director. The moguls like Louis B. Mayer and Jack Warner had run the studios, but they had in-house producers to oversee the day-to-day activity of production. For MGM, there was Irving Thalberg and for a few years David O. Selznick; and Warner Bros. had Hal B. Wallis, who was involved in more than 350 productions. Like movie stars, these hardworking individuals were company men who did not participate in the profits of the films they produced, though for the most part they were treated extremely well and received bonuses.

In 1919, Mary Pickford, Douglas Fairbanks, D. W. Griffith, and Charles Chaplin founded United Artists (UA) so they could distribute their own films and benefit from the profits. This was short-lived because sound effectively ended the careers of Pickford, Fairbanks, and Griffith; and Chaplin only made four movies from 1928 to 1940. United Artists continued as a distribution company and was used over the years by Walt Disney, David O. Selznick, Samuel Goldwyn, Alexander Korda, and Walter Wagner, the original group of independent producers. However, by the end of the war, United Artists had almost ceased to exist. Then, in 1951, Arthur Krim, Robert Benjamin, Max Youngstein, and two other partners worked out a deal with Pickford and Chaplin to take over operations. What they did changed the movie industry.

As Max Youngstein explains it, United Artists would put up half of the money for a film once it met approval, and the production company would put up half. The production company was given complete freedom to make the film, United Artists would distribute it, and both sides would split the profits equally. This allowed movie stars the opportunity to make films and reap the rewards. Burt Lancaster was one of the first, creating Hecht-Hill-Lancaster productions. Maverick directors such as John Huston, Stanley Kramer, Otto Preminger, Billy Wilder, and Blake Edwards with the Pink Panther series also seized this opportunity. The independent producers included Sam Spiegel, Joseph E. Levine, and Harry Saltzman and Albert Broccoli with the James Bond 007 films, which got the studio through several bad years. United Artists was also responsible for Sergio Leone's spaghetti Westerns and backed such television shows as *The Fugitive, Outer Limits,* and *Gilligan's Island.*

With film production opening up again in Europe after World War II, independent producers made motion pictures with international audience appeal. Sam Spiegel with Horizon Productions is the only producer with four films on the AFI's one hundred greatest list: *The African Queen, On the Waterfront, Bridge on the River Kwai,* and *Lawrence of Arabia.* Joseph E. Levine with Embassy Pictures Corporation was a master at putting package deals together, like *Zulu, The Carpetbaggers* and *The Lion in Winter,* and taking chances on offbeat films like *Darling, The Producers* and *The Graduate.* Dino De Laurentiis started by importing Hollywood stars to appear in Italian productions, like Kirk Douglas in *Ulysses* and Anthony Quinn in *La Strata,* and then relocated to America with movies like *Serpico, Death Wish,* and *Three Days of the Condor.*

Roger Corman, it can be argued, might be the most influential producer-director of this era. With American International Pictures, he tapped into the growing youth market by making films that brought thrills and chills to the drive-ins. In the 1950s and early 1960s, drive-ins represented almost one-fifth of the theaters in America. Baby boomers were the first generation in which almost everyone had cars when they turned sixteen, and drive-ins were popular meeting places. Corman is best remembered for a series of Technicolor films starring Vincent Price and loosely based on tales by Edgar Allen Poe, like *The House of Usher* and *Pit and the Pendulum.* His autobiography is *How I Made a Hundred Movies in Hollywood and Never Lost a Dime,* and his cult favorites include *The Little Shop of Horrors* and *The Wild Angels.*

As a producer, Corman kept the budgets very low, shot in a few weeks (sometimes a few days), found sensational material that appealed to the youth generation, and hired young filmmakers who were hungry to make a first-time feature. In the 1960s, film schools like NYU, UCLA, and USC were educating students to make industrial training films, *if they were lucky.* George Lucas remembers a teacher at USC telling students that if they wanted a real career they needed to change majors immediately. During this changeover era, Corman proved to be the only bridge between the film schools and the studios.

He hired a vast number of inexperienced filmmakers that went on to revolutionize movies and establish the New Hollywood in the 1970s. This long list includes Francis Ford Coppola, Martin Scorsese, Ron Howard, Peter Bogdanovich, Jonathan Demme, James Cameron, John Sayles,

John Cassavetes, directing a scene in **Husbands** (1970), became the spirit of the American Independent Film movement.

Jack Nicholson, Robert Towne, Peter Fonda, Bruce Dern, Dennis Hopper, and Robert De Niro. As Scorsese remembers his experience, Corman gave the director a budget, a completion schedule, and a camera and then stayed out of the way. Because of this hands-off approach, the director also had to line produce his own film, a tough but invaluable experience.

Another director-producer started an independent tradition that is still alive today. John Cassavetes is considered the pioneer of the American *cinema verité* movement. Like Orson Welles did for most of his life, Cassavetes took acting jobs to raise money to shoot ultra-low-budget personal films that were mostly improvised and shot "in the moment." This one-man movement was an extension of the French New Wave and Italian Neorealism, in which filmmakers took to the streets to make movies that looked more like documentaries and treated the camera like a pen to tell autobiographical stories. For his first film, *Shadows,* made in 1959, Cassavetes could not find a domestic distributor so he took the movie to the Venice Film Festival where it won the Critics Award. Later, European distributors released the film in the United States.

Francis Ford Coppola established American Zoetrope in 1969, along with George Lucas and other young filmmakers, with the intention of making cinema verité films shot in San Francisco, away from the "suits" in Hollywood. The failure of *THX-1138* forced Coppola to take outside writing and directing jobs to prevent the collapse of this dream project. This led to *The Godfather, Part 1* and *2*, but he would continue to return to his independent roots with *One from the Heart* and *The Outsiders*. In a complete reversal of fortune, Lucas formed Lucasfilm for his next feature, *American Graffiti*, which was executive produced by Coppola. The success of this low-budget feature was followed by the *Star Wars* trilogy (1977–1983), making Lucas the most successful independent producer in film history.

Since 1978, the American independent movement was kept alive by the Sundance Film Festival. A year later, Harvey and Bob Weinstein formed Miramax Films. The success of these two organizations led studios to create their own in-house independent companies, like Sony Classics and Fox Searchlight Pictures. Increasingly, the line between independent and studio productions is blurred because most boutique companies are now under the financial umbrellas of Warner Bros., Disney, and other major entertainment corporations. Adding to this is the increasing number of movie stars, like Tom Cruise and Brad Pitt, and directors, including Steven Spielberg with Amblin Entertainment, who have formed their own production companies after big box office hits and entered into multipicture deals with studios.

## The Modern Studio System

> We are in the transportation business. We transport audiences from one place to another.
>
> —Jerry Bruckheimer

What does not kill you makes you stronger. This appears to have applied to the studios that are still standing. There are six major studios remaining from the Golden Era. Columbia is now Sony and occupies what is left of the MGM lot in Culver City. Paramount, Universal, Warner Bros., Disney, and Fox are still on the lots they built eighty years ago. MGM and United Artists are still producing, in large part because of the James Bond franchise, but sadly are shadows of their former glory days. With the exception of Disney, all these studios are part of giant entertainment conglomerates. Because of Disney's motion picture division, theme parks, television networks, merchandising, publishing, and the acquisition of Pixar, it is the only studio that is a self contained entertainment empire.

These studios are like miniature cities—or frequently referred to as kingdoms—with communities of independent production companies under an exclusive agreement to develop and produce feature films and/or television programs. Disney has such an agreement with Bruckheimer Productions, plus has acquired Miramax Films and Pixar Animation. Warner Bros. is part of Time Warner, which also includes New Line Cinema, Castle Rock Entertainment, Turner Entertainment, HBO, the Cartoon Network, DC Comics, and the Atlanta Braves. Fox is owned by Rupert Murdock's News Corporation, which includes Fox Broadcasting Company and Fox News. And Paramount, owned by Viacom, recently purchased DreamWorks SKG.

The five events that changed the studios are very apparent today Each division of production has its own guild or union, which over the decades has been responsible for the recruiting and training of the finest talents with the objective of making professional quality motion pictures. Though the studios and guilds have historically been uneasy bed partners, this relationship has generated a large pool of professionals to work on the increasingly large film production and the expanding number of television programs.

Battles have been fought over residual payments for television reruns, VHS and DVD sales, home box office, and most recently movie downloads on the Internet. No single studio could afford to keep in-house the talents that are part of the guilds, like was once possible in the early sound era. Thus the inevitable formation of the guilds, which was bitterly opposed by the old studio moguls, has benefited the studios by keeping the costs tied into picture-by-picture agreements.

Though the divesting of theater ownership from the studios almost destroyed the studios in the early 1950s, this action also proved to be highly fortuitous. With productions being drastically cut back because of the rise of television, the extra financial burden of maintaining the existing theaters, plus building new cinemas for widescreen presentations, the studios would have certainly collapsed if they had kept their theater chains. Today the studios can open in thousands of theaters in one day without having to worry about maintenance and repairs. The multiplex began as an independent effort by owners to divide existing theaters into smaller groups. This eventually allowed the owners to contract with several motion picture companies and, in turn, gave these companies a way to open wide with potential blockbuster features.

Once the old studio guard faded out, the resentful attitude about television quickly disappeared. Disney was the first to see the enormous value of television for promotion, starting with *Disneyland* and *The Mickey Mouse Club*. Now every studio is involved in television production, which generates more revenue from sponsor advertising than box office revenue for the motion picture division. Starting with Desilu Productions taking over and renovating the rundown RKO studio, the reason the old studio sound stages are still standing is because of long-term rentals to television productions.

During the studio era, the number of independent producers in Hollywood could be counted on one hand: Samuel Goldwyn, David O. Selznick, Walt Disney, and Walter Wanger.

Starting with United Artists in the early 1950s, actors free of long-term contracts, maverick directors, and an increasing crop of young independent producers created production companies. Today almost every successful movie star, director, special effects wizard, or producer has established his or her own production company. The rewards of a hit film are so lucrative there is the need to start a company to avoid a large percentage of the profits being collected by Uncle Sam. But the deep-seated reason is artistic control. After an actor, director, line producer, and occasionally a writer and cinematographer, have "paid their dues" working on assigned projects until they hit pay dirt with a breakout production, the desire is to create personal projects and maintain a large amount of control over the productions. This crossover began with writers like Preston Sturges and Billy Wilder, both at Paramount, who took cuts in salary to direct their first features.

Studios offer development contracts to the most successful of these individuals and companies, working out agreements for first right of refusal on projects. In turn, the studios negotiate arrangements for office space, operating staff, sound stages, and other niceties. They do this in exchange for the potential marketing and distribution of productions that come out of this development process, which includes a big percentage of the gross revenue and a large slice of the licensing deals. In many ways the studios have not changed that much since the early years because of these exclusive arrangements. The business has become far more complicated with two-hundred-million-dollar productions and releases in thousands of theaters internationally. But in many ways the process has come full circle. The remaining studios are still dream factories controlling the lion's share of the motion picture and television industry.

Like any battlewise hierarchy, to avoid small encampments of competitive forces, the studios have learned to invite potential rivals inside the secure walls of these super fortresses. Thus, Machiavelli is alive and well in modern Hollywood, and *The Prince* is still recommended reading to enter this profession. But the lasting appeal of the studios, it can be argued, is very simplistic. The studios represent the very beginning of the motion picture business, and the dream of most ambitious filmmakers is to be inside these walls and part of this heritage.

## Inside the Studio

> "There is nothing duller on screen than being accurate but not dramatic.
> —Darryl F. Zanuck

There is still evidence of the past inside the modern studios. Sound stages are busy. Sets are being built. Technicians hurry about. But the primary business is television production. Now most films are shot on location, except for special effect scenes done in sound stages against a blue screen. Because of tax incentives and a bigger return on the dollar, Hollywood has experienced an increase in runaway production to other states and countries since the late 1980s. In the modern studio, movies stars no longer rub elbows in the commissary and extras do not crisscross the back lot dressed as cowboys, Roman soldiers, and femme fatales.

Ernest Hemingway wrote that Paris during the Jazz Era was a movable feast in the mind. This metaphor can also be used in regard to the studios, not because films can be made anywhere in the world but because people endeavor to make great films. The reason the glamorous image of the old Studio System remains has little to do with bigger-than-life movie stars and everything to do with the motion pictures these stars made. The real legacy of this system is a pursuit of excellence in craft and storytelling.

The motion picture industry is structured around great artists. In the Studio Era, MGM might have had the largest roster of movie stars, but it also had the best composers, arrangers, choreographers, art designers, costumer designers, writers, and directors available. The one thing the studio moguls did was to seek out the finest. Granted, this was during the Great Depression and talent was thankful for work, but these individuals were well rewarded for their creative efforts. One of the most remarkable and lasting features of the studios, which is usually underappreciated, is the pursuit of excellence in the studio movies. The major studios always strove to put quality on the screen in every aspect of production.

This was during a great financial hardship in the country during which audiences would be delighted to see any form of escapist entertainment, and the studios could have easily cut corners on production values. Instead, throughout this era the look of the films improved tremendously. The studios invested fortunes in large musical numbers, creating sets on back lots, lighting stars perfectly, and getting the finest musicians. This led up to the landmark year of 1939, which is considered the greatest year for motion pictures ever, with *Gone with the Wind, Mr. Smith Goes to Washington, Wuthering Heights, Gunga Din, The Wizard of Oz, Stagecoach,* and many more.

All of the studio moguls came from impoverished childhoods and were immigrants or sons of immigrants. There is every reason to suppose that these men would skimp on production costs and shoot as quickly as possible. But they did not—it was the complete opposite. This does not mean they did not scream and yell about costs and overages, but the budgets were generous for each production. Coming from merchant backgrounds, the competition for quality goods might be part of the reason.

The real reason, though it probably can never be proven, is that audiences responded to the high-quality look and sound of films. This is despite the fact that only a small fraction of these audience members had any concept of lighting,

Art director Richard Day designed the enormous, realistic set for **Dead End** (1937), directed by William Wyler and shot by legendary cinematographer Gregg Toland.

costume materials, realistic three-dimensional sets, musical orchestrations, or how to write memorable dialogue. Even in the late 1960s and 1970s when most of the studios were struggling to survive, money was poured into epic motion pictures like *Ben-Hur, Spartacus,* and *Lawrence of Arabia.* The true battle between film and television, as far as the old studio bosses were concerned, was over the quality of production: Movies were thoroughbreds and television shows were saddle horses. To the studios, television had become a haven for down-and-dirty B-movie directors and actors.

Foreign films made a stir because of their revolutionary style, but many had bad sound recordings, poor musical scores, and natural lighting, like *Open City* and *Breathless.* However, the American-made films released through the studios that reflected the influence of this international movement, like *On the Waterfront* and *Paths of Glory,* copied the radical camera techniques and improvised storytelling, but the cinematography and sound were always first-rate. People may leave a studio film complaining about the cookie-cutter story, but there are rarely adverse comments about the technical aspects of the movie.

Today, all the creative and technical talent that at one time were under contract are now members of the guilds and ready to work. For over twenty-five years, the great composer Alfred Newman worked exclusively for Twentieth Century Fox. Now John Williams selects the films he wishes to score, no matter which studio is involved. With all this excellent talent readily available to make a motion picture, what the studios have become is an open-pit mine for original ideas. These fresh ideas come from writers with a "new voice," young directors that have gotten attention with a low-budget, eye-catching movie or students that have made an early reputation at a film school.

## Today's Total Filmmaker

> "When people ask me if I went to film school I tell them, no, I went to films."
> —Quentin Tarantino

The foreign film movement represents a remarkably small number of directors in different countries who made personal films under primitive conditions. They shot on real locations, using mostly existing light, mixing professional and amateur actors, and selecting subject matter that focused on problems of individuals, usually without the paint-by-the-numbers of Hollywood movies. Most of these films, unfortunately, are rarely seen today, with the exception of *Seven Samurai, La Dolce Vita, 8½,* and *The Seventh Seal.* Even films like *Breathless, The 400 Blows,* and *The Bicycle Thief,* which had a profound effect on moviemakers around the world, are infrequently shown even in film classes.

At the height of the foreign film movement, these movies were seen by a limited audience, but this audience just happened to be all the young wishful directors, writers, and actors that later became the dynamic force of the New Hollywood. What the foreign films meant to them was that old studio rules of "seamless" moviemaking could be broken; but, more important, they proved that inexpensive films would be shot on the outside—and the good films would attract the attention of studios. Though almost none of the foreign directors of this movement—like Fellini, De Sica, Goddard, Bergman, and Kurosawa—were enticed to work in America, their influence is widely acknowledged by all of the directors that reshaped the studios in the 1970s.

This movement became the foundation for today's independent films. And this independent movement is divided down the center with a thick red line. There are directors like John Cassavetes, John Sayles, and Woody Allen that choose not to cross this line and remain independent their entire careers. They want the freedom to make personal films that may only find a small audience.

And there are directors like Stanley Kubrick, Francis Ford Coppola, Oliver Stone, Bryan Singer, and Sam Raimi who used independent films (this would also include movies in the horror genre) as a calling card to get into the Studio System to make big-budget motion pictures. Recently, it has become common to see directors that cross over both sides of this line, like Ang Lee, John Woo, Robert Rodriguez, Spike Lee, and Quentin Tarantino.

Some of these directors learned their craft in film schools or working in television; others begged and borrowed the money and went out and shot a film. With all of these diversified directors, there are two common denominators: They have a deep understanding and appreciation of film history, film genres, and the styles of legendary directors; and they know the business of filmmaking.

It is vitally important to understand this, because to break into the movie business, a hopeful filmmaker is competing with the best of the best *in every area*. With the possible exception of the oil industry, there is no other business as competitive as motion pictures. Most schools simply do not teach film as a practical vocation. Film is usually taught as a general history or hands-on work with digital cameras, usually without comprehensive training in the visual language of film. Thus, urban legends abound about breaking into the business, but most of these legends are spawned from movies and television shows and become dead ends to the unprepared student.

There is an almost universal feeling by young filmmakers that *someone* in Hollywood is waiting for his or her Orson Wellesian first-time movie. There is an ounce of truth in this because one of the chief goals of producers is to find "the next Steven Spielberg," which is an often-quoted phrase. But what is neglected in most schools is training students how to get a film to that important *someone*. With every class in Filmmaking 101, there should be companion courses in Finding an Agent or Entering a Film Festival.

In the arts, especially in education, there is a reluctance—or even bias—about teaching the business side of the individual arts. In motion pictures this is not only a handicap; it is a death wish to assume it is unimportant. Whether it is screenwriting, directing, cinematography, or any of the other creative occupations, understanding the business is not an elective, it is essential knowledge.

A screenplay might show a knack for clever, fast-paced action that is a good compelling read. But the screenplay is something different for everyone that looks at it. The cinematographer wants to know how many scenes are during the day and how many are at night. The costume designer needs to know how many characters there are and have a rough idea what those characters are like. The line producer wants to know all this, plus the number of locations to break this information down into a working budget. Though this might not be the reason a writer sits down to create a great story, eventually a screenplay becomes an invitation for someone to invest upwards to one hundred million dollars or more.

The journey to get a film made begins by forming a company.

# Tales about the Film Business:
# Steven Spielberg and Peter Jackson

The two most inspirational tales for young filmmakers are the stories of amazing rise to fame and fortune of Steven Spielberg and Peter Jackson. But both of these tales are one-shot wonders. As a teenager, Spielberg hopped on the tour tram at Universal Studios and snuck onto the back lot for a personal walking tour. He met someone who was so impressed by a young man with such an intense love for movies and old Hollywood that he gave the youngster a three-day pass. After three days, Spielberg found a way to keep coming onto the lot, where through a series of fortuitous circumstances he met the right people who eventually gave him a chance to direct an episode of *Night Gallery.*

Today, if someone tries this—and there have been many—they are quickly escorted off the lot. Spielberg did this at the right time in the right place, during a period when young ambitious directors were a rarity in the studios. Film schools had not yet become the proving ground for new filmmakers, so Spielberg's little visit to the back lot of Universal was a novelty. Spielberg has said the important thing about this approach to breaking into the system was that, "I knew what I was doing." In other words, he was prepared: He had a background in making short films, an encyclopedic knowledge of the movies, and a maturity that allowed him to talk with high-powered adults.

Jackson had a bigger hurdle. He lived on the other side of the world from Hollywood in a small New Zealand town. He had made a few extremely low-budget horror films, but this was during a time when everyone was making horror films to break into the movies. His one Hollywood venture, *The Frighteners,* was a box office disappointment. *Heavenly Creatures* was a powerful film that received an Oscar nomination for writing but was only successful with the critics. In the movie business having films that underperform is a major stumbling block in getting a green light for future productions.

There was nothing Jackson had done up to this point that would convince a production company to give him three hundred million dollars to make three epic special effects films in three years. He originally pitched *The Lord of the Rings* as two films and had prepared a previsualization demonstration on how he would approach the hundreds of CGI effects. After listening to Jackson's vision of the film, the executives at New Line Cinema made the decision to do three films.

In other words, he was prepared: He had a background in making films, also with an encyclopedic knowledge of the movies, and knew his subject matter impeccably. As he later said, "This is a giant undertaking, but I consider this a personal film. It's my film of a lifetime. I read the book when I was eighteen years old and thought then, 'I can't wait till the movie comes out.' Twenty years later, no one had done it—so I got impatient."

If there is a lesson to be learned from these two directors, it is that film is a lifelong occupation and it is not possible to know too much about the subject. The teaching starts with the first movie a future filmmaker watches; and, despite the fact that there are a growing number of excellent films schools, it is primarily a self-taught profession. Opportunities are often once in a lifetime, so to know the business of filmmaking is vital in convincing investors that a project will have merit and that it will stay on the right course.

# FORMING A PRODUCTION COMPANY

## Weekend Filmmakers

All films are alike—some just cost more than others. With each film, there are actors (or voiceover talent), a director, a cinematographer, cameras, locations, costumes (even if they are what the actors bring to the set), editing equipment or software, and a time schedule. There also is the expectation of having people see the final production.

If the film is very low budget, perhaps funded by a student loan or a new credit card, there are several things that could happen that could quickly alter the lives and aspirations of everyone involved. A fearless, young, inexperienced stuntman will volunteer to roll down some steps. There might be a pan from a couple kissing to a billboard for Virgin Airlines. And it is decided during editing that "Born to Be Wild" should play under the opening credits.

What might happen is that the stuntman will break his collarbone, Virgin Airlines will demand that its logo be removed, and there will be a lawsuit over the use of copyrighted music without permission. Because there is no corporation, insurance, or legal counsel, the happy-go-lucky student who organized the two-weekend film shoot will either have to declare bankruptcy or turn to his or her parents for a major financial bailout.

Granted, this is the worst-case scenario, but all of these mishaps, and many more, have befallen filmmakers. An injury is the most common and usually involves a stunt, like a fake swing that goes astray. The other two examples might fly under the radar if the film is for a class project and not entered into festivals. However, the idea that a big corporation will not come after a little film is a dangerous excuse to tempt fate.

If the film has scenes that are considered R-rated or undesirable, which might taint a corporate image, major corporations literally have the proverbial army of lawyers on staff that for a few hundred dollars can file an injunction to prevent the film from being shown until changes are made. And not only are songs copyrighted, but the use of old-time standards is a big business that can generate millions of dollars a year from licensing rights.

On the flip side, a state film commission could have a contact for local stunt people. If asked, and perhaps treated to lunch, one of these professionals might give tips on how to fall safely and if the location site selected sends up any red warning flags. After reading the screenplay, a corporation might give permission to use a logo or business location because the limited high school or college audience that might see the film is one of its target audiences. The music is a little harder, because the artists do not control the rights. So, an appeal to Ringo Starr for "Yellow Submarine" will only result in a polite rejection. But deals have been worked out with licensing companies for "needle-drop rights" and for secondary fees if the film is accepted into a festival or finds a distributor.

These examples are how to work around problems for a small film, a personal endeavor that does not even have a shoestring budget from which to work. There are thousands of these films made each week, and through some undefined miracle most avoid catastrophes and legal entanglements. These short films are invaluable learning experiences. The best "teacher" is to go out each weekend and shoot a three-minute movie, always looking for a new challenge by experimenting with camera angles, directorial styles, or film genres. Making small films and making big mistakes are learning experiences like none other. But these films are for personal growth and never will be distributed or most likely seen outside a living room or classroom.

For any film project beyond this, a corporation needs to be formed.

## The First Steps in Forming a Company

> I hope we'll never lose sight of one thing—that it was all started by a mouse.
> —Walt Disney

Throughout the following on forming a production company, the phrase "the filmmaker" is used instead of "the producer." The various roles and titles for the producer are discussed separately. In the past, it was usually the producer that formed such a company. Today, production companies are formed regularly by an enterprising individual who wants to make a film but does not always see himself or herself solely as the producer. Quite often, the filmmaker is a director who has formed a company and is in search of someone to accept the responsibilities of being the producer.

To form a production company requires three things: (1) legal representation, (2) an outside accounting firm, and (3) start-up money to cover these expenses. There is a long list of the different business forms that can be used, and it is important to sit down with an attorney that has experience in the entertainment field to go over the options. Finding the right attorney and law firm might turn out to be the single most important decision made regarding the formation of a motion picture company.

## Entertainment Attorneys

> Today everyone is a star—they're all billed as "starring" or "also starring." In my day, we earned that recognition.
> —Bette Davis

Entertainment attorneys tend to be found in cities with flourishing film or television production. Therefore, it is not surprising that Los Angeles and New York have the largest firms, followed by San Francisco, Chicago, Dallas, and Miami. Most of the firms in these cities are deeply rooted inside the film industry. As expected, such firms can be very costly. But for the formation of a production company, there are many attorneys outside these locations that can effectively put together the legal documents required for an investment corporation to produce one or more feature productions.

Most law firms that specialize in entertainment advertise or are listed in information provided by state film commissions. The commissioners cannot recommend a firm, but they can tell you how long the firm has been around and perhaps what local companies have been represented by them. With a first-time production company, the start-up dollars are difficult to raise, and most likely the person forming the company is the one investing his or her hard-earned dollars. So, an attorney that is willing to waive certain fees is very appealing.

The key point to consider is that in reality the motion picture community is controlled by a small number of people that interact with each other constantly. Thus, an attorney or law firm that is part of the mainstream of this business will have connections with the heads of studios or production, distribution, television, games, and licensing companies. These connections for networking a new film are invaluable; but, as expected, they often come at a high price, demanding a sizable retainer. The larger, well-established firms have a full plate and are not looking to cut fees for a new company with no track record.

Interviewing with different entertainment law firms provides a powerful and often frustrating education about how the film business works. Rejection is part of the business, so this is one way to toughen up quickly. The reason to visit as many firms as possible is to discover what their operating philosophies are. This might sound like a fancy term but it does exist. Some firms focus on mainstream motion pictures and discourage clients from crossing over to less profitable independent productions. Large firms can afford to help start-up companies, but the attorneys of such firms have an obligation to their successful clients. So if something does not happen quickly, a new client might be greeted with an abrupt lack of enthusiasm, along with a depleted start-up account.

The one common denominator in the entertainment business is a great idea. And protecting the idea is vitally important. Because "ideas" cannot be copyrighted, there has to be a "tangible medium of expression," like a screenplay. Once a copyright is obtained, the author—having legally become the "owner"—can then enter into an option arrangement with an individual or small group of people that has formed a company. A terrific screenplay or the exclusive rights to a novel, graphic novel, or nonfiction property, combined with a strong business proposal, can perk the interest of a prestige firm because there is the sweet smell of success.

## Forming an Entertainment Company

> I've been to Paris France and I've been to Paris Paramount. Paris Paramount is better.
> —Ernest Lubtsch

The attorney that forms and oversees the development of a new company is a powerful force, but there are legal limitations. The attorney *might* either waive up-front legal fees or postpone payment until the company is operational. But the attorney cannot waive the fees for filing the legal documents required for a company. Nor can the attorney find investors for the company's projects. This becomes a conflict of interest because the responsibility of the attorney is to see that investment dollars go through the proper legal formalities. To oversee this, plus pitching the business proposal to potential investors or fellow business associates, removes the impartiality and is a situation begging for a lawsuit or action from the state bar association.

An attorney can suggest a strategy for finding investors and can advise on the business background of potential investors. The attorney's main responsibility is to assist the producers in putting together the business plan that is ultimately given to investors for consideration. This plan must conform to strict regulations dealing with time lines, the correct methods for approaching investors, financial accountability, and overseeing the standards of business practices.

Investors are attracted to potential business partners who are represented by strong, well-established law firms. However, on a first-time film project, finding an attorney that will keep start-up expenses down and give good sound advice is difficult but not impossible. There are many new attorneys trying to establish a business practice that might welcome a filmmaker with a wonderful new project. Normally, attorneys will not charge for an initial consultation, but the occasional fees for such a consultation are generally low. The wise filmmaker should meet many attorneys the first time out. One of these meetings hopefully will result in the ideal match, and the overall search will certainly test a first-time filmmaker's true interest in this field.

## Production Accounting

> You're an accountant. You're in a noble profession. The word "count" is part of your title.
> —Max Bialystock in *The Producers*

Finding an attorney to file corporation documents and put together an investment package is the first step in getting investors for a project. The next step is to find an outside accounting firm to oversee all the financial matters and to file quarterly financial reports for the investors. The outside accounting firm needs to have a good long-standing reputation; thus, the selection of this firm might be the deciding factor for investors to come on board for the project. Such firms can also bring investors to the table.

The motion picture company should have an in-house production accountant to oversee the daily expenses. This individual will work closely with an experienced line producer or production manager to put together the operating budget for a motion picture, plus serve as watchdog for every step of production. The production accountant will collect receipts and invoices daily and apply them to the proper budget lines. This person will also send up warning flags when certain funds are rapidly being depleted, thus potentially causing overages. During a production, the production accountant will receive daily updates on budget lines; plus, he or she will review every invoice that comes in to ensure that there are no mysterious items or mistakes with payments for contracted services.

The production accountant will review all documents with the outside accounting firm for verification and reporting to the investors. For obvious reasons, investors prefer to have an impartial accounting firm put together the financial reports. It cannot be overly stressed that for a new production company all financial matters must be strictly adhered to for reporting purposes. Taking precautions at every step is a wise habit to cultivate. If one line item is low because of unexpected circumstances, then go through the process of getting permission to borrow from another line item that still has ample funds remaining. As long as this does not create a budget overage for the production and the proper steps are taken, this should not be a problem with the investors.

If a new production company's records do not jibe with the outside accounting firm, this could prove to be the kiss of death for raising future funds on new projects. The accounting firm's obligation is to report such discrepancies to investors. In a worst-case situation, the outside firm could sever relations with the production company creating a bad reputation that will be exceedingly difficult to shake off. Every filmmaker is working toward the funding of the next and possibly bigger project. Proper accounting practices are the gateway to the hard-earned dream. If the filmmaker comes in on or under budget and the accounting is in good order, then the investors are satisfied that they have been well looked after. Even if the film does not make money or only breaks even, the investor has had a good experience because everything has been done professionally.

## A Few Important Thoughts about Investors

> " I believe in mortality, but not in inflicting it on myself. "
>
> —Sam Spiegel

There are many myths about investors in motion pictures that have wreaked havoc on the best-laid plans of filmmakers. The biggest myth is that investors get involved in movies to lose money so they can write it off on their taxes. Completely untrue. Investors hope to make money, which is why most of them have money in the first place. Their expectations are based on the business proposal they sign off on. If the proposal has targeted a certain financial projection through documented research, then this is the amount the investor is anticipating.

It is important for a filmmaker to think like an investor. If the investment is for the construction of a three-story office complex with advanced rentals projected at 50 percent, then it is assumed that such a structure will go up as planned, on schedule, and according to the blueprints. If the structure ends up being only two stories, with 20 percent advance rentals, then the investor has a good right to be upset. This example involves a physical structure, on a piece of carefully chosen land, built with steel and glass. The substantial difference between investing in a building and investing in a motion picture is that a film has none of these tangible dynamics and the final product can be burned on a DVD for less than a dollar.

This lack of a physical form is what sometimes creates the gulf in thinking between investors and filmmakers. Instead of having 250 tenants on long-term leases for $1,000-a-month rent, movies are sold 250 seats per screen for $8, half of which probably goes to the distributor. A first-time investor most likely thinks that a motion picture is closer to slot machines than a roulette table with its even or odd payoffs. What does not change is the presumption of professionalism.

If an investor sees that the contractor who was hired to put up drywall has inflated the cost, then the contractor should not be surprised when fired. This is a physical operation and it should be immediately obvious if the project is not meeting the basic requirements. With motion pictures, it is exceedingly difficult to assess the quality of work by a director, writer, or cinematographer until the first rough cut is turned in. This means that an investor in a motion picture is taking an enormous gamble based on the trust that everyone involved is professional and knows their jobs inside out.

This establishment of *trust* is the most important thing for a filmmaker to nurture when searching for investors (usually a lifelong pursuit). Investors give money to the filmmaker the same way they would to a building contractor. But because there are no foundations to pour that can be inspected, the investor is taking the risk that everyone the filmmaker hires is the best possible.

The violation of this expectation is what destroys—or at least derails for a long period—many filmmakers at the beginning of their careers. The more white lies that are perpetrated to the investors about the background and talent of people hired for a motion picture, the more chances the soufflé will fall. Every time a filmmaker hires an inexperienced friend who has always wanted to indulge in pyrotechnics, or hires a costume designer who has only done *The Fantasticks,* or casts an untrained relative in a major acting role, they are taking a risk. These are white lies that might severely affect the bottom line of the budget because of overages and sheer incompetency.

Movie history is littered with white lies. Orson Welles told his investors he was going to do a faithful adaptation of Franz Kafka's *The Trial.* Robert Altman told Warren Beatty not to worry about the sound on *McCabe & Mrs. Miller.* And Francis Ford Coppola said his daughter, Sofia, could carry a major role in *The Godfather: Part III.* Nevertheless, these films got made and became part of movie lore. What does not make it into the history books are the thousands of first-time movies that never had a life past the first screening.

The most important and unquestionably the most difficult thing for a filmmaker to learn is that he or she *does not* have any close friends or relatives. There are only the right people for the jobs. For every Joel and Ethan Coen, there are thousands of brothers that are no longer talking to each other or have a rough cut of an unfinished film in the bottom drawer of a file cabinet. The filmmaker must learn to think, as unglamorous as this might sound, like a cigar-chomping drill sergeant who gathers only the best people to become involved in an almost insurmountable task. There is one rule in the movie business that is as absolute as the speed of light: Every film can be your last one.

The other myth about investors is that they only get involved with motion pictures because of the glamour, spotlights, and movie stars. This is not a myth; it is a nightmare. It is not unheard of that an investor with no experience in the business thinks of movie people—and, consequentially, all people in the arts—as children who have never grown up. Thus, it is the investor's job or self-appointed responsibility, to oversee the investment through all the stages. Unfortunately, there is more than a grain of truth in this wide-eyed child

metaphor and many people in the arts have brought it on themselves. Not having an elementary understanding of the business of entertainment is an invitation to jump into a swimming pool without water.

On the other side, a good reason for a filmmaker to understand the fundamentals of the movie business is for protection from the wrong investors. To become involved with an investor that wants to hang out during production or be introduced to the lead actress should be avoided at all costs. When an investor shows up in the middle of a production grinning like a Cheshire cat, it changes the climate on the set. People begin to play at their jobs instead of doing their jobs. The legendary director John Ford would stop everyone when a person from the front office wandered onto his set. He would introduce the cast and crew to the person and then tell the person to leave and never return. To a certain extent, everyone has to be John Ford on their set.

One of the hardest things for a filmmaker to do is turn down money from a potential investor. An investor that micromanages every aspect of a production and thinks he or she has the right to do this is probably the wrong investor to get in bed with. This underscores the importance of choosing the right business form for the company, such as a limited liability company (an "LLC"). Pursuant to the Operating Agreement, the interference of an investor is generally limited, if not completely eliminated.

Movies are like a Catholic marriage; if the filmmaker enters into a production with an interfering investor, it is a very thorny arrangement from which to exit. Finding the best investors is like casting a movie. If you have a gut reaction someone is not right, take this impulse seriously. If you can wait for the right actor before starting a production, then also take the extra time to find investors that respect the intense process enough to not interfere—and then earn that respect by doing good work.

## Completion Bonds

A completion bond is insurance that guarantees the investors that a motion picture will be completed as originally proposed. This insurance is not a policy on artistic values. As long as the film is on schedule and within budget, there should be no issues of shutting the production down. However, if the production runs into significant problems due to weather, injuries, or a director losing control of the film and going into overages, then the investors have a right to step in and make significant changes.

If an unavoidable calamity like a storm or fire stops the film, then the insurance will cover the extra expenses because of the "act of God" clause. On the other hand, if a director falls behind and loses the confidence of the production team, then the completion bond will pay for an established director to take over the production. In the worst case, if a production is plagued with problems and footage cannot be cut together, then the bond will allow for the production to be shut down and the investors repaid.

Most studio motion pictures are self-guaranteed. These films are under constant scrutiny by the production executives, and any overages or replacements are dealt with internally. Completion bonds are part of the line item budgets of most independent productions, even features released and distributed by the major studios. There are several films by Orson Welles that are legendary because they were seized by the investors and still rest in vaults in some distant country.

These were acts by unhappy investors who did not have a completion bond on the production. It is always best to finish a film, even with a new director and major cuts in the story line, because there is still an opportunity to recoup part of the investment through a direct-to-DVD release. Bad movies sometimes take on a life of their own by becoming cult favorites.

However, a film that is not completed is a total loss. The completion guarantor might repay the investors or bank involved, but even with this there is a loss in the interest the money would have generated elsewhere; plus, the tax reporting becomes a nightmare. Then there is the bad media reporting that often harms the reputations of everyone involved in the production. Also, if the completion bond agreement is not carefully worded then certain situations might not be covered, thus converting the loss back to the investors. Terry Gilliam's ill-fated production of *The Man That Killed Don Quixote* became embroiled in such a legal entanglement, which is painfully revealed in the documentary *Lost in La Mancha*.

## The Sad Truth about Start-up Money

One of the unbreakable rules of the motion picture business is, Never use your own money. The other rule is, Unless you have to.

Start-up money is the hardest and often most complicated to find. To put a retainer down for an entertainment attorney to start the first step in motion by filing the documents for a new corporation can easily amount to five thousand dollars or more, depending on the firm. The Catch-22 is that investors cannot be solicited until everything is filed and a notice is published. And depending on the charm or visionary enthusiasm of the filmmaker, the attorney might waive some of the start-up fees, but the attorney cannot pay for the filing fees because this would be a conflict of interest. This is where most beginning filmmakers get in over their heads very quickly. The services of a reputable accounting firm will also require a retainer to show good faith. However, because the filmmaker does not have any investment money at this point, the hiring of the accounting firm can wait a little while. And because the company papers have not been filed, and there is no accounting firm, a bank will only loan money on personal credit. This is where the personal financial hole begins.

The pursuit of start-up money forces the ambitious, green filmmaker to appeal to a wealthy uncle (if the filmmaker is fortunate to have one), put together a pool with his friends, or use his or her own money. Robert Townsend allegedly maxed out his credit cards to make *Hollywood Shuffle* and lived to tell about it. But this tale has been the downfall of thousands of student filmmakers since. The hard truth is that if the filmmaker cannot afford a few thousand dollars, then the filmmaker should not be trying to make a movie. However, this argument has never stopped anyone.

There also is the approach of finding a "good person" that will loan the start-up money on a production, with the agreement that the generous soul will be paid back with either money from the investors or first money back on the production. If the repayment of a loan is in the budget and it is not cut due to negotiations with the investors, then the person will see the money back, possibly with a prime percentage. Most investors will not argue over having the person receive first money back, because this is high risk and anyone that enters into such an agreement deserves a financial perk. Another solution to finding start-up money is to enter into a partnership.

## Partnerships

> I started at the top and worked my way down.
> —Orson Welles

A partnership is an agreement, whether written or verbal, between two or more individuals who agree to share responsibilities on an endeavor, in this case a film, by pooling talent and financial resources. They will likewise share in the profit or loss. A partnership also can be with another group involved in a co-venture, which is very common. Often the credits on a motion picture begin with the titles of such partnership arrangements.

For a filmmaker with a great project, becoming a partner with a person who has the start-up money and financial connections can be mutually beneficial. Walt Disney was fortunate to have his brother Roy. John Ford had Merian C. Cooper. Ron Howard has Brain Grazer. To find a working relationship in which one person directs and the other produces is the ideal Hollywood marriage.

Proof that long partnerships can exist in Hollywood, director Ron Howard and producer Brain Grazer celebrate their Oscar wins for *A Beautiful Mind* (2002).

Unfortunately, Hollywood is not known for its long-term marriages. What might seem like the ideal partnership to start with can turn sour quickly. To form an alliance with someone because he or she has ready cash for start-up expenses is not a good partnership. A partner is someone who knows as much—if not more—about motion picture production as the filmmaker. To have someone that writes a few checks and is then expected to disappear only invites hard feelings.

The best partnerships are based on respect and the proximity effect, that is, working long hours together without wanting to kill each other. There also needs to be a constant sharing process. The filmmaker should share his ideas and knowledge about motion pictures and at the same time listen to brass tacks about the business aspects of production. Like the courting process before marriage, it is wise to take a potential partner out to dinner a few times.

If the conversation begins to stall or it is obvious that the other person has never seen *The Godfather* or *The Usual Suspects* (nor obviously possesses any critical knowledge related to movies and filmmaking), it might be best to call it a night before things get too serious. Then again, if a conversation ensues about what makes great motion pictures tick and four hours quickly pass, this might be, as Bogart says in *Casablanca,* the start of a beautiful friendship.

## The Company

> " Making a film is like putting out a fire with a sieve. There are so many elements, and it gets so complicated. "
>
> —George Lucas

To make a motion picture, there must be a business structure that protects both the investors and the artists. Filmmaking is a seemingly endless process of accountability. Money is raised to make the film, the film is shot, and the revenue is divided—sometimes for decades after the original release. This process of supply and demand has been part of the motion picture business since the beginning and is similar to most businesses. The obvious difference is that each film has it own unique qualities. This is equivalent to General Motors never making the same car twice. The variety in production is what attracts investors to the movies—and what scares them the most.

From the 1930s to the late 1950s, a small group of studios controlled the motion picture business with a corporate structure like that of General Motors. Production money was borrowed from banks against the track record of past films, and stocks were sold based on the accumulated financial success of the studios. The need to reflect a healthy bottomline led to a pattern of moviemaking in which popular genres like musicals, comedies, and westerns were run off the production assembly line in greater numbers than dramas or social issue films. In fact, these prestige films, as they were referred to by the moguls, were possible because of the high box office revenue generated by escapist entertainment motion pictures.

This movie juggling act worked in large part because the studios owned the theaters and could market prestige films along with crowd-pleasers. After the major studios were forced to sell off theaters in the late 1940s, fewer risks were taken with movies that might not bring in big crowds. Motion pictures with something serious to say fell to the independent producers. These producers usually made one film at a time, thus did not have sufficient collateral for bank loans. Instead, they relied on investors for working capital.

An independent producer like Sam Spiegel, who made *The African Queen, On the Waterfront, The Bridge on the River Kwai,* and *Lawrence of Arabia,* was part circus barker, con man, and business entrepreneur. He was a maverick producer, along with Stanley Kramer, Harold Hecht, and Merian C. Cooper, during the transitional period of the Studio System. Spiegel would spend years raising money for his next production, which often meant that on the eve of a new production key funding would still be falling into place. This is still the time-intensive routine of the modern-day independent producer who, in order to put a deal together, must rub elbows with savvy Hollywood insiders along with individuals who have no background whatsoever in motion pictures. This experience can become a true dance macabre.

The Supreme Court in 1915 decided in *Mutual Film Corporation v. Industrial Commission of Ohio* that motion pictures were a business and not covered by the First Amendment, while all other art organizations had the right to freedom of speech. This remained until 1952 when the Court unanimously overruled its earlier decision with *Joseph Burstyn, Inc. v. Wilson*. This change did not affect how independent producers could incorporate. Obviously, a not-for-profit status could not be used to secure millions of dollars on a high-risk endeavor. For decades, independent producers used a corporate shell that is essentially the same as major corporations.

The limited liability company (LLC) has become the business structure of preference in the movie industry. An LLC is a hybrid of a partnership and a corporation in which the owners are shielded from personal liability. In turn, all profits and losses are directly passed to the owners without taxation of the company itself. LLCs have been used internationally for a long time, but because of changes in corporation tax laws they have grown more common in the United States. As with a standard corporation, the articles of organization need to be filed within a certain state. The advantage with an LLC is that there are fewer formalities to be observed than in comparison with the paperwork demands of a corporation. For independent productions, an LLC is easy to work with, especially with investments of five million dollars or less.

## The Path of an Investment

> **" Anyone who doesn't believe in miracles isn't a realist. "**
> **—Billy Wilder**

The path of a single investment is complicated and demands attention to ensure that it stays within the parameters of the contract and tax regulations. The investment can be ten thousand dollars, a hundred thousand, or a million or more. The management of the investment does not change much as the amount increases. Overseeing this is the primary duty of the entertainment attorney or firm. Because each investment will take about the same amount of time to manage, the ideal situation is to have a single investor cover all production costs. This rarely happens, and even if it does this investor might represent several other parties.

The investor is given a budget showing the detailed expenses of a production. The budget for a motion picture should be calculated by an individual with years of experience in this highly specialized area. This person is usually a line producer or an assistant director who has a working knowledge of studio and independent features plus television. The Producers Guild of America (PGA) or the Directors Guild of America (DGA) could recommend several qualified individuals, or there are a number of motion picture directories that carry contact information. It is always best to find a compatible fit with a project. Look at credits for films made within a comparable budget range and then seek out the line producers or assistant directors involved in them. If they are not available, most likely they will know someone who is.

The fees will vary, but normally it costs about five thousand dollars for a budget and scene breakdown. There is software for budget and scheduling, and there are very thick books that list expenses and rates, which usually are updated twice a year. There is an old wise saying: Whoever controls the budget *is in control.* This is very true. An excellent training experience is to use the available software and put together a rough budget. Then find an experienced professional to review and fine-tune it. This will cut down on cost but, more important, will provide an invaluable understanding of the demands of a production and what is essential.

## Budget Considerations

The single most important thing to do before preparing any budget is to *lock down the screenplay.* As unglamorous as it sounds, a screenplay contains information about every aspect of the physical production. This includes locations, the time period of the action, the number of extras and principle roles, costumes, and effects and, in addition, will give ideas about permits, travel, catering, and insurance for the cast and crew. Every time a few scenes in a screenplay are changed, it also changes the budget.

To hire someone to constantly revise the budget and schedule is costly—though, in reality, this happens because a screenplay will go through changes during the process of finding the right director, leads, or even a production manager. With this in mind, a budget should reflect the development, preproduction, production, and postproduction expenses, plus office management and supplies directly related to the production. Listed within these expenses should be a line item for budget revisions. As a matter of course, an overall cushion of 10 to 15 percent should be built into the budget to protect it from unforeseeable circumstances. Prices will always fluctuate during the preproduction and production phases, especially related to travel. If everything goes smoothly, then this cushion will reflect that the production came in under budget, which always impresses investors.

## The Investment Agreement

The role of the investor should be clearly defined in an agreement. That "agreement" will actually consist of multiple documents. An investor will generally receive the Business Plan, the Budget, the Private Placement Memorandum, and the Subscription Agreement. It is better to address any potential elements of conflict on paper than to have disruptions on the set because the dividing lines were not clearly set forth. The agreement will define the duties for the producer and creative staff to deliver the film on time and as promised but also establish the conditions in which investors have a right to step in, such as budget overages, scheduling problems, or circumstances that fall under "acts of God."

Others issues include who has the right of final cut or changes to script on location. These should stay with the director and/or the producer unless the production gets into trouble with runaway expenses or the first cut is a disaster. Another critical factor is the content of the film and the potential rating. If the investors signs off on a screenplay that is PG-13, but the director's cut receives an R-rating, this is a serious problem because it throws off anticipated revenue projections.

Another critical issue is budget overruns. If there is a built-in cushion to the budget, this hopefully will cover individual line item overages. However, issues that demand additional capital investment resulting from production troubles with weather, unexpected cost increases, accidents, or other unforeseen incidents that delay a shoot should be stipulated in the original agreement. Will the investors cover these overages up to a certain agreed-upon amount for a higher percentage of the gross net? If not, then the producer will have to locate other investors. This is difficult because the only enticements left are probably from the producer's share of the potential revenue. Bringing in additional investors during a troubled shoot is the hardest way to find money.

## Division of Revenue

When the film starts to generate box office revenue, depending on the distribution deal, money does not necessarily immediately flow to the production company. The distribution company can take all of the first revenue until its expenses for marketing and exhibition are met, which can range anywhere from 30 to 70 percent of the gross revenue depending upon the arrangements. If the distribution company works out a deal with the production company that each gets 50 percent of all gross revenue, this means the production company receives fifty cents on every dollar. But unless the production company has business clout because of star power or other favorable situations, this equal sharing arrangement is rare.

When revenue is received by the production company, investors will receive all of it until their original investment is paid in full, plus generally a 10 percent premium. However, for simplicity's sake, let's say the investors have agreed to 50 percent of the production company's gross revenue. Under these terms, the film needs to generate four million dollars to repay a one-million-dollar-investment, that is, half goes to the distribution company and the other half is split between the production company and the investors.

The long-term involvement of the investors can work in several ways. The investors might continue to receive their full percentage for the life of the film, which can be an undetermined number of years. Or a deal can be structured so the investors receive their full percentage until a certain ceiling is reached, such as five times the original investment. After this, there might be a sliding scale whereby the investors' percentage of future revenue will drop. However, the most common scenario for low-budget films, especially those that have received honors or "good buzz" at festivals, is for both parties to sell out to the distribution company, who will then take all the risks.

The revenue received by a production company is by no means profit. If in the course of production payments were deferred to guilds, or back-end percentages were offered to the director or cast members, these expenses must be retired in good faith. For tax reasons, the last thing a company wants is to show a large profit with no money going out. Revenue is typically applied to the development of other motion pictures or television projects though option deals, hiring writers, and overhead expenses, including staff, legal fees, and accounting. The producer who has put the deal together, negotiated the contracts, and who oversaw all aspects of production and post-production, receives a fixed salary along with the rest of the staff. However, if the film is a hit and makes ten times its original budget or better, then most likely there will be raises, bonuses, and profit sharing.

Then the process of finding investors for the next film starts all over again.

## Not-for-Profit

> Don't pay any attention to the critics; don't even ignore them.
> —Samuel Goldwyn

Not-for-profit or nonprofit corporations are typically created for theatrical companies, museums, education institutions, medical foundations, and other charitable enterprises. Not-for-profits rely upon the generosity of the public, patrons, and grant organizations to supplement general operating expenses, rather than the monetary benefit of directors or members. The formation of this type of corporation is not a practical way to secure money for most motion picture productions. With a not-for-profit, there cannot be investors, because any potential profits are rolled back into the company and staff salaries are fixed. Individual investors and business companies give donations for tax purposes or a strong belief in the cause that the not-for-profit corporation was formed to promote and support.

However, not-for-profits are an important part of the film world. Most festivals and film schools use this business structure to raise money, sometimes up to 70 percent of the yearly budget. Also, many documentary filmmakers find underwriting by using the not-for-profit status. In theater, there is a wide divide between productions. Regional and children's theaters are not-for-profit, along with most regional Actor Equity companies. The kinds of productions from these groups range from Shakespeare to musicals to experimental new works. On the other end of the scale, Broadway productions, most national touring companies, rock concerts, and extravagant Las Vegas shows are created as for-profit corporations. This high profile theatrical entertainment includes *The Phantom of the Opera, The Lion King,* and The Rolling Stones.

As a bit of speculation, part of the widening gulf between theater and film comes from the security of the not-for-profit corporation. Until the Great Depression, theater in America had been a for-profit endeavor, as it had been throughout history. Shakespeare wrote thirty-eight plays in thirty years, plus ran the box office, performed, and was able to retire in comfort. Traditionally, many companies were owned by a famous actor who served as director and producer, and counted the box office receipts after a performance.

After World War II, regional theatrical companies began to pop up across the country because major cities wanted the prestige of local professional productions. This often meant building, managing, and marketing a large performance facility, in addition to paying performers and a production staff. To keep prices affordable for the general public, and competitive with motion picture prices, theatrical productions were lucky to break even and pay staff salaries. To maintain a performance hall was impossible. Thus, these theatrical companies embraced the not-for-profit status, as did most art organizations.

Throughout the 1970s, theater was still a very active force in American culture. With increased local support and corporate underwriting, box office prices were kept down and most children grew up going to plays. Then, as the major grant organizations grew more influential, there was a shift in who was funded. Companies that were perceived as too profitable did not always get rewarded. Instead, groups that were struggling by doing the classics, alternative theater, or new works received the grant prizes.

Though this might be perceived as a debatable observation, not-for-profit theatrical companies saw the course of survival in *not* being too commercially successful. These companies were gradually conditioned to avoid popular theater fare for plays that reached specially targeted audiences. If a company almost broke even at the end of the season, it was often denied grant requests. But a company that had to pass the metaphorical tin cup to underwrite 50 percent of its yearly budget was determined worthy of outside support. Typically, these companies were ballet, modern dance, symphonies, and opera. The need for constant funding changed the nature of most stage plays. The companies that received grants produced shows that fit within the tight guidelines of grant proposals.

This perpetual pursuit of fund-raising has subtly changed the way of thinking and operating in the theatrical arts, which is in total contrast to film. There is the obvious contrast of trying to raise twenty-five thousand dollars to produce a stage production of a new work, when in the age of the blockbuster a new studio feature release is considered a failure if it only grosses twelve million dollars its opening weekend. This gulf is increased further when students can get a theater degree but never take a single business course in box office management or how to form and run a not-for-profit corporation. The unspoken attitude is that there is no need to focus on the economics of running a theater company, because the board of directors is comprised of successful VIP business people that aggressively fund-raise to meet the projected loss on productions.

There is no question that a company with 250 seats will struggle to make ends meet in a competitive for-profit world. Likewise, companies that stage topical, multicultural productions, children's theater, or new works will not survive without support. These forms of limited-appeal entertainment (which is not intended as a disparaging term) find it almost impossible to attract investment support. What has been potentially lost is that throughout the twentieth century, theater has been a stepping stone into film and television and now it is not.

During the Studio Era and the early years of live television, which was based in New York, there was a balance between light entertainment and serious drama. *White Christmas, Sabrina,* and *Rear Window* came out in 1954, the same year as *On the Waterfront* and *The Caine Mutiny.* With television, *I Love Lucy* and *Twilight Zone* were on the air with *Omnibus* and *Playhouse 90.* Broadway and off-Broadway theater once supplied the great actors, writers, directors, designers, and composers that had highly successful movie careers. This began to change after the major television networks relocated to Los Angeles for the production of the hour-long series and sitcoms. With this transition, new faces began to come out of film schools.

## Universities and Film Schools

> I am very concerned about our national heritage, and I am very concerned that films that I watched when I was young and the films that I watched throughout my life are preserved.
>
> —George Lucas

Universities are big businesses that function as miniaturized bureaucratic city–state governments. Department chairs answer to the dean of the college, who in turn answers to the provost, who is responsible to the president, who reports to the board of regents. They operate as not-for-profit

organizations that perpetually seek funding from the private sector and corporations like financially starved sharks. There are a few exceptions that are for-profit, like the University of Phoenix. These citadels of learning grew up in the Middle Ages and still reflect the freedoms from which they evolved. Sometimes trying to find basic information becomes a Kafkaesque journey. This is not meant as a critical remark but as an accurate observation in which almost any professor will agree.

Traditionally, the arts in universities exist in protected environments, the last refuge of the old patronage system that provided security for composers and artists during the Renaissance. Here students learn the basics of an art form and exercise their creative muses with hands-on projects. This is the ideal climate to experiment, break a few established rules, fail miserably, and then hopefully succeed with personal projects; projects that are not yet mega-dollar driven. But even in this cocoonlike atmosphere, there are still fundamental questions to ask when it comes to student film production.

A long ways from their days in the fledgling film departments of UCLA and USC, Francis Ford Coppola visits George Lucas and his friend R2D2 on the set of **Star Wars** (1977).

## Insurance

How much of the student production is covered by the blanket insurance policy of the university? It is assumed that if a production is connected to a course there is no concern about insurance coverage. Hopefully this is something about which the professor of the course or the chair of the department will be knowledgeable. Insurance will probably cover activities on campus but not necessarily off campus in the local community. Colleges often have different riders attached to the blanket policy that covers special activities on classrooms and labs but might not cover all activities that are part of a film production.

## Permissions

Because a student is making a film "just for a class," does this allow him or her to use the logo of a local business or international franchise or copyrighted music without permission? The answer is a resounding no. But of course it happens constantly. There are no reported instances in which a student has been forcibly apprehended by FBI agents during a class screening for using "Misirlou" by Dick Dale and His Del-Tones as background music. The only real problem with the everyone-does-it approach to student filmmaking is that it omits an important educational lesson in the labyrinthine process of securing rights, something that cannot be conveniently ignored for an independent production shot with the hope of finding a distributor.

Then there is the issue of on-campus permissions. Are all buildings on campus available for student productions? Does the college housed in a certain building have the right to give permission to shoot in this space, or must this permission be granted by a special department? Did someone alert the campus police department or security about the shoot? Hopefully common sense prevails, but there are certain circumstances that are like Sirens beckoning to young directors looking for that touch of *cinema verité*. Thus, to shoot a scene in a biology lab after hours or on the weekend might not be covered, and unauthorized areas should not be looked upon as invitations for rebel filmmakers to climb fences or to sneak into elevator shafts.

In this day and age, it is exceedingly unwise to run across campus with actors firing blanks as part of a staged shootout or to enact a mock kidnapping to just to capture real-life shock reactions from fellow students. These are only a sample of issues that might cause an outcry from university officials. The public image of a university is sacrosanct. A film company that wants to shoot on a campus must submit the screenplay for approval. If the script is about drugs, sex, and graphic violence, not surprisingly, these are not images the university wants to be seen by people around the world. The smart student will make a short that reflects a unique and personal viewpoint and not be another post-noir imitation of *Reservoir Dogs*.

## Copyright and Other Issues

Who owns the copyright on a student film? The University of Southern California holds the copyright on student films. This is due to the power of USC to promote student projects directly to the film industry. This promotional clout is one of the key reasons students apply to this internationally known film school. However, not all schools can claim George Lucas as an alumnus. Only a select few film programs have this high visibility to catch the attention of industry professionals.

The legal debate over the ownership of copyrights stems from the dual situation of students creating and shooting projects with equipment provided by the school. One argument is that cameras, lights, and editing equipment are the tools of the artist, the same as brushes and paint. The other argument is that watercolors do not sell for a million dollars. A student grateful to the university for jump-starting a career in the film industry will probably turn around in later years and give back to the place that was his or her cultural learning ground.

The issue is over student projects that are feature length and can be submitted to festivals. A ten-minute film is a calling card to show off a student's abilities if the student is fortunate enough to make professional contacts. In the 1990s, shorts like *George Lucas in Love* and *405* became pop hits because of the Internet and started a land rush to make short films that would catch the attention of industry titans. None of the shorts that became an overnight cult phenomenon made the filmmakers wealthy or led to lucrative contracts. The Internet popularized the short film but the landslide of shorts that followed overwhelmed industry insiders. This early love affair with the Internet has waned. Now only a few lucky filmmakers attract the cherished one minute of fame for an inventive short subject.

The film school has become a magnet for the motion picture industry. If the school has a high reputation, then industry professionals will watch the winners of the student film competitions in search of new talent. Thus, if the school attracts major attention, then the school owning the copyright makes sense because it can funnel the student projects toward a professional outlet. As a result, a hundred students are not making a hundred inquiries to DreamWorks at the end of each semester. There is one showcase for industry executives or representatives. This approach is neat and direct and saves time, which is a precious factor in the film business.

A ten- to twenty-minute short is the perfect demo for a student. To really refine a film to ten minutes or less is a daunting challenge. A short today is up against incredible international competition. The reality is that features, if they are lucky, sometimes only have ten minutes of memorable footage. A feature film is a very different animal and not a good calling card unless it is placed in a festival. The goal of winning an honor at a festival is to find a distributor. This scenario becomes a problem, because the school has supplied the equipment for the student to make a full-length entertainment piece that might attract a significant financial reward to the student and not the school.

Checking on a school's philosophy about copyright ownership is only one of the considerations for finding the right film school. It is very wise to kick the tires of a school that has a focus on film. This is still an evolving form of education, unlike theater and the other arts. Students who attend UCLA, USC, or NYU have a decisive advantage over other students. The film industry is only a few miles away, so important guest lecturers or professors work directly with the students. Former graduates that have made a name in the industry often have a soft spot for the next generation of young filmmakers. The reputation of the school is highly important. It means the faculty has been doing something right in preparing students for the professional world, whether in the mainstream or independent production.

In the last decade, film programs have grown very rapidly, which is both good and bad. Some have developed out of theater departments where film courses might have spent many years as ignored stepchildren. It is important to check out the dean's support of film and the chair's background in either film studies or production. Go online and read the résumés of the staff. This does not mean every professor will have strong film credits. There are many excellent teachers that know the subject and know how to motivate students to superior work. Ask a lot of questions.

Take the time to see how effective the department has been at placing students in good positions. Does the school have relationships with studios, television networks and production companies for apprenticeships or job placement? And what kind of filmmaking does the school teach? There are some programs that have an anti-Hollywood philosophical slant toward filmmaking, meaning they focus on art films and frown on films with the trappings of commercial blockbusters. Ideally, a good school will encourage all forms of filmmaking and at the same time give students an awareness of the classic motion pictures that started it all.

## The Next Steven Spielberg

There is one person that everybody in the film industry looks for: the underdog that appears out of nowhere with a brilliant short or an ingeniously clever screenplay. Film schools until the early 1970s were not taken seriously, but then Lucas and Francis Ford Coppola put them on the map. Since then, a school—either far away or next door to Hollywood—can have the world knocking at its door because of one student.

Film history is full of tales about a single individual that spun moviemaking off in a new direction. Alfred Hitchcock, Orson Welles, Elia Kazan, Ingmar Bergman, Federico Fellini, Jean-Luc Godard, Dennis Hopper, Francis Ford Coppola, Steven Spielberg, George Lucas, and Quentin Tarantino are just a few directors that altered the concept of film forever. The student whose name might appear next on this list needs to be focused and ready for the opportunity. Universities often tend to overly praise students and consequently not fully prepare them for the hard knocks of breaking into the business. A student can use the tools and talent provided by a film school, but a true understanding of film is still a personal journey self-motivated by the hunger to learn everything possible with a tenacious determination.

# PART TWO

# DEVELOPMENT

A movie is three good scenes
and no bad scenes.

—Howard Hawks

# CHAPTER THREE

# STORY DEVELOPMENT AND RIGHTS

> 66 Nobody knows anything. 99
>
> —William Goldman

## Motion Picture Development, Part 1: The Property

A piece of exceptional writing that has the potential of attracting millions of dollars from enthusiastic investors is known by the unexciting, battleship-gray title of *property*. This is the starting point and the creative flint for any motion picture or television show. It is known simply as *the story*. The story can originate from a novel, nonfiction book, magazine article, short story, screenplay, or a treatment that is only one paragraph long. The essence of the story will eventually be boiled down to its bare bones. For example, in *TV Guide*, a classic movie that makes audiences laugh or cry and is full of unexpected plot twists and memorable dialogue is reduced to one sentence: "Heartbroken nightclub owner gets second chance at love in war-torn Casablanca."

A story that is fresh and unique to the movie-going public is potentially worth a king's ransom. Everybody potentially wants it. The ultimate ownership of the story is what transforms it into a *property*. Like ocean-front real estate in Malibu, a story can fetch high dollars for a writer that sits down and conjures an original idea or a new twist on an old genre. Instead of land, the development becomes an *intellectual property*.

To prove ownership of property in Malibu, the owner must register it with the state land office. The ownership of a story, put into the form of a screenplay, novel, graphic novel, or nonfiction book is secured by registering it with the Library of Congress, Copyright Office.

If the writer is lucky and has a good agent, this work can be sold outright to a studio, producer, or anyone with investment money. Once the story is sold it becomes the legal property of the owner, just like the sale of land. If the script has what is referred to as a "high concept" for a feature motion picture, it becomes the lure for movie stars, directors, and production companies.

So far, this process of writing and selling a story might appear straightforward. A good story should pop out like a vein of silver to anyone that reads it. If tangible objects have certain qualities that make them valuable and these qualities are recognized worldwide, then a good story must have familiar features that are obvious to everyone. This is when screenwriter William Goldman's legendary, battle-worn observation comes in: "Nobody knows anything."

If there was a surefire formula for stories, then bad movies would never be made. But somehow *Jaws: The Revenge, Howard the Duck,* and *The Adventures of Pluto Nash* were given the green light and large budgets, but *The Usual Suspects, American Beauty, Braveheart, Shakespeare in Love, Million Dollar Baby,* and *Brokeback Mountain* languished for years and were turned down by most studios before finally being made.

On any given day, hundred of writers are *pitching* story ideas to executives, which amounts to tens of thousands a year. Yet, the studios make less than one hundred movies a year, and this number has been decreasing. The movie industry is a global empire built on great stories that have been magically transformed into great movies. Yet, in recent years, with all these bright ideas available, the majority of the screenplays nominated for Academy Awards as original screenplays or adaptations not only do not stand the test of time, they disappear from popular viewing within a year.

To stack the number of stories that are turned into movies next to stories that have been optioned but never made is like putting a country cottage next to the Empire State Building. There are writers with homes in the Pacific Palisades that have made a fortune on options for story ideas—but never had a screenplay produced. The astounding thing, to go back to Mr. Goldman's observation, is that nobody buys a bad story idea. Everything that is optioned is a jewel in the beholder's eye. But for some unexplainable reason, most of these jewels turn into glass. To restore it to its original glister becomes a process known as *development.*

## Development: The Search

> Some films are slices of life, mine are slices of cake.
> —Alfred Hitchcock

In *To Kill a Mockingbird* (1962), Gregory Peck as small southern town attorney Atticus Finch attempts to calm an angry lynch mob, as his children witness the life-changing incident.

Development is the ultimate scavenger hunt. Every news story, magazine article, novel (new or classical), nonfiction book, graphic novel, comic book, old movie, play, biography, or personal family history is a potential movie. This does not include all the screenplays making the rounds, screenwriting Web sites, and option deals based on pitches. The search is frustrating and aggravating but, with a little fool's luck, highly rewarding. It is frustrating and aggravating because upon initial inspection most stories sound like potential movies.

Watch the news, and within thirty minutes there is social injustice, a new twist in the war against terrorism, political wrangling, disappearances, unsolved murders, natural disasters, and corporate greed, plus a human interest story about a pet dog that barked so much he scared off a potential kidnapper of a three-year-old child.

Upon first glance, all of these stories could make riveting, heartbreaking movies. But there is one classic problem handed down to us by the ancient Greeks: A great story needs a beginning, middle, and an end. The story about the brave barking dog is just that, a story about a barking dog—unless there is an element that makes it a full-blown story. For example, imagine *To Kill a*

*Mockingbird* without the children. The story would focus on the trial, which ends in a guilty verdict for a black man. The man is obviously innocent; but as tragic as this situation is, the events are sadly familiar to audiences.

What makes *To Kill a Mockingbird* a great story *is* the children. A young son and daughter are being raised by a dedicated father, Atticus Finch, during the hard years of the Great Depression after their mother's death. They are still innocent and live in a play world of childish imagination. The real story is about the painful loss of this innocence as they witness injustice perpetrated by the white citizens of their little southern town.

This is what *the search* in development is all about: to find a unique angle in a story. Potentially any story, even the seemingly most insignificant one, can be exceptional. It is all about how it is told and the point of view of the writer. If *Schindler's List* was told from the sole perception of Oskar Schindler, the movie would be about a man who sees terrible hardships but plays it safe by not exposing his compassion for the Jews being murdered around him, whereas the real heart of the story is about a group of Jews *who learn to trust a Nazi.* This is shown through Ben Kingsley's character, Itzhak Stern, who is the ultimate Doubting Thomas. So when Stern learns to like and eventually respect Schindler, it means something to the audience.

To test a good idea, ask the following questions: What is unique about it? What emotions will audiences experience if it is done well? Then there are other questions: Is it a story worth the investment of millions of dollars, even if it is a small independent film? Is the story worth spending two or three years fighting for and trying to get it produced? The answer to these latter questions is an immediate *yes* if the story takes fire and becomes an obsession. Before this happens, there must be a discovery about what the central core of the story is. This is when Goldman's infamous phrase raises its ugly head. After three thousand

years, there is still no magic formula about how to do this.

In the Galleria dell'Accademia in Florence, where the statue of *David* is housed, there is a hallway with large blocks of marble that Michelangelo started working on but never finished. Emerging from these blocks are beautifully sculpted arms and bits of human torso, but none of them are complete. Michelangelo wrote that inside every piece of marble there is a magnificent statue—and it was the artist's duty to find it. These unfinished works are amazing to study. But to Michelangelo they were like half-finished pieces of paper torn out of a typewriter by a frustrated writer.

If Goldman's observation is to be tested, then another artist should be able to finish the sculpture and receive acclaim without anyone recognizing the difference. But will it be as remarkable as if Michelangelo had completed it himself? Or will the best part of the sculpture be the arm that the master originally carved? There you have it. To live in a world where nobody knows anything is a maze of perpetual confusion.

## Structure and Point of View

> Once a month the
> sky falls on my head,
> I come to and I
> see another movie
> I want to make.
> —Steven Spielberg

To tell a story without structure is impossible. Every story begins and ends. There is no better definition of structure than this. It is a process that is made up, controlled, and manipulated, even if it is a documentary. The problem rests in that no man's land called the middle, that is, the Second Act. This stretch of land either becomes a tired old formula full of bombed out landscape or a place of suspense and excitement. In the pursuit of doing something that is fresh and unique, even if it is the retelling of an old genre tale, a few notions need to be discarded.

A screenplay has a fixed structure by its very nature. Sometimes writers try to deliberately avoid this structure because they do not want to write the typical "Hollywood trash." This is a noble objective, but it is also like claiming to write the world's longest haiku poem—after three lines, it is no longer a haiku. The popcorn clichés in movies should not be blamed on traditional structure.

For example, a masterpiece of the Italian Neorealism movement is *The Bicycle Thief,* directed by Vittorio De Sica. It is a devastating story about the hardships of a poor family in Rome after the war. There are no stars. Most of the actors were common people De Sica discovered on the streets. And the film was shot for a fraction of a Hollywood feature. Yet it has one of the most memorable, heartbreaking endings of any motion picture. *The Bicycle Thief* works because it is perfectly structured, and De Sica has cleverly manipulated the audience every step of the way.

If the idea of manipulating people does not sound artistic, then the whole purpose of art is missed. Every time people in a movie theater laugh out loud, or jump in surprise, or hold back a tear, this is the direct result of an artist setting them up. This goes back to the question of what an audience should feel, what is the emotional journey of the film? Should the audience leave the theater uplifted, with a smile on their collective faces? Or should they be teary eyed? Thoughtful and pensive? Outraged? Excited? Or perhaps have an overwhelming desire to hug the first stranger they see?

All of these reactions are the result of an assortment of clever old tricks. Knowing what you want the audience to feel is the pulse of the movie. It gives the film a purpose and direction. And to achieve this, "mind games" are played with the audience. Not playing these games successfully

***The Bicycle Thief*** (1948), directed by Vittorio De Sica, captures the look of post-War Italy, but the film's emotional power comes from carefully crafted story structure.

will result in audiences leaving the theater with the exasperated look of wasting eight dollars.

Once the decision has been made about the mood of the film, which is often an immediate gut reaction, the next thing to be determined is how the story should be told. What is the dramatic point of view? A linear structure is the form of most films, that is, starting on a particular day and moving forward in time. In *To Kill a Mockingbird,* the action begins on the day Atticus is approached by the local judge to defend Tom Robinson, a black man accused of raping a white woman. The point of view of what happens focuses on Scout, his daughter. In *The Bicycle Thief,* the film opens on a day when the father gets an opportunity for a better job—if he has a bicycle. The emotion center of the story is from point of view of his young son.

Within a linear structure, there can be the flashbacks to reveal information about one of the characters or the re-creation of an important event. Or a film can open in the present, flash back for the entire story, and end back in the present. This creates a bookend for the story. Perhaps the most famous example of this is Billy Wilder's

In **Pulp Fiction** (1994), director and co-author Quentin Tarantino plays with time and order to tell three different overlapping crime tales in a nonlinear format.

*Sunset Boulevard.* which opens with a shot of a dead man floating in a swimming pool; then the dead man proceeds to narrate the film through a long flashback that leads up to his murder—told entirely through his point of view.

Other films reveal information through flashbacks to provide insights to the main characters. *Forrest Gump* opens in the present, flashes back for almost two-thirds of the movie, returns to the present, and continues in a linear structure to the end. *GoodFellas* opens with a lengthy flashback or remembrance of the past with a voice-over. In both of these movies, the points of view are from the principal character. However, in Akira Kurosawa's classic *Rashomon*, the flashbacks tell four people's version of an incident involving murder, with four radically different, self-serving points of view.

Since the 1990s, the story line of a screenplay has been turned on its head. Movies like *Pulp Fiction, Go, The English Patient,* and *Memento* have mixed up the time order of the scenes and even told the story backward. There are rare examples of this in the past. *Citizen Kane* is told in a series of overlapping flashbacks by five people, plus a newsreel. The French New Wave classic *Last Year at Marienbad* moves backward, and even employs

*flash forwards* to interweave a love story. *Annie Hall* jumps back and forth in time, as Alvy Singer recalls the one woman in his life he never got over. And with the exceptions of *Memento* and *Annie Hall*, these films have multiple points of view.

These films work because *the story* demands an unorthodox approach. This seemingly disjointed approach is a difficult juggling act because each scene must fit perfectly into the puzzle, but it can have a very powerful effect on the audience. However, to mix up scenes just because Quentin Tarantino did it does not mean this is the right approach for an interesting story. With each of these films, the story was structured in a linear fashion, and then sequences were moved around to release important character information a little bit at time. In the case of *Memento*, the story is perfectly linear—only told backward.

Storytelling comes from an oral tradition than unfolds in a linear structure, with the central character being the hero, like Ulysses. So, a good way to start is to sit down with a tape recorder and tell the story. This can help map out the direction a story naturally wants to take. It will also give clues about the point of view of the story. In *Annie Hall*, the story jumps around like someone telling a tale of lost love to a stranger. Occasionally, the Woody Allen character, Alvy Singer, leaves out something and has to go back and pick it up. This is common when people tell a story about something that happened to them during a day. But upon closer examination, each sequence in *Annie Hall* is there for a specific reason; there is nothing random about the structure.

Going back to Michelangelo, the point of view is critical to finding the complete figure hiding inside the marble. If this discovery is made correctly, the audience is left with the feeling that there is no other way to have told the story. *Pulp Fiction* would be an anthology movie with three seemingly unrelated stories. *Annie Hall* would lose its personal charm if told straight and become ordinary. And *Memento* would be deadly dull if told in a linear fashion. However, *To Kill a Mockingbird* and *The Bicycle Thief* would lose their emotional centers if the story lines jumped around—as would almost all films.

Most films give the impression of being told by an omnipotent third person with the characters performing on a large stage. A basic element of a great story is to have a principal character that *forces the action forward. The Silence of the Lambs* is done without a voice-over and only two brief flashbacks. The story has a classic linear structure, and the camera work is passive, with a documentary approach—or so it would seem. Clarice Starling is the central character because it is through her journal that we get to know all the other characters, include the nightmarish Dr. Hannibal Lecter. The director Jonathan Demme cuts away from Starling to show "Buffalo Bill" Gumb, but this is an old Hitchcock trick to build suspense and heighten the danger when Starling finally encounters him.

Because the story follows Starling, Demme uses subtle camera placements to make the audience identify with her and occasionally shows the action through her eyes. Most shots of Jodie Foster are at a slightly upward angle to give her a greater presence in the male-dominated world she is working in. On her close-ups, she is looking almost directly into the camera lens, with the reverse-angle shots letting the audience see through her eyes—again, little tricks to bring the moviegoers into the drama, letting each person watching the film experience some of the fears and excitement inside the principal character—which arc usually emotions common to everyone.

During the development process, finding the dramatic structure and point of view of a story can turn an overly familiar tale into something fresh and exciting. Every story has this potential; it is just a matter of finding it. But for some inexplicable reason, these simple observations are allegedly what *nobody knows* and everyone is searching for.

> " I enjoy playing the audience like a piano.
> —Alfred Hitchcock "

If a writer woke up one morning with a million-dollar story idea and then was told he needed to walk into a room full of complete strangers and tell his story—well, the writer would think this was absolutely crazy.

Welcome to Hollywood. This happens a hundred times, maybe a thousand times a day in producers' offices around the world. It is called a *pitch* or *pitch session*. As the word suggests, this is a process of pitching an idea and seeing if anyone wants to catch it. This is when it is important for a writer to have taken at least one film acting class, because the pitch process is performance art.

A new writer going out in the wilds of the corporate jungle for the first time is usually given three minutes to pitch a story concept. There are screenwriting expos where thousands of hopeful writers will pitch three-minute ideas over a two- or three-day period to maybe a hundred production or development assistants. Just by sheer volume, the process has an incredible numbing effect on the listener. This is where the acting lessons come in. It is not a matter of telling a good story and having someone recognize the box office potential. This is telling a story while balancing with one foot on a tightrope, without a net below, and juggling flaming torches. In other words, be excited about your idea, because if the idea does not excite you—then it won't excite anyone.

A very common reaction to this process is: Wait a minute, this is not fair, some people tell stories better than other people. After all, in a perfect world, a writer should be judged on his or her *writing*—period! Both of these observations are unquestionably correct, but this means nothing in Hollywood.

The process of pitching story ideas is the direct result of highly successful screenwriters like William Goldman and Shane Black. Goldman back in 1969 sold his spec script *Butch Cassidy and the Sundance Kid* for $400,000, which would amount to a cool million today. Then, in 1987, Black, fresh out of UCLA at the age of twenty-two, sold *Lethal Weapon* for $250,000. Over the next nine years, he sold three more spec scripts for $1 million, $1.75 million, and $2 million. This, along with a few other urban legends about writers who had met with similar windfall fortunes, set off the second California gold rush. Only this time it was *spec screenplays*, and the rush has only gotten bigger over the years. And both of these writers did it with—*their writing*.

This is when the pitch comes in. Reading the tidal wave of screenplays year after year is impossible, even for the most hands-on producers. Readers are hired to plow through the endless piles of screenplays and write coverage on each one. But there are several problems with the screenplay, the biggest being that the formatting demands of a script do not always capture the excitement a writer feels when trying to fill up pages with carefully selected words. The overly used but true phrase that a screenplay is a blueprint for a movie is absolutely true. A well-written screenplay can move like gangbusters, but it is still full of impassive slug lines and the action lines need to be lean and short on descriptions.

The oral tradition of storytelling is probably the oldest of all the arts. There is nothing like hearing a good story from an enthusiastic spinner of yarns. Pitching a good idea for a movie has been around since the very beginning. The first flickers were nothing more than an idea turned into action. There were no scripts or treatments. Try to find anything resembling a screenplay for the comic two-reelers of the Keystone Kops or Buster Keaton. Eventually the pitch became a selling tool. Julius and Philip Epstein met with David O. Selznick and pitched *Casablanca* for hours in hopes of getting Ingrid Bergman for the lead, which was not an easy feat because there was no finished screenplay.

Pitching an idea to a producer for an hour or more takes the same amount of time as it does to read a script. Writers with track records, or those that have recent hits, are given the privilege of lengthy visits to elaborate on new story ideas. Pros are the best resources for a producer seeking the next blockbuster. A writer (or a writing team) familiar with this exclusive, high-pressure brand of performance is a modern Homer in a royal court.

The writer will sit or wander about a plush office and tell the three acts of the story in vigorous details. But it is the toughest audience in the world. The performance has to be recalibrated dozens of times if the producer or executives show a flicker of boredom. Often the writer is interrupted with troublesome questions or observations that indicate the story might not be completely baby-new or original. This is why over the years pitches have gotten shorter as the number of spec scripts have grown.

## The Three-Minute Pitch

> " Give me any two pages of the Bible and I'll give you a picture. "
> —Cecil B. DeMille

The three-minute pitch, the same length as a song, is pure snake-oil salesmanship. It is a lively description of Act One, establishing the major characters and ending with the setup, thus creating a cliffhanger for the listener. A good mental concept is to imagine that you are on the top floor of the Empire State Building and Steven Spielberg steps into the elevator with you. It is just the two of you, and you have until the elevator descends to the ground floor to tell him your idea. (This is only a mental exercise, remember.) The desired effect is to have the listener request a copy of the screenplay when the pitch is over. Here are a few things to consider:

**Step 1.** Give a one-line overview of the story to establish the genre and the general story arc. This is called the *tagline*—and it can be two lines, but keep it brief, to the point, and memorable. This is often the hardest writing of all.

**Step 2.** Describe how the story begins. This is the hook that grabs the audience during the first ten minutes.

**Step 3.** Introduce the principal character. Do not use star names, but a line or two of clever character background will give the listener a strong casting image to work with.

**Step 4.** Introduce the protagonist and give a few well-phrased clues to show off the uniqueness of the character. This can range from criminal masterminds to great white sharks.

**Step 5.** Then tell how these adverse forces are headed toward a collision course. This is the meat of the story that will fuel the second and third acts.

**Step 6.** End with the *conflict*, which completes the *setup* or Act One. This is the moment when the principal character's life is taken out of his or her control until the resolution or showdown of the movie.

## Conflict

This sometimes is the hardest plot point for writers to understand. A conflict must *take control away from the principal character*. This motivates

action as the character attempts to regain control. A person dying is not dramatic conflict; it is a sad part of real life. An estranged son trying to come to terms with his dying father is dramatic conflict (*Five Easy Pieces*). A wife leaving her husband is real-life conflict. A wife leaving her husband *and her son* is dramatic conflict (*Kramer vs. Kramer*). A New York cop visiting his estranged wife in Los Angeles on Christmas Eve is not conflict. A New York cop in a building taken over by ruthless robbers on Christmas Eve *and his estranged wife is one of the hostages* is conflict (*Die Hard*).

### Bad Three-Minute Pitches

This egg-timer approach to tantalizing someone with a story works best with high-concept ideas—ideas that have the smell of buttered popcorn about them. Independent film ideas are often not served well by this approach. Movies like *Fargo, Sideways, Lost in Translation,* and *Eternal Sunshine of the Spotless Mind* would definitely not make good three-minute pitches. And movies that have nonlinear plot structures could end up being more babble than coherent storytelling.

### Three Essential Things to Remember

*Number One*   Rehearse, rehearse, and rehearse. To stroll into a producer's office and wing a pitch is asking for a loud gong to chime and the trapdoor in the floor to swing open. Rehearse the pitch with friends, relatives, and fellow writers to get comfortable and find ways to tighten the presentation. Stand in front of a mirror and tell the story to yourself and afterward consider if you would have optioned the idea based on what you just saw. The "cottonmouth factor" will slow a story down in a room full of glaring executives. The cool nerves of a writer can quickly fray if not well rehearsed. An invitation to give a pitch is an opportunity worth taking seriously, and the people who listen to pitches daily know who has prepared and who has not.

*Each Dawn I Die* (1939) and *The Shawshank Redemption* (1994) show how genres are reinvented but keep many of the original characteristics, in this case an ambitious warden locking horns with a troublesome prisoner.

***Number 2*** Know the whole story—and rehearse the whole story. There is no sadder sight than a writer who has pitched a terrific setup but is then asked by the listener to keep going and tell the whole thing—the look of fear is unmistakable. If the writer is not prepared to comfortably continue with the tale, all the good karma previously established goes straight into the trash can. Think through the story and know the plot points.

***Number Three*** If the story sounds like the plot to another movie—*fix it.* Genre movies have certain notable characteristics, so genre films are easy to pitch because the listener has an immediate inside track to the structural makeup of the story. Every genre has an established look and familiar characters; but because most genres were popularized during the Studio System, the plotlines have become cookie cutters for stories in which the writer must add something new to the formula. The great genre films have many of the same earmark ingredients, so the filmmaker must reinvent the genre with unexpected twists and three-dimensional characters that make the experience fresh and emotional to a new generation of moviegoers. Compare *Each Dawn I Die* (1939), an early prison genre film, with *The Shawshank Redemption* (1994) to see how much they are alike and how vastly different they are. Keep working your pitch

until it is transformed from the commonplace to the exceptional.

## Motion Picture Development, Part 3: Treatments

> If Hollywood didn't work out, I was prepared to be the best secretary in the world.
> —Bette Davis

Treatments come in three basic sizes: one page, five to ten pages, and full length or "the bible." During the silent era, before the formal screenplays emerged with the coming of sound, a writer, director, or producer would jot down ideas for a movie. These notes were similar to a short story and were the guidelines for the plot and character action. Sometimes the notes were just that, a checklist of sight gags for a two-reeler comedy. Exactly when these notes became known

## *Casablanca* in Three Minutes

Casablanca is a neutral city on the eve before America enters World War II. We open by getting to know a few of the colorful characters, from pickpockets to smugglers to frightened refugees to coldhearted Nazis.

In Casablanca, everyone goes to Rick's Café, an oasis in this turbulent time, for drinks, music, and backroom gambling. There we meet Sam the piano player, a crazy Russian bartender, and others who have fled their beloved homelands for the chance to reach America. One of the frequent guests is Capt. Renault, an amusing but corrupt French official. On this night, he is there to arrest a nervous, bug-eyed little man who has mysteriously scored two letters of transit—the only official guarantees out of Casablanca.

Enter Rick, a man everyone admires and envies but a man with a dark past, a man whose heart has turned to stone because of a woman. Rick agrees to hold the letters of transit in his café for safekeeping—for one night only. But later that evening, the little man is arrested in a raid and later killed by the Nazis. Now Rick has the letters, the most desired items in Casablanca because they mean freedom to whoever possesses them. In the bustling black market, they are worth a king's ransom.

Then, unexpectedly, the woman who left Rick in Paris, the only woman he truly loved, walks into his café—with her husband. The husband is a legendary member of the French underground, but he is trapped in Casablanca unless a miracle happens. His only hope is the letters of transit held by Rick—who has no intention of giving them up.

as treatments has been lost in time, but the term appears in memos from studio moguls in the early 1930s.

### Full Treatment or "The Bible"

When sound arrived, the studios hired writers on long-term contracts like they did actors and directors. The writers quickly fell into two categories: Adaptations or Original Stories. More than any other aspect of film production, the studio screenplays were truly an assembly-line product. One writer might dream up an original idea; a different writer would do the screenplay; and additional writers might come in for specialty touches like love scenes, action sequences, or comic bits.

The Academy Awards divided the writing honors into Adaptation and Original Story from 1927 to 1934. An adaptation was a screenplay based on another source, including an original story treatment. However, an original story could either be a completed screenplay or a treatment for a screenplay. To eliminate this confusion, starting in 1935, best Screenplay and best Original Story awards were presented. So a movie could be nominated in two writing categories. For example, *Mr. Smith Goes to Washington* was nominated for best Original Story (it won) and best Screenplay (lost to *Gone with the Wind*). Thus, the writer of the full treatment for *Mr. Smith Goes to Washington* won in his category, but the writer of the actual screenplay lost in his.

Then, from 1940 to 1956, there were three awards given: Original Story, Screenplay, and Original Screenplay. This last category was later listed as Story and Screenplay, meaning the same writers thought of the idea and wrote the screenplay. Then in 1957, the Original Story was eliminated, and since then there have been two

Dalton Trumbo (wearing glasses), whose uncredited screenplays would win two Oscars during the Blacklist Era, waits for the train to take him and the other Hollywood Ten to prison for contempt of court.

categories, one for screenplays "based on material from another medium" and the other for screenplays "written directly for the screen." However, the credit for original story did not disappear; it was folded into Story and Screenplay. Today, a writer can still get credit in this category for a story idea but not be listed for writing the screenplay.

The most famous example of a writer winning for Original Story is Dalton Trumbo, who was blacklisted during the 1950s. His original story treatment for *Roman Holiday* won and was accepted by his "front" Ian McLellan (who actually co-wrote the screenplay but lost). And three years later, his original story treatment for *The Brave One* won under the alias Robert Rich. The Oscar went unclaimed because no such person existed. Trumbo was finally given the award for *The Brave One* in 1975, but the mystery about *Roman Holiday* was not revealed until McLellan's death. Trumbo's widow was given his posthumous Oscar in 1993.

A full treatment or "scriptment" as it sometimes referred to, is essentially a novella. It is around sixty pages long and describes in a narrative form each scene of the movie. Unlike a screenplay, there are no restrictions on the length of character or scenic location descriptions. In fact, biographical background and the dramatic mood of the scenes are encouraged, thus making for a much more compelling read than a screenplay.

During the Studio System, almost every potential motion picture had a full-treatment workup. Novels were usually bought for the title and general story line. A studio writer was assigned to whittle down the story and all the sub-plots to a tale that could be told in two hours. There were sections with dialogue to give a flavor of the characters' language, but the job of creating all the dialogue was saved for the next phase when the screenwriter took over. Often (as still happens) the end result is only "inspired by" the novel.

Once the full treatment was approved by the head of production, the characters and story line were locked down. Only minor adjustments could be made to the story after this; thus, the long treatment was given the nickname "the bible." This was a producer's tool. Everybody took their marching orders from "the bible," especially the actual screenwriter and production manager. What was described in the treatment had better be on the screen, unless the head of production signed off on the changes. By the late 1960s, this procedure changed as freelance writers turned in original screenplays instead of full treatments for motion pictures.

## One-Page Treatment

What is still used in motion picture development is the short treatment. The one-page treatment is deceptively hard to write, and a writer might spend as much time playing with this as an entire screenplay. This is a bare-bones description of the story. It has a lot in common with the three-minute pitch. In fact, a one-page treatment can be described as "the dialogue" for a short pitch. A pitch is usually more informal in the language, whereas a treatment is a polished piece of writing. They both cover the same ground and are designed as teasers to interest a party in reading the screenplay.

# Tips on Writing a One-Page Treatment

- The treatment should be single-spaced in Times New Roman, using a 12 font.
- The title of the screenplay should be centered in **bold** at the top of the page.
- One space centered under the title is the credit line:

  An Original Screenplay by [Writer's Name]
- Do not use this format if the story is an adaptation; this is only for original ideas. An adaptation is a separate issue covered under intellectual property rights.
- Go down two spaces and begin writing the treatment.
- Do not go over one page.
- Try to leave space at the bottom for contact information.
- Keep working until the story is as tight as possible.
- Do not spend time describing the main characters; this is all about story.
- However, give your principal character a powerful one-line description but not physical; focus on one aspect that would make the character compelling to play.
- Give the names of your main characters if this helps streamline your narrative.
- Do not suggest stars for any of the roles.
- Do not use dialogue unless it is a potentially quotable phrase, for example, "Make my day."
- Do not use profanity in your narrative; save this for the screenplay dialogue.
- Do not try to fit in the subplots; stick to the main story.
- A three-minute pitch covers the story until the setup (moment of conflict).
- A one-page treatment generally covers the arch of the whole story, however.
- Do not give the climax away; leave this as a cliffhanger for the reader.
- Try to use your title several times in the description so it sticks in the reader's mind.
- Open with a plotline or tagline, that is, a one- or two-sentence overview of the story.
- Skip a line and start a new paragraph that distills the setup into roughly two hundred words.
- And then in short paragraphs describe the action leading up to the climax.
- Again, leave readers curious about what happens (let them read the screenplay to see how everything ends).

The reason a one-page treatment is potentially difficult to write is because it funnels a 120-page screenplay down into less than four hundred words. These words need to sparkle. This does not mean "purple pose," it means that these well-chosen words have to summarize the dramatic conflict of the screenplay with vigor. What the reader is looking for is an acorn that will grow into a feature motion picture. This might be an overused metaphor, but it is precisely what a short treatment is meant to convey.

After the treatment is finished, put it away for a week and then re-read it. Keep working until it is as smooth as possible. Though it is tempting, do not write about the anguish or unusual psychological makeup of your main character. The one-page treatment is a tool to sell a *story*, not a biography. A really good treatment is a perfect piece of writing in which every word has been carefully selected for maximum impact.

# Moving Target

### An Original Screenplay by Ron Newcomer

## Plotline

To avenge the murder of his longtime friend, a person he considered the father he never knew, Eddie Martin lures the killers into lethal traps in small numbers, until the man responsible is forced to come out of hiding. Then, at the most dangerous moment in his life, he meets the woman he has been looking for all his life.

*　　*　　*

Eddie Martin is a business partner, close friend, and bodyguard to a man named Big Sam. In fact, Sam, an old school curmudgeon that has a love for high adventure out of the pages of Hemingway, has over the years become the father figure that Eddie never knew. Eddie spent years in covert operations for the Special Forces but had lost his direction in life when he accidentally ran into Sam. He always credited his stubborn old friend with giving him back the desire to live.

When Sam is brutally killed, Eddie promises him that he will avenge his death. This is not an idle promise. With his military background, Eddie is perhaps the most dangerous man alive. With nothing to lose, he starts his revenge by stealing the blood money from the men responsible for Sam's violent murder. This sets into motion a nonstop chase from New York to Key West. To lure some of the men responsible into the open, he calls in his whereabouts daily, setting traps for the hit men that show up in small teams. His plan is to dwindle down the odds and eventually draw out the one man responsible after no one else is left standing.

Sam and Eddie had talked about going deep-sea fishing in Key West, like Hemingway. As a personal tribute to his dead friend, Eddie takes a break from exacting vengeance to go fishing. He rents a boat run by a young woman named Mandy, who has become prematurely hardened by the unfulfilling day-to-day life she has been leading. Eddie finds that his personal homage to Sam is bittersweet without his old friend around to argue the finer points of life. He is prepared to get back to the business of revenge when some of the hit men discover where he has been hiding.

During a shootout, Eddie inadvertently involves Mandy in his deadly game. With no options left, she is forced to go on the run with him. What happens next, over a series of violent narrow escapes, begins a gritty, film noir Cinderella story. Eddie discovers that at the most dangerous moment in his life, he has met the woman he has been looking for all his life. Now, with the best hit men in the world after them, all he has to do is to make sure he doesn't lose someone else that he deeply cares for a second time.

*Moving Target* is a rapid-fire crime story that keeps pushing the accelerator to the floor. It is peppered with raw humor, swift violence, and an off-beat love story of two opposites that attract with unexpected consequences.

## What's in a Name?

The reason the names of main characters might fit into this tight format is because a well-thought-out name has a lot of descriptive power. The name given to a certain character reflects his or her personality. With just a name, the reader can envision a character type. Here are a few examples: Captain John H. Miller (*Saving Private Ryan*), John McClane (*Die Hard*), Atticus Finch (*To Kill a Mockingbird*), Elwood P. Dowd (*Harvey*), Margo Channing (*All About Eve*), Harry Lime (*The Third Man*), Ripley (*Alien*), John Foster Kane (*Citizen Kane*), Jack Sparrow (*Pirates of the Caribbean*), and Scarlett O'Hara (*Gone with the Wind*).

## Narrative Style

Another way to get more mileage out of a one-page treatment is to write in the "literary style" that suggests the genre of the movie. This should be subtle but in a style that hints at the tone of the story. This will help translate to visuals in the reader's mind. If the story is a fast-paced action or crime thriller, write in short sentences with "tough guy" words (*but no profanity*), like a passage out of a Raymond Chandler or Stephen King novel. If the story is a comedy, then make your sentences light with occasional touches of humor, like Erma Bombeck or P. G. Wodehouse. If the story is a period piece, set perhaps in ancient Rome or during the French Revolution, then use fuller sentences, suggesting a touch of Alexandre Dumas or Charles Dickens.

## Five- to 10-Page Treatment

If the one-page treatment is successful, then hopefully the reader(s) will ask for a screenplay. A longer treatment, which can be five to ten pages, is really a tool for the writer. This process is twofold. Writing the story out in detail will force the screenwriter to imagine all of the dramatic action. The one-page treatment is a compact version of the story with no frills. The longer treatment should expand on this and outline if not each scene then each sequence of the movie's action, including subplots.

As with the one-page treatment, stick to the story and not the makeup of the characters. In a screenplay, character is defined—or redefined—by action. One of the reasons *Crime and Punishment* has not been made into blockbuster (with all due respect to Mr. Dostoyevsky) is because there are about two pages of action and seven hundred pages of character conflict. It is a great novel, a masterpiece of literature, and a perfect example of the differences between the two art forms.

Imagining all of the plot points in a longer treatment is a test of how strong the story is. Stories usually hit a writer in creative spurts. By describing the action over five to ten pages will reveal potential potholes, dead ends, and the ghost of old movie clichés. By working out all the shaky plot moments, not only is the story stronger but the writer now has the ammunition to keep talking if a producer likes the three-minute pitch and cannot wait to hear more.

The second reason to write a longer treatment is protection. The Writers Guild of America (WGA) will allow members and nonmembers to register treatments. There is no copyright protection for a short treatment, unless it is a full-treatment sixty pages or more and filed as a novella. With the WGA it is the same fee to register a one-page treatment or a ten-page treatment. A short treatment gives an overview of a story, and there can—and always will be—other writers with similar ideas. A longer treatment has worked out story problems and takes on the vision of a single writer. Thus, to register a longer treatment gives extra protection, just in case.

# Proposal for a Television Series

> "I hate television. I hate it as much as peanuts. But I can't stop eating peanuts."
>
> —Orson Welles

A proposal for a television series is comprised of a show overview treatment; brief episode treatments; biographical profiles; and, ideally, a full pilot episode. This format is used for sitcoms and episodic hour-long series. There are variations on this format, depending naturally on the track record of the individual pitching the concept.

## Title Page

The title page has the name of the series, the person or persons presenting the proposal, and contact information.

## Series Overview

This is a one-page treatment that gives a sense of the characters, the genre, and the ongoing story line of the series.

## First Episode Treatment or Pilot

This is a five- to seven-page double-spaced treatment detailing the story line that will launch the series, outlining the act structure of the show. If the show is a dramatic series, then the ending can be a cliffhanger. *Hill Street Blues* (1981–1987) was one of the first night-time dramas to use a continuing story line. Until then, hour-long shows had a self-contained plot for each episode because there were few opportunities for audiences to catch a missed show. This changed with the boom in syndication marketing. Now many television series are like old-time Saturday matinee serials that leave the viewer in suspense each week, such as *24, Lost, Heroes,* and *Battlestar Galactica.* In addition to the treatment, it is best to have the completed pilot script. The pilot will showcase the writing style and the interaction between the main characters. Many ideas can sound alike in a treatment; thus, a pilot script will clearly demonstrate a fresh approach to a popular genre.

## Brief Biographies of Major and Reoccurring Characters

Starting in the order of importance, give the name of the character, followed by a brief single-spaced description of his or her personality. Do not go into the physical descriptions of the characters because this can limit the casting possibilities—many television directors and producers love to cast against type. In no more than fifty words, give a short biography of each character, focusing on the personality traits that might weave into the plot of future episodes. Like the novel, television series can explore characters in greater detail over a long time period. *M\*A\*S\*H, Cheers, Law and Order,* and *NYPD Blue* ran for more than ten years. Look at all the changes the characters in these series went through—and how they also remained remarkably true to themselves.

## Summaries of Eight to Twelve Episodes

The concern for any television series is to have enough story conflict to carry it for years of good ratings. The description of each episode should be about a hundred words, single-spaced. These are short teasers to let the reader know the series has lots of material to mine, or "legs" to continue. If the proposal is for a sitcom, this becomes difficult because each show is a self-contained story situation. There can be spillover story lines, like with *Frasier* or *Friends,* but each episode is a self-contained story. Because most American sitcoms, going back to *I Love Lucy,* are about domestic situations, this field has been plowed over and over. However, sitcoms have been pronounced dead many times, but then a *Home Improvement* or *Everybody Loves Raymond* comes along and revitalizes the genre. If the proposal is for episodic hour-long television, this is a

# 2033

### Series Treatment by Ron Newcomer

## Tagline

*2033* uses the potential evolution of real science and technology to project what crime investigation might be like in twenty-five years. The focus is on Vladimir Jabokov, Head of International Criminal Technology in Los Angeles, and a group of eccentric professors and scientists from around the world who form a think tank to predict the next wave of crime and terrorism. Each of these individuals is a specialist in a certain field—and each has a dark personal history that at times threatens to compromise the cases he or she is involved with.

## Synopsis

To certain radical organizations, *2033* is the true year of the Apocalypse because it represents the two-thousandth anniversary of Christ's death and resurrection. Vladimir Jabokov realizes the significance of this year will trigger a series of widespread terrorist attacks. The sophistication of these attacks goes way beyond suicide and car bombings or the threats of suitcase nukes. In the years leading up to *2033,* America has become ultra secure along its borders as a backlash resulting from a series of homeland attacks dating back twenty years. Eyes-in-the-Sky now scan every inch of the United States for illegal aliens and smugglers. Cell phones, map navigators and personal computers are monitored daily to track the whereabouts and activities of the vast majority of citizens. Technology has made America safe—and it is this technology that is the target.

With technology terrorism, anything supported by a satellite or a computer can be compromised. This means every conceivable aspect of daily life that is taken for granted can be shut down in the blink of an eye. Lights, cell phones, airplanes, and Wall Street all depend on computers; but this technology has grown so fast it has left a giant underbelly vulnerable to a new generation of tech weapons. A group identified as "Twenty Thirty-three" is behind a series of attacks using highly trained children to instigate them. Vladimir and the members of his think tank with International Criminal Technology find themselves in the front lines of this wave of techno-terrorism. They must somehow outthink an enemy that has planned these attacks for decades.

Using science fact, each episode of *2033* explores what crime-fighting methods might really be like in the world of tomorrow. The thrust of the series is the continual effort to stop "Twenty Thirty-three." In addition, each episode will have a complete story line involving the future methods that could be used in crime scene investigation, forensic science, police enforcement, the legal system, politics, entertainment, and international security. The principal characters are a band of eccentric geniuses who approach their jobs with humor and take great delight in frustrating the traditional channels in an increasingly bureaucratic government. They have been handpicked because their past experiences give them unique insights—but some of these experiences have given them emotional scars that might jeopardize their powers of objective reason.

little easier to write because there is not the restriction of focusing on primarily domestic situations. With so many cable channels now producing series, almost any genre is waiting for innovative reinvention.

## Motion Picture Development, Part 4: Assembling the Screenplay

### Is There a Script Doctor in the House?

> " If I wasn't the head of a studio, who would talk with me? "
>
> —Harry Cohn

Harry Cohn, the head of Columbia Pictures during the Studio Era, once remarked, "I have a foolproof device for judging whether a picture is good or bad. If my fanny squirms, it's bad. If my fanny doesn't squirm, it's good. It's as simple as that." To which Herman Mankiewicz, the co-author of *Citizen Kane* and infamous raconteur, replied, "Imagine. The whole world wired to Harry Cohn's ass!" Whatever his methods, it is undeniable that Cohn knew a good picture when he saw it, including *It Happened One Night, Mr. Smith Goes to Washington, His Girl Friday, Gilda, From Here to Eternity, On the Waterfront,* and *The Bridge on the River Kwai.* Like the old studio moguls, Cohn grew up in the movie business and his decisions were absolute.

As the moguls retired or passed away, there was no one else quite like them to fill the gap. These men had literally invented the popular movie genres and formed the Dream Factories that turned out something for everyone. By instinct, they knew what worked and what needed work. There are stories that after Walt Disney's

Though Walt Disney, seen here with a good-humored Donald Duck, is not perceived as a tough studio mogul like Harry Cohn or Louis B. Mayer, he shared with these industry pioneers the ability to develop a great story.

death the lights in the production conference rooms would be on late at night as anxious executives tried to figure out "what Walt would do."

The studio heads that followed did not come by this knack for the movie business as instinctively. As the old Studio System faded, the empty offices were filled with production companies that co-produced under the studio logo. These companies were given *development deals.* The arrangements can be complicated, depending on the box office track record of the company or producer. This, of course, is what matters the most. In the simplest terms the studio advances money to the production company to come up with prestige projects that could be made into successful features.

Because writers were no longer under long-term contracts with studios, this began the process of getting stories from the growing number of *spec scripts,* or screenplays by independent writers that wrote without up-front fees with the hopeful speculation they could sell something. Because many of the younger writers were still green, with no moviemaking experience, and because during this transitional period books and workshops about screenwriting did not exist, the properties that were bought or optioned had a core of good ideas but needed rewriting—or so someone with a production company believed. The rewrites were given to old pros with screen credits.

Looking back on the Studio System, there is the feeling that these men did *know something.* Irving Thalberg, Louis B. Mayer, Darryl Zanuck, David O. Selznick, Harry Cohn, Jack Warner, and Walt Disney certainly had misses, but overall they possessed a magic touch for making good films, many of which still endure a half-century or more later. When the old system died, so did the assembly line for creating in-house screenplays. After this era, story ideas and screenplays were brought from the outside and squeezed through a process of development. This process is akin to piecing together the Frankenstein monster.

Once a production company secures a property, the original writer might be given the opportunity to work with the producers and perhaps the director on a rewrite. If the writer is without experience, this process can be incredibly intimidating and can result in quick burnout. Then another writer is brought in to fix the problems (or the perceived problems) with the story. This is where the development process is infected with bugs. There has never been a writer in the recorded history of Hollywood that took a flat fee and then said, "The original screenplay worked perfectly and should be left alone."

Instead, the replacement writer, sometimes referred to as a script doctor, sews on a new arm to the Frankenstein monster. Sometimes this is enough, and sometimes the other arm falls off and thus this writer has to be replaced by yet another writer. Several writers later, the producer might decide to take a crack at the screenplay—after all,

this is the way David O. Selznick made *Gone with the Wind.* (Selznick, it should be pointed out, had been writing coverage and punching up scenes on screenplays since he was fourteen years old, giving him an edge over almost any producer before or since.) The inherent problem of a producer donning a writer's cap is that the individual responsible for objectivity is suddenly not in the captain's room steering the ship.

The process of rewrites, if it is not controlled by a strong producer who knows where true north is, can spin ludicrously out of control. Directors' wives begin making suggestions, actors improvise dialogue, and the process becomes a creative donnybrook. What can get lost very quickly is the original vision of the story or screenplay. Whatever was in the original had enough flash and sparkle to excite someone to option or purchase the property in the first place.

If the story is well-structured and every scene pushes the action forward, then to tamper with this structure will potentially throw off the balance of the story or cause characters to change motivations. To sit around with producers, their assistants, the director, and perhaps the line producer, cinematographer, and (hopefully) a writer, analyzing a screenplay can be an enlightening process if done with a clear comprehension of the story's journey. Or it can become a free-for-all in which everyone wants the screenplay to bend to certain specialized viewpoints. Thus the Frankenstein monster ends up with four arms and two heads.

Playing god with a story idea is intoxicating. Because almost everyone has grown up watching motion pictures and television incessantly, the "perfectly structured story" often gives the false illusion of being commonplace. Because *anybody* can tell a story, the next leap is that the art of storytelling must be easy—which is an assumption that effectively annihilates three thousand years of great writing. One of the reasons the renowned critic Pauline Kael stopped reviewing movies is because she felt the onslaught of mediocre to bad television shows had numbed the public's senses to great movie themes. This will always be an invitation for an argument, but there are certainly seeds of truth in Kael's concern.

From 1934 to 1948, people in America saw an average of one movie a week in theaters. With a short, cartoons, and newsreel, this was a visit of about three hours. By 1950, with the spectacular rise of television, people were suddenly watching the equivalent of three hours of shows per night. This could include the evening news, a couple of sitcoms, and an hour-long dramatic series. For those that stayed up late, there were old Hollywood movies. *Captain Kangaroo* and other kid programs started the morning, followed by soap operas and quiz shows. Thus, some people were watching—off and on—up to eight hours of television a day, when only a few years before this would have represented an entire month's worth of scripted entertainment.

Because the number of television shows increased so quickly, audiences accepted the inevitable fact that if one episode was not funny, it probably would be better the following week. If this drop in standard fare occurred for several weeks, then a new show would replace it. As this acceptance for inferior programs grew, and with so many shows to watch weekly, bad writing became a normal part of the viewing process. But because it was free, hey, what the heck.

Kael would probably agree that this onslaught of formula programming has left most people apathetic to the introspective dramas that were once the mizzenmast of classic theater. Now, everything has the illusion of being the same and this has gradually eroded the audience demand for story excellence. For centuries, playwrights were booed if they wrote something inferior. Today, movie patrons complain if the picture is out of focus or the sound distorted but usually not if the story fizzles.

This fizzle is the very thing that should have been fixed during the development process. On a motion picture production, in which years are spent developing a single script, this illusively easy fix, which is so obvious *after* a film is released, is notoriously hard to achieve. There is a long list of movies that spent millions on writers to fix scripts that only resulted in acorns wrapped in brown paper. To get a sample of how different people working on the same project do not always produce *Casablanca,* find a short story and have a half-dozen people adapt it into screenplays. In the end, every script will be slightly different; and, remarkably, some will be excellent and others terrible—despite the fact they are all from the same story.

The one constant in good movies seems to be a strong producer with a writer's sensibilities. A producer that knows how to find the inner workings of a story will instinctively know—a good percentage of the time—when something is off track. The trouble is that this type of producer is very hard to find. Individuals like David O. Selznick, Hal B. Wallis, Darryl F. Zanuck, Richard Zanuck, David Brown, Kathleen Kennedy, and Brian Brazer have remarkable track records. If it is possible to discover what they all have in common, then perhaps a pill for the perfect producer could be created. Maybe it is something simple. Brown says he has a secret weapon, "I read."

## Motion Picture Development, Part 5: Copyrights and Ownerships

> What I don't like are pompous, pretentious movies.
> —Peter Jackson

Once a screen or television play is completed, it can be copyrighted. This is done by contacting the U.S. Copyright Office with The Library of Congress. The Web address is http://www.copyright.gov and it costs forty-five dollars to register an original work. Expect several months before receiving written confirmation. However, the work is under copyright protection once the registration payment clears. Because this process is lengthy and somewhat expensive, a writer is wise to spend extra time polishing the material so the copyrighted version represents the work that will be shown to agents and producers.

In motion picture and television, a copyright is transferable. In theater, the playwright retains the copyright. After an original screenplay is sold, the legal ownership of the copyright is transferred to the studio or production company. The copyrighted work will remain with the production company thereafter, unless the project goes into turnabout and then the copyright is transferred to the new company.

If the contract is worked out properly, the writer can retain partial ownership of certain elements found in the original work, in particular, the major characters. If the production is successful and a sequel is made, then the writer is entitled to creative and financial participation in the new project. The intellectual property rights to a work can become a cash cow to a writer for decades. This is a highly specialized legal field, and once again it is recommended for a writer to consider having an entertainment attorney review a contract before signing.

## WGA versus Copyright

> " I'll give you a definite maybe. "
> —Samuel Goldwyn

Another form of protection for a writer with a new script is to register it with the Writers Guild of America (WGA). The Web address is http://www.wga.org (be sure to put "org" because

wga.com is for the Western Growers Association, which will not get a writer very far in the movie industry). Both members and nonmembers can register treatments, scripts, and even storyboards with the WGA.

The registration is not the same as a copyright, because it does not give the writer legal ownership of the work. What the registration does is to show that on a specific day the work was registered by the writer. This gives the writer the reasonable expectation that the story idea will be protected thereafter if pitched to a producer or the script is submitted for consideration. The cost for nonmembers is twenty dollars. A writer cannot copyright a short treatment, which can range from one to twenty pages, but a treatment can be registered with the WGA. This allows the writer to pitch a story idea before the script is completed. And because the fee is low, a writer can register the treatment or script after significant changes are made.

For WGA members, there is legal advice available, especially if it appears that a story idea has been used without compensation or story credit is being unfairly withheld. Nonmembers are not entitled to this service. However, because a dispute about the original source of a story idea can involve hundreds of thousands of dollars and perhaps years in court, it is uncommon that a story is "stolen" and produced. Most beginning writers are happy with a minimal payment for a script, which will certainly amount to less than hours of attorney and court fees.

An old, cheap way to protect a story idea or script is to send it registered mail to the writer's home address—*and never open the package.* It is still wise to register and copyright a completed script, but this is another method of protection. The only drawback with this approach is that over the years many writers forget where they have stored the package. Thus, the purchase of a small file cabinet might be a good investment.

> " I'll either become a very rich and famous man, or die like a dog in the gutter. "
>
> —Sam Spiegel, Independent Producer

An option is a shortterm contractual agreement that gives a studio, production company, or producer a window of opportunity to advance a project through the steps of production. An option can be on a story pitch, original screenplay, published novel, unpublished novel, short story, magazine article, video game, song, or any other forms of authorship. As long as the work is under copyright protection and not in public domain, someone can offer the writer or the writer's estate, an option deal.

If a literary property is in public domain, like *The Three Musketeers,* then a writer is free to adapt the work and seek a copyright on his or her screenplay. In general, any work that is over a hundred years old will probably be in public domain, but there are many exceptions. Sometimes a writer would wait until late in life, revise the work, and take out a new copyright. Works created after January 1, 1978, can apply for copyright protection that lasts the lifetime of the author plus seventy years.

If someone translates *The Three Musketeers,* they own a copyright on their version. This is something to consider if writing a screen version, because it would be copyright infringement if the writer lifted dialogue directly from the new translation. The same is true with classical music. Though Beethoven's work is in public domain, any orchestra that records it owns a copyright on the recording. And, of course, if a work is in pub-lic domain there is nothing preventing another screenwriter from adapting Alexandre Dumas' classic novel at the same time. In turn, a producer is free to option one or both versions.

Sometimes an author's work is purchased outright, depending upon the appeal of the property. This is most common with a trilogy of a series. A purchase takes a lot of up-front money, like with Warner Bros. and the Harry Potter novels, or United Artists with the James Bond spy thrillers. There tend to be complex contracts that have contingencies for the potential sales of future novels in the series. By current standards, the Bond series was relatively inexpensive, especially considering that it included what is now referred to as spin-off sales and merchandising. James Bond video games have reportedly grossed as much as the movies.

An option allows the producer or production company to risk a small up-front investment on a property with the expectation of securing all of the production funding within an agreed-upon time period. A standard spec screenplay option agreement is for six months with another option to renew for an additional six months if there has been forward movement with the production. If the writer feels after a year the production process has stalled, then the writer is free to pursue other possibilities.

However, if the producers have met the goals outlined in the agreement, then the property goes to the next step of the option deal. The next phase most likely would be a full contract with the writer and a first payment for the work. This contract should meet the criterion set forth by the Writers Guild of America, or a sister guild in another country, clearly stating the payment arrangements for the writer's work, additional payments for possible rewrites, and details about special rights.

An option deal comes in all shapes. It can be for six months to a year with a new script, or for several years, like J. R. R. Tolkien's *The Hobbit.* Likewise, there can be a wide range of payments, from a handshake to a hundred thousand dollars or more depending upon the circumstances.

Ideally, there should always be some exchange of money, even if it is only a dollar. This gesture creates a mindset that the option is being taken seriously as a business transaction. The important matter is the wording of the option, because if the arrangement is not clearly stated it could create a legal entanglement over the ownership of the property. This is where good entertainment attorneys earn their money.

A screenwriter does not have the freedom to adapt a copyrighted work in the hope of persuading the original author to give him or her an option. It is illegal to adapt or use any portion of a copyrighted work without permission. An ambitious writer or producer can certainly approach the owner of the copyright to seek permission or negotiate an option arrangement. But this can become a very complicated world.

The first step is to discover who controls the copyright. If the work is published, then correspond with the rights department of the publishing house and inquire who the current legal contact on record is for the writer. This could be the original writer, but most likely it will be an agent or attorney that represented the writer or the estate if the writer has passed away. This representative should be able to give information as to whether the work is currently under option or not. If the work is available, then the representative should be able to negotiate an option on the original writer's behalf, or at least forward the terms of the agreement for the writer's approval.

Beware; once the terms "motion picture" or "television" are used, these negotiations can get very steep and expensive. An interested party without production funding in place will probably find these inquiries frustrating, no matter how talented the screenwriter might be, even with proclamations of being faithful to the original work. If the rights are being held by an estate, then these rights often boil down to financial compensation for the benefit of the existing relatives or relations.

Occasionally inquiring about rights to a famous writer's work can have a happy ending. Frank Darabont as a film student was able to meet with Stephen King and impressed the legendary writer. From this meeting, Darabont received permission to adapt the novelette *Rita Hayworth and the Shawshank Redemption.* After the success of *The Shawshank Redemption,* King gave him permission to make *The Green Mile.*

During his life, Dr. Seuss refused to merchandise his characters and only allowed Chuck Jones to make a few animated shorts out of his work. However, after his death, the rights fell to his wife who was willing to make lucrative negotiations, including big-budget, live-action motion pictures. Likewise, J. D. Salinger has vehemently refused to sell any of his stories to Hollywood, especially *The Catcher in the Rye,* after his disappointment with *Uncle Wiggily in Connecticut* being turned into the movie *My Foolish Heart.* There is speculation that the reason he has not published for almost fifty years is to avoid copyrighting his works until his death, thereby preventing Hollywood from gaining control of his writing for a hundred years.

## Development Hell

> It's no use talking to me about art, I make pictures to pay the rent.
>
> —John Ford

As the term implies, this is a state of seemingly endless mental torture that Dante would relish writing if alive today. The difference between *The Inferno* and Development Hell is that the unfortunate characters in Dante's world are stuck there forever and know it, but in Hollywood there is perpetual hope that the green light will be given and production will finally start—but it doesn't for manifold reasons that seem incomprehensible. Actually, the reasons are very simple: lack of funding, script problems, casting problems, lack of funding, turnabout of management at a studio, an out-of-control budget, and, of course, lack of funding.

What is frustrating to the people stuck in Development Hell is why these reasons play out the way they do. One director might love the script, but, due to funding problems, things are put on hold, which forces that director to drop out. Meanwhile, the next director hates the script. The heads of a studio are solidly behind a project, but then the summer box office plummets and pink slips rain down. A budget is given the ok, but then oil prices skyrocket or the peaceful South American location is suddenly overrun with rebels and the budget shoots up 15 percent. A star agrees to a project and funding is raised based on star power—but an act of God forces the star's current production to be extended and the star bails, which, of course, causes a funding problem.

A good script attracts a director, a good director attracts a star, a director and star package interest studios, and this combination helps raise production funds.

## Closing Thought

Be careful whom you get in bed with. The idea of having an option is very appealing to an unproduced writer. The process becomes intoxicating, especially with the dream of having the project going the distance and ending up a motion picture. However, if the project is green-lighted, the producer might start tampering and make major changes. Thus, the writer could quickly become an outsider in the process and even see the original script altered so much that screen credit might go into arbitration. It can be a tough call, especially on a first-time project.

In the long run, common sense and gut reactions are invaluable qualities for a writer to nurture. Anyone with a thousand dollars can file documents and become a production company overnight. In this aggressive business, there are people who *are* producers and others that talk like producers. It is a form of self-preservation to be aware of this and learn to distinguish between the two. A little research before meeting with a producer and pitching an original idea is time well spent.

# CHAPTER FOUR

# SCREENWRITING

I just
make pictures
that I
would've liked
to see.

—Billy Wilder

## The Screenplay Is Born

People are impressed if writers say they are working on a screenplay; but unlike poetry, the novel, or the short story, the screenplay is a highly structured tool to make a movie and not the stuff for pleasure reading. Screenplays are often called the "blueprints" for movies but this is not totally correct. Blueprints are *visual* drawings of a large project, and screenplays are words sparingly used to tell a highly structured story without visual reinforcements. The comic book and graphic novel would make ideal screenplays because they combine visuals with words. However, until everyone can draw with the fluid style of legendary artists like Jack Kirby or Frank Miller, the format of the screenplay will not change.

By 1928, a year after *The Jazz Singer* ushered in sound to motion pictures overnight, most of the format features of the modern screenplay were in existence. The screenplay is the product of producers, not writers. This is important to the understanding of why a screenplay looks the way it does. Writers slowly evolved the structure of plays, poetry, and the novel over centuries. But a screenplay is designed to give pertinent information to a variety of creative personnel involved in a film production, including the director, line producer, cinematographer, production designer, location scout, principal actors, and extras.

Yet, with all the mechanical features built into the screenplay, a well-written screenplay can be a thing of beauty. A perfectly crafted screenplay can trigger a movie inside the mind of the reader. During the Silent Era, most "photoplays" looked like short stories. Because there were only snippets of dialogue in these scripts, the writer's responsibility was to tell a story that highlighted movement and emotional reactions. These photoplays were like purple prose checklists that described the physical action of a story. They were exciting to read, much like the dime novels popular at the turn of the twentieth century. Because dialogue was the least important element of a photoplay, what evolved was a literature of visual storytelling—a literature of pure action.

Sound hit the movies unlike anything in the history of the arts. Literally, after the New York premiere of *The Jazz Singer*, it was obvious by audience reaction that silent movies were ancient history. There was

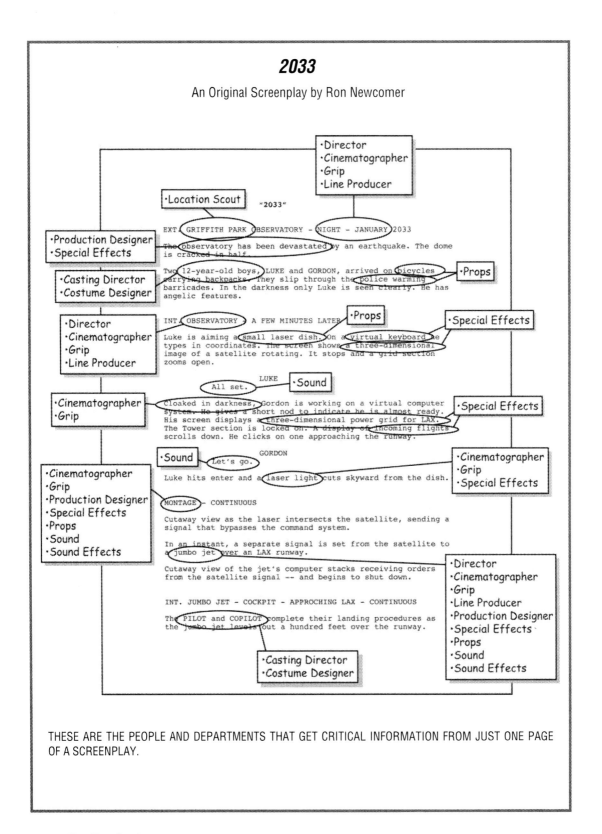

# 2033

An Original Screenplay by Ron Newcomer

·Director
·Cinematographer
·Grip
·Line Producer

·Location Scout

·Production Designer
·Special Effects

·Casting Director
·Costume Designer

·Director
·Cinematographer
·Grip
·Line Producer

·Cinematographer
·Grip

·Cinematographer
·Grip
·Production Designer
·Special Effects
·Props
·Sound
·Sound Effects

·Props

·Props

·Special Effects

·Special Effects

·Sound

·Sound

·Cinematographer
·Grip
·Special Effects

·Director
·Cinematographer
·Grip
·Line Producer
·Production Designer
·Special Effects
·Props
·Sound
·Sound Effects

·Casting Director
·Costume Designer

"2033"

EXT. GRIFFITH PARK OBSERVATORY - NIGHT - JANUARY 2033

The observatory has been devastated by an earthquake. The dome
is cracked in half.

Two 12-year-old boys, LUKE and GORDON, arrived on bicycles
carrying backpacks. They slip through the police warning
barricades. In the darkness only Luke is seen clearly. He has
angelic features.

INT. OBSERVATORY - A FEW MINUTES LATER

Luke is aiming a small laser dish. On a virtual keyboard he
types in coordinates. The screen shows a three-dimensional
image of a satellite rotating. It stops and a grid section
zooms open.

                    LUKE
       All set.

Cloaked in darkness, Gordon is working on a virtual computer
system. He gives a short nod to indicate he is almost ready.
His screen displays a three-dimensional power grid for LAX.
The Tower section is locked on. A display of incoming flights
scrolls down. He clicks on one approaching the runway.

                    GORDON
       Let's go.

Luke hits enter and a laser light cuts skyward from the dish.

MONTAGE - CONTINUOUS

Cutaway view as the laser intersects the satellite, sending a
signal that bypasses the command system.

In an instant, a separate signal is set from the satellite to
a jumbo jet over an LAX runway.

Cutaway view of the jet's computer stacks receiving orders
from the satellite signal -- and begins to shut down.

INT. JUMBO JET - COCKPIT - APPROCHING LAX - CONTINUOUS

The PILOT and COPILOT complete their landing procedures as
the jumbo jet levels out a hundred feet over the runway.

THESE ARE THE PEOPLE AND DEPARTMENTS THAT GET CRITICAL INFORMATION FROM JUST ONE PAGE
OF A SCREENPLAY.

no time for writers to fuss with a new writing style, so the producers stepped in. Sound ushered in the Studio System and Hollywood quickly became a dream factory where each studio turned out a movie a week. Though there were large indoor stages (which later became known as sound stages), most silent movies were shot outdoors with lightweight, hand-cranked cameras. Suddenly everything had to go indoors to a controlled technical environment or a back lot where miles of cable provided electricity for lights, motor driven cameras, and sound equipment.

Now scripts had to have not only dialogue but sound effects written in. Enormous sets were built on sound stages that had exterior locations, like desert sand dunes, forests, or city streets, which in the past would have been shot on actual locations. With a backlog of films waiting to be shot, this meant that the construction of sets became a critical time factor, in which one day of rescheduled shooting meant a sizable financial loss to the studio. Thus, scripts had to clearly indicate locations so sets could be started months in advance.

For the director of photography, it was important to know if a set was going to be used for a day or night scene, because it took precious hours to wire units for lights. In addition special filters, film stock, and lighting equipment had to be ordered to create the dramatic mood of the scene. Even the difference of a few hours in a story resulted in major lighting changes on a set. The visual language of a scene had to let the audience know if it was noon, late afternoon, early evening, or midnight and if it was raining or intensely sunny. This meant that scripts also had to clearly state the time of day and even the weather.

The line producer had to have all this information, plus know exactly how many actors and extras were in a scene, if there was any second-unit shooting to establish real locations or outdoor action (which was shot without sound like silent movies), and how many scenes took place in a single location. The line producer also needed to have a general idea of how each set was dressed and the number of hand props to be used by actors.

Even the actors got involved in the birth of the screenplay. Not being used to dialogue, many complained they could not tell the difference between descriptions and the words they needed to memorize. They likewise wanted to know when a speech carried over to the next page or just ended abruptly. The solution was that all the dialogue, along with the character's name, was tabbed in from the left margin to the center of the page—unlike the stage play, in which the dialogue extends from the left margin and the stage directions are interspersed.

Within a few months after *The Jazz Singer,* scripts went from reading like short stories to becoming detailed outlines that had slug lines for time and place, the capitalization of key words for actors, music and sound effects, continuations, and pithy descriptions of locations and action. Somehow, in the midst of all these technical demands, the writer was responsible for clever dialogue and memorable characters.

There was a complete turnabout in the motion picture industry with sound. Writers were brought in from Broadway because they had a knack for dialogue, and many of the silent writers were out of jobs. This resulted in a replacement of writers that knew the demands of the movies with writers that had no idea how a film was made but could write snappy dialogue.

This is when the underpaid production secretary became one of the most vitally important individuals on a production. She (most were women in this time) would get the scripts from the Broadway writers, which looked like theatrical scripts, and add all the essential language the producers were looking for. Often, these busy secretaries cut down long, overblown descriptions and thinned out verbose stretches of dialogue.

Thus, the screenplay is the only art form created by producers, designers, technicians, and actors *and then* given to the writer to somehow make cinema magic. It is the equivalent of juggling a dozen objects in the center ring of a circus and adapting *A Tale of Two Cities* at the same time.

## Then and Now: The Changing Role of the Screenwriter

In Billy Wilder's ***Sunset Boulevard*** (1950), William Holden plays an ill-fated B movie screenwriter who is a victim of the impersonal Hollywood assembly line system of screenwriting.

> ❝ To make a great film you need three things—the script, the script and the script.
>
> —Alfred Hitchcock ❞

Irving Thalberg, David O. Selznick, Darryl F. Zanuck, and other legendary Hollywood moguls professed great admiration for writers. But this did not prevent them from constantly changing a writer's blood, sweat, and tears or bringing in other writers to punch up a sequence or two or more. Because screenwriting was a new art form, there were no schools or books to teach writers this craft in the early part of the twentieth century. It took many years for writers to grasp the peculiarities of the screenplay, and the only way to learn was to work on movies. Even masters like Dudley Nichols and Ben Hecht that literally invented the art of motion picture writing had their scripts punched up or rewritten by other writers, as they did likewise.

The image of an assembly line is an accurate metaphor. One writer might tediously labor over the first draft of a screenplay adapted from a novel or play. Then the script would be given to another writer to tighten the story line, another to add comic touches, another to finesse the love scenes, and another to give the star memorable lines. Some writers learned to live in this boiling pot; others were broken by it. This has not changed much over the decades. Unlike playwrights in the theater who have sole ownership of their final script, there is no single screenwriter whose lifetime work has not at some point been tampered with by another writer under orders from a nervous producer.

There is one significant difference between the writers during the Studio System and the writers of today. The old studio writers fleshed out every detail of a motion picture, even at times giving camera directions. This was a period when the producer was in complete control and the writer—*not the director*—was responsible for describing every aspect of the motion picture. A writer (or series of writers) would spend months hitting the keys of an Underwood typewriter. Pages would be turned in to the producer for the movie, memos would fly back and forth, and then began weeks of rewriting. A writer would be expected to describe not only the action but also the scenic composition of each scene. This process might take half a year to complete and refine. Then two weeks before production began, *the director* would come on board and his job was to follow the script exactly as written.

There were directors that had a hand in this process, like Frank Capra, John Ford, William Wyler, and Howard Hawks, but once the producer approved the final shooting script even these men rarely made changes. A good example of this process is Ernest Lehman's screenplay for North by Northwest, one of Alfred Hitchcock's most famous thrillers. Lehman and Hitchcock hit upon the idea of a crop duster with machine guns trying to kill Cary Grant, but it was Lehman who wrote the shot-by-shot action that finally ended up on the screen.

When the Studio System began to collapse in the 1950s, writers went from being full-time employees to freelancers. Instead of working with a producer to carefully flesh out the minute details of a motion picture, the writer now had to write spec scripts to sell to producers. Because these scripts were looking for homes, the last thing this new generation of producers wanted was to be told how to shoot a motion picture.

This was a complete turnabout from the old days. In this era, the director was the *auteur* of a motion picture, not the producer. A writer would work with the director on polishing a screenplay before turning it over to the producer. The producer still had the right to demand changes but was no longer involved in the daily supervision of the script. And these changes were mostly about expenses, not about story structure and character development.

William Goldman's *Butch Cassidy and the Sundance Kid* is often cited as the turning point in screenwriting. When Goldman first started writing scripts in the mid-1960s, he could not find a single book on the subject, and the old studio scripts were often deadly dull to pour through. Goldman decided to make his script a whopping good read. He streamlined the action, giving a few short sentences to set up a scene, and focused on the character development and dialogue.

There were no long descriptions of sets and costumes and only occasional references to camera work. It was a fast, entertaining read. In fact, it read with the speed of a movie. Each page took about a minute to get through. There had been other screenplays published before this, like *La Dolce Vita,* but the paperback edition of *Butch Cassidy and the Sundance Kid* became a best seller. A new wave of hopeful young writers used this as a model. The screenplay almost overnight went from being a laborious outline for a motion picture to (in the right hands) a fun two-hour excursion.

## The Hollywood Melodrama

> " All movies are westerns.
> —Reportedly said by George Lucas "

Starting with the first American narrative motion picture, *The Great Train Robbery,* the prevailing structure of the studio screenplay has been a linear, three-act melodrama. The *American Heritage Dictionary* defines *melodrama* as "a dramatic work marked by exaggerated emotions, stereotypical characters, and interpersonal conflicts." The *Wikipedia Encyclopedia* describes melodrama as "a play, film, or other work in which plot and action are emphasized in comparison to the more character-driven emphasis within a drama."

The typical screenplay is like loading a musket. Essential information about characters and plot are compacted into the opening act of the story, and once ignited, the action flies in a straight line toward a predetermined target. This is the format for every Western: conflict = action. For example, in *A Fistful of Dollars,* a stranger rides into town and gets entangled in a blood feud between two warring families. All alone, facing overwhelming odds, the stranger plays the families against each other, building to a showdown.

In *Star Wars,* a group of young rebels take on the superpowers of the Empire, finally forcing a showdown with an impossible mission to blow up the Death Star. In *Die Hard,* a barefooted New York cop with just one gun takes on a gang of ingenious, lethal criminals, finally confronting the leader in a one-on-one showdown. (In the movie, John McClane uses the handle "Roy," short for Roy Rogers, the King of the Cowboys.)

Today, the word *melodrama* conjures up the image of a villain dressed in black, tying a helpless

In **High Noon** (1952), Gary Cooper goes it alone in one of the oldest traditions in American films—the shootout in the final reel.

damsel to a railroad track, as the hero dressed in white races to the rescue. A melodrama forces action. And the movies are built on action. In a general sense all stories are melodramas because a story demands *conflict* and conflict results in action. In the *Iliad,* Paris kidnaps Helen, resulting in the long siege of Troy. In *Hamlet,* the ghost of a father tells his royal son that he has been murdered, thus setting in motion a bloody act of revenge. *Hamlet* might be revered for its great language, but plotwise it is akin to *A Fistful of Dollars.*

The melodrama is a perfect fit for the movies. In a play, characters talk about what they are going to do, usually resulting in a final scene of action. In Shakespeare's age, the theaters were small and the acting took place on a bare stage. This allowed the Old Bard to move quickly from location to location, relying on the audience's imagination to supply the scenery. In movies the talk became action, allowing the characters to move over vast terrains and encounter many perilous plot twists.

This applies not only to Westerns but to all movie genres. In *Some Like It Hot,* two musicians witness a gangland massacre and are forced to disguise themselves as women and join an all-female

band for safety. In *Field of Dreams,* a man hears a voice telling him to "build it and they will come," starting him on an odyssey to find certain people so that Shoeless Joe can play baseball again. And in *Erin Brockovich,* a down-on-her-luck woman happens upon suspicious real estate documents with medical records and decides to tackle the legal army of a giant corporation.

In movies, a melodrama tells a story in a three-act structure that fits neatly into a two-hour feature. The characters might be pulled from *stock* or described as stereotypes, like the brooding lover, the corrupt official, the heartless Nazi, the mysterious woman, and the dashing hero of the resistance forces; but in the right hands, this becomes *Casablanca.*

Screenplays have many rules and restrictions, and the stories for film are almost always pulled from theatrical trunks that contain tried-and-true plots. Screenplays are also mistaken as deceptively simple, to the point that millions of people think they have a good idea for a movie. The truth is that screenplays are incredibly difficult to write— *successfully.* An untold number of people have written (and are currently writing) 120-page screenplays. Of these, maybe one in a thousand will be *successful* and none will equal *The Godfather.*

This may appear as a depressing observation, but the fact is that most screenplays are pale copies of other screenplays. And in this multitude of intermarried scripts, the characters are indeed stereotypes and the plots predictable. The trick and challenge of writing a unique screenplay are working within the confines of the three-act structure, borrowing from the endless rows of familiar character types, and yet finding new riches in these overworked mines. The solution to this literary Gordian Knot is two interrelating factors: Find original twists to old plots, and populate a fictional world with characters that become real to an audience. This boils down to *conflict* and *character development.*

> " Audiences don't know somebody sits down and writes a picture; they think actors make it up as they go along. "
>
> —Joe Gillis in *Sunset Boulevard*

In Alfred Hitchcock's **North by Northwest** (1959), one of the favorite themes of The Master of Suspense is the man in the middle, where an innocent person is wrongfully accused of murder and must go on the run to find the actual killers, all the while being pursued by the police.

The classic definition of conflict is direct and to the point: *Something happens* to the principal character that changes his or her life and forces action. For some reason, this becomes confusing to new writers. Whatever happens must be something outside of the character's control. If the character finds he is dying, this is the course of real life and not a conflict. In the movie *D.O.A.,* a man discovers he has been poisoned and has twenty-four hours to find his killer. This is *conflict.* If a woman works as a waitress to support her sick son and has rude customers, this is unfortunately real life and not a conflict. But if the waitress finds herself inexplicably falling in love with her most obnoxious customer, then this is *As Good As It Gets* and it is conflict.

Conflict is a manufactured occurrence that interrupts a character's normal life, sending it in a radically new direction. In Greek tragedies, the gods shower down misfortune to playfully mess with characters' lives. Oedipus blinds himself. Ulysses meets with a violent storm that drives his ship off course. In the Old Testament, Job endures all kinds of agonies he has no control over. And Faust makes what he thinks is a reasonable deal with the Devil and sells his soul for knowledge.

Most people travel through their lives without encountering the kind of conflicts that are commonplace in all literature. Missing the game-winning pass in football, getting a divorce, having a loved one die, or being held up at gunpoint are not conflicts. These are the rough-and-tumble things that happen in each day to a vast number of people. Somehow these individuals will resume their normal activities. The vast majority of the world population are not confronted with something so unexpected it changes the course of their lives overnight, forcing them in a new, uncharted direction. They go to the movies to experience this.

The stories of people who have encountered true conflicts in life often make the news or have books written about them. Soldiers awarded the Congressional Medal of Honor have experienced real conflict: they are usually young, nervous boys who had to make a quick decision by taking immediate action, thus changing their lives and the lives of people around them.

## Character Creation

Scarlett O'Hara, Rick Blaine, George Bailey, John McClane, Luke Skywalker, and Atticus Finch are all fictional characters that seem real to audiences. A great character (combined with the right performer) transcends the frame of movie screens and become the stuff of immortality. Here are sixteen things to consider when creating memorable characters:

1. Is the character male or female?
2. What is the name of the character?
3. What is the genre of the story? (Each genre has certain "rules" for characters.)
4. What is the personal past history of the character?
5. What are the influences of the time period the character lives in?
6. What is the geographic location of the story and how does it influence your character?
7. What are the character's friends and acquaintances like (public versus private)?
8. What is the potential for the character to be a hero *or a villain,* that is, what are the "character flaws" to overcome?
9. What is the mission or journey the character is "forced" to take?
10. Does the character have a sense of humor—or not?
11. What is the sexual orientation of the character?
12. What are the character's favorite things?
13. Does the character like animals, and if so what is his or her favorite?
14. What was the last thing of importance the character did before the story began? (How long ago was this?)
15. Is the character worth our time to get to know? (What will the audience remember about the character?)
16. All of these questions are just an exercise—unless the writer puts in real-life experience.

Conflict is not always a negative situation. *Field of Dreams* is a good example of a conflict that is life-changing but positive in its trajectory. Forrest Gump discovering he can run like the wind is another. But the rule remains the same; in each of these stories, *something happens* to the main character to dramatically manufacture a change of life. Lindbergh flying nonstop from New York to Paris is a real event that had a positive, life-changing outcome.

In real life, people are not accidentally mistaken for spies, like Cary Grant is in Alfred Hitchcock's *North by Northwest*. But this is a perfect example of why people love to go to the movies. Cary Grant plays a "normal guy" who suddenly finds himself on the run from both the real spies and the police for a murder he did not commit. On screen, the average guy sitting in the audience is transformed into a handsome, dashing leading man whose hair never gets messed up. Then in the blink of an eye, this character is thrust into nonstop high adventure that includes a beautiful, seductive woman; a brilliantly diabolical villain; hair-raising escapes; and a happy ending. But without *conflict,* Cary Grant's character would have continued his unexciting work-a-day routine indefinitely—just like most of us.

# Character Development

> I don't think plot as a plot means much today. I'd say that everyone has seen every plot twenty times. What they haven't seen is characters and their relationship to one another.
>
> —Howard Hawks

Characters in a novel, play, television show, or movie can achieve lasting fame the same way Caesar, Da Vinci, and Einstein have. Oliver Twist, Hamlet, Charles Foster Kane, and Columbo are examples of fictional immortality. They are real in the public's mind. A remarkable character with the right actor can lift a well-written story to greatness. Clark Gable is inseparable from Rhett Butler, and Kiefer Sutherland will probably be best remembered as the personification of Jack Bauer.

If a screenplay is the blueprint for a production, then strong characters are the creative glue that binds everything else together. This is the phase of filmmaking, with a writer alone in a room, that is arguably the most important, because casting, directing choices, costumes, cinematography, and even the marketing campaign revolve around bringing to life someone new that audiences can identify with and talk about.

Without strikingly real characters, *The Godfather* would have been a routine gangster shoot 'em up. However, in the first scene when Don Corleone makes "an offer he can't refuse," it is obvious this is not a dusted-off stock character but a complex individual in a dark and dangerous world. Marrying a richly developed character with the right actor, like Marlon Brando, is the basic formula for movie immortality.

A good character is not snappy dialogue. Like a real person, a fully developed character has a past, present, and a future—even if it turns out to be a short-lived one. The character has learned from hard knocks to be either good or bad, and he or she has friends and associates who populate this fictional world. Like people, good characters are defined by what they will or will not do. What are their standards and morals, and how are these personal codes chipped away at as the story unfolds? In *The Godfather*, Michael Corleone is the golden child of the family, the one member who might become a respected public figure. Instead, he turns out to be a monster that kills without remorse.

A great character is often a gift to a writer. A character might spring to mind out of the creative ether, be a present from a Muse, or be inspired by a real person. This includes the personal experiences of the writer. Ernest Hemingway said all his main characters were really himself. William Faulkner wrote many complex characters that were based on people he knew or were part of his family history. And J. R. R. Tolkien created hobbits and wizards that have a truer sense of reality than most living people.

Even if an idea for a character is a momentary flash of inspiration, this is only the infancy stage. A three-dimensional character is forged by copious thinking and the right story. A character can quickly emerge as Frankenstein's monster, a being sewn together by borrowed parts that utters stilted dialogue and lumbers through the story squashing the dramatic fire of scenes. In fact, there are thousands of these characters on exhibit late each night, stuck in the purgatory of forgotten movies.

To create a good character, the writer needs to make up a background history. Most likely, 98 percent of this information will never make it into the completed story. But what is vitally important is that the writer has a complete vision of the character, and the behavior of the character is the sum total of these small personal facts. If properly fleshed out, the writer will instinctively know if the character will shoot or run to fight another day or if the character will fall in love at first sight or resist passionate temptations. In other words, the character develops a mind of its own.

## 1. Male or Female

The first step in creating an original character is to decide if "it" is going to be male or female. This might seem like an obvious choice, but a character must be believable in the time frame of the story. Today it is immediately accepted to see a woman as a soldier, cop, lawyer, political figure, or CEO of a major corporation. In the 1950s, and the years before, a woman in these positions would

have been the exception to the norm. If the story is about a woman that is ahead of her time this approach works. But if the story is a film noir thriller, then a female cop is going to take a lot of explaining to justify. This does not mean it cannot or should not be done, but the audience will want to know "how come." This twist on historic truth might take a long speech or several scenes to justify, so the question becomes: Does this help the story or slow it down? Admittedly, it would be nice to have women appear in any part in any time period, but this sadly is not what history tells us.

## 2. Character's Name

Next is to name your newborn character. Names are extremely important. Margaret Mitchell originally wrote *Gone with the Wind* with her lead character named Pansy O'Hara. This probably would not have prevented the novel from becoming an international best seller, but it certainly would have diluted the image of the character better known as Scarlett. This applies to real life. Try to imagine, if Albert Einstein name was

At the end of *Alien,* the only survivors are Ripley (Sigourney Weaver) and her cat; in *Aliens* (1986), James Cameron put her at the center of the deep-space military mission, opening the doors for women to become action heroes.

A character's name can immediately create an image in the moviegoer's mind, like Bond, James Bond.

Harry Bumstead instead. Would a bright person then be called a "Bumstead" instead of an "Einstein"? Unlikely.

Remarkably, most people look like their names. Does the image of a name serve as a model for a person growing up? That is one of life's mysteries. But in fiction this is an element controlled by the writer. During casting, an actor might get the role because his or her personal appearance invokes the character's name. Peter Falk *is* Columbo. Clint Eastwood *is* Dirty Harry. And Paul Newman *is* Cool Hand Luke. To mix these actors up with different character names would create a mismatch. Eastwood just does not look like a Columbo, and Falk would give a whole new meaning to Dirty Harry. Names become inseparable with certain actors. After almost a half-century, many moviegoers still see Sean Connery as *the* James Bond.

In movies, there is no need to name a character unless the name is going to be used as part of the story—or if it helps the writer to create an image. However, everyone in a screenplay, whether in a sight gag or with one line of dialogue, must have some kind of name. A name, even if it is a descriptive one, is needed for budgeting, scheduling, contracts, and credits. Some films might have two hundred speaking roles. In a stage play or musical, thirty roles is a large cast. The names on the final credits are often amusing and inventive. Besides obvious identifiers like Policeman #1 and Policeman #2, there might be Death Star Trooper, Man Killed by French, and Scuttled Ship Helmsman.

## 3. Genre

Every film genre has a cast of characters. And every film will eventually be pigeonholed into a genre. The reason it is important to research and view as many films as possible in a certain genre before writing is to became familiar with the characters and see how the genre has changed over the decades. The Western was a fast-action morality tale of good versus bad for almost forty years. Then movies like *Stagecoach*, *Red River*, and *High*

Film noir has distinct traditional story elements; in Billy Wilder's **Double Indemnity** (1944), there is a femme fatale, a love-bitten chump, late-night meetings in shadowy rooms, a perfect crime that goes sour, and a couple of dead bodies.

*Noon* took the established characters of the outlaw, cattleman, and town sheriff and gave them complicated backgrounds.

These were the same characters that had been on the screen for decades, but gradually with each film their personalities took on a greater sense of reality. This would continue for another forty years until *Unforgiven*, when what was once the traditional hero coming to the rescue was now a man composed of an even mixture of good and evil. Still this film has character types that reverberate back to the Silent Era, like the sidekick, the sheriff, the saloon keeper, the prostitute, and the young ambitious gunman.

Each genre has a long past, and there are certain movies that redefined the nature of the characters in the genre. Often the last successful film in a certain genre will become the starting point for a writer. But there are also hundreds of other films in each genre that can serve as an inspiration for a new twist on an old story. This is not a process of copycatting a story—it is background education for the writer. A scenic designer will study art deco if the time period of the movie is the 1930s. A costumer will research the dress styles of Ancient Rome if it is a film about Caesar and Cleopatra. A cinematographer will study the artwork of a certain time period to get ideas how to light a scene. A writer has the same responsibility to research the past.

Presenting familiar characters in a genre satisfies audience expectations. The cowboy hero usually had a sidekick who was often the comic relief. William Boyd as Hopalong Cassidy had Gabby Hayes. Clint Eastwood as Bill Mummy had Morgan Freeman. The tradition of the characters is still there, but the relationship, personalities, and ethic heritage have changed dramatically. If a writer is going to take on the Western genre, *Unforgiven* will be a big influence, but a wealth of other themes in this genre can be explored. The writing can be more humorous, like *Butch Cassidy and the Sundance Kid,* or a revisionist look at the West, such as *Little Big Man.*

*The Usual Suspects* and *Pulp Fiction* are part of the legacy of film noir and crime films that go back to the early Sound Era. This remains one of the most popular genres because of the mixed bag of characters. Many noir films are about a big robbery or heist, the kind of deal that will allow the members of this criminal underworld to retire to a respectable life. But the heist needs specialized people to pull off precision steps in the master plan. The gathering of this gang brings together people with wildly different backgrounds that are forced to work together.

There is the mastermind, often a scholarly type with a foolproof plan; the kingpin who bankrolls the operation; the woman, or femme fatale, who plays everyone against each other; the dirty cop who wants a cut of the action; the weasel-like character who is often the yes-man to the kingpin; and the guy looking for a way out. This last character is the antihero, a man with a troubled past, perhaps an ex-boxer down on his luck or someone trying to go straight in a work-a-day job that joins up because this is finally a sure thing. These characters will double- and triple-cross each other, and the big plan will always go south at some point, which is what the audience enjoys watching over and over again.

*Pulp Fiction* plays with these character types but breathes fresh life into them by making the hit

Norman Bates in **Psycho** (1960), is tormented by unnatural events from his childhood that cast a long shadow over his actions as an adult.

men average guys talking about simple pleasures and local gossip. *The Usual Suspects* also plays with these characters but switches around the traditional roles creating unexpected surprises. Both films borrow plots from classic noir thrillers like *The Asphalt Jungle, The Set-Up,* and *Double Indemnity,* but the characters, who have been around for a hundred years or more, seem timeless because writers have found new angles to explore.

The decisions about the name and sex of the characters and the genre they will inhabit are the basic building blocks used in starting the writing process. The remaining factors are what will give the character an individual personality—the kinds of traits that can make them real to moviegoers.

## 4. Past History

Where does the character come from? What was his or her childhood like? What kind of parents did he or she have? Was he or she raised by an aunt or a stepfather? Did the character have a good childhood or was the character miserable, always moving around and never making long-term friends? Everyone is the sum total of past experiences. When writing a story, the vast majority of a character's experiences will never be shown or talked about. But a comprehensive knowledge of a character will guide the writer; and ultimately, bits of the past will become the driving forces behind the character's decisive actions. Writing a short biography of the character will establish an image of this newly born creation. This allows the writer to have a sixth sense about the dramatic reactions of the character during the writing process.

## 5. The Times

Robert Graves observed that we are all influenced by the times we live in, even if we are against what is happening. This is absolutely true of characters in a story. Most often characters get swept up in the rolling history of a time period. In *Casablanca,* Rick tries to ignore the winds of war only to become caught up in world events. Scarlett O'Hara's selfish little life is turned upside down because of the Civil War. Don Corleone tries to keep the five families from trafficking drugs only to become a victim of change. And any character in the early part of the twenty-first century will be affected by the events of 9/11. History is full of these critical moments, from Waterloo to the Battle of Britain to the assassination of President Kennedy.

The writer can use personal remembrances of significant historical events and then by careful research apply these insights to past events. This is a form of "Method writing" where, like in acting, personal experiences are integrated with the feelings of the characters. People's problems and happiness in every age have been the one constant in history. Every movie reflects the time period during which it was made, as well as the period being depicted on screen. For example, during the Great Depression, movies were often pure escapism, but during the Vietnam conflict films tended to show the death of heroes with a growing sense of vio-

The horrific images of 9/11 will remain forever with the people that saw them, becoming a defining moment in history.

lence. The more a writer researches a time period, even if it was only twenty years ago, the greater the sense of realism because of the attention to historical and cultural details.

## 6. Geography

Location is an inescapable factor in a character's life and habits. In movies there are often two reoccurring themes: small towns and big cities. When Mr. Smith leaves his small town and goes to Washington, D.C., he is an easy prey for the big city politicians. Both Steven Spielberg and George Lucas like the small town theme, perhaps because of the influence of Frank Capra's *It's a Wonderful Life* combined with their own upbringings.

*America Graffiti* shows kids in a small town talking about going off to college. In *Star Wars,* Luke Skywalker comes from a small farming community and dreams of going to cadet school. In *Jaws,* a small seaside town is feeling the financial pinch of a great white shark. And Captain John Miller in *Saving Private Ryan* is a small-town English teacher caught up in the invasion of Normandy.

On the other end of the scale, Martin Scorsese sets many of his films in the big city

In Frank Capra's ***It's a Wonderful Life*** (1946), the small American town becomes both an entrapment and heavenly salvation for George Bailey.

where corruption and murder are a way of life. *Mean Streets, Taxi Driver, GoodFellas,* and *The Departed* are the flip side of small-town life. In Scorsese's world, characters move and operate in—to use a film noir description—a big city jungle that at times is like a hell on Earth. This contrast between small towns and big cities is a favorite in literature. Oliver Twist runs away to bustling, corrupt London. And Holden Caulfield has a life altering experience roaming the back streets of New York in *Catcher in the Rye.*

Alfred Hitchcock uses the small-town theme in *Shadow of a Doubt* and then turns around and sets *Strangers on a Train* in the big city. In film, geography helps to define a character. This certainly does not mean all city people are bad and town people are good and generous. In the novels of William Faulkner and the plays of Tennessee Williams that have been made into motion pictures, the small town is often infected with prejudice, harmful gossip, and political corruption.

The contrasting influence of geography can happen in the same city. A person from Little Italy is very different from someone raised on Park Avenue. This is popularly known as being from the wrong side of the tracks and becomes a very real insight to character behavior. Though someone is from the same city, he or she can still be a stranger to the exclusive parts of that city's society. The stranger-in-a-strange-land theme is found in *Sayonara* with Americans in Tokyo after World War II, or *Butch Cassidy and The Sundance Kid* with cowboys in Bolivia in the late 1800s. This theme goes back to Homer's *Odyssey* and continues with the Tarzan novels and almost every adventure, war, and science fiction tale.

## 7. Friends and Acquaintances

A person's acquaintances are not always friends. There is often a big line drawn been friends and everyday acquaintances. A person in a professional situation, school, government job, the military, or a religious organization might be in constant contact with many acquaintances. But it is possible that none of these acquaintances have been invited to dinner at the person's house. Police Chief Gillespie played by Rod Steiger in the racially charged mystery *In the Heat of the Night* tells Sidney Poitier as Virgil Tibbs he is the only person to step foot in his house. Here is a man who is the public law enforcer in a small southern town, yet he has no social connection with the men he works with or the local officials. Instead, he invites a stranger he has come to respect—a black detective—to have dinner with him.

Most people have a public persona that might be very different from their private demeanor. This becomes an important element in telling a story. The principal characters in a story tend to be bigger than life. This causes them to behave one way in public and another way entirely behind closed doors. Politicians, policemen, military officers, movie stars, and, of course, criminals deal with scores of people daily, but these high-profile individuals might have just two or three people they call close friends. This may or may not include the spouse. Sometimes jovial public figures can be abusive and cold to family members in the privacy of their homes.

To get into a powerful person's inner circle is a recurring theme in stories, and it is usually highly fraught with danger. Eve and the Serpent

Leonardo DiCaprio as an undercover policeman plays a deadly game as a friend to Irish mafia boss Jack Nicholson in **The Departed** (2006).

Darth Vader is a classic example of a man who starts out performing heroic deeds but gives in to the dark side of his character and ends up a villain.

might be the first, and Cleopatra getting Caesar's undivided attention is probably the most famous. In *Notorious*, Ingrid Bergman's character is a spy for the FBI who is asked to have an affair with a Nazi industrialist. In *Silence of the Lambs*, Jodie Foster as Clarice Starling tries to win the confidence of convicted serial killer Hannibal Lecter. In *All the President's Men*, Bob Woodward played by Robert Redford meets in dark parking structures late at night with "Deep Throat," his exclusive inside source for the Watergate scandal. And in *The Departed*, Jack Nicholson as mobster Frank Costello makes a fatal decision to treat Billy Costigan played by Leonardo DiCaprio as a son, not suspecting he is actually under cover for the Boston police department.

## 8. "Character Flaws"—Heroes, Villains, and Antiheroes

Everyone has character flaws that range from jealousy to self-doubt to hunger for power to moments of dishonesty. Nobody is perfect. People learn from mistakes. But in storytelling, because of the compression of time, one mistake might be one too many. Shakespeare played with every possible "character flaw." Othello is blindly jealous of Desdemona. Hamlet cannot make up his mind. Lady Macbeth convinces her husband to take a bloody shortcut to the throne. And Falstaff is always making up lies. The Bible is full of lost souls in search of redemption.

Great stories are about people who are either overcome or overwhelmed by their personality defects. *The Red Badge of Courage* is about confronting cowardliness. *All the King's Men* is about the corruption of political power. Overcoming a character flaw is the stuff that makes heroes, and it pops up in movies all the time. Hans Solo overcomes his lust for wealth and returns to help defeat the Empire. Private Hudson in *Aliens* overcomes his fear of big bugs and starts blasting away. And Shooter puts down the bottle and gets his act together in *Hoosiers*.

Giving into a character flaw is what makes villains—at least in the movies. It is one of the elements closely entwined with the melodramatic structure of most Hollywood films. Darth Vader, naturally. Hannibal Lecter clearly embraces his bad side. In *Amadeus*, Antonio Salieri is a nice man until Mozart shows up. And Mrs. Iselin in *The Manchurian Candidate* has traded possessive motherhood for political power.

All of these characters have qualities for the category of the *antihero*. This is the prevailing personality of contemporary cinema. Film began in a time when many of the arts were moving away from realism. There was expressionism, surrealism, and symbolism in painting, literature, and the theater. For decades, film was part of this movement. Silver screen reality was bigger than life, stylized in black-and-white cinematography.

Directors like Alfred Hitchcock, F. W. Murnau, and Carl Theodor Dreyer used this new medium as a hatchery for visual symbols.

In the early days of sound, many actors became symbols themselves. Edward G. Robinson and James Cagney represented tough-guy, fast-talking gangsters, images they later struggled to change in the public's mind. Throughout the 1930s, movies closed the doors on the Depression outside and audiences were treated to righteous men, heroes, mothers, and ideal family life in movies like *Mr. Deeds Goes to Town, The Adventures of Robin Hood,* and the Andy Hardy series.

Then world events caught up with movies, and by the end of World War II directors were trying to capture realism using documentary techniques. From this, the antihero was born. In effect, the antihero is everybody, a blend of good deeds and occasional questionable behavior. Everybody has thoughts about what they would do if they discovered a bag of money in the middle of a street that fell out an armored car, or they have quietly considered how to get rid of an extremely rude person by making the death look like an accident.

An antihero is someone who is tempted to surrender to a darker path. Sometimes this is giving into the vice of corruption and other times it is a dangerous flirtation with human desire. Temptation is a strong and powerfully motivating force. In the movies, it adds to the dramatic suspense because there is an uncertainty about how far the main character will teeter on the edge before regaining a sense of balance. Is Humphrey Bogart in *The Maltese Falcon* going to lie to the police to cover up for the woman he loves or turn her in for cold-blooded murder? Is Marlon Brando in *On the Waterfront* going to stay deaf and dumb about the corruption he sees or give evidence against the mob? But the issues do not always have to be murder and brute force. In *Lost in Translation,* Bill Murray plays a married movie star past his prime who is tempted by the young innocence of Scarlett Johannson.

## 9. The Journey

***Spiritual***   A character's journey in a motion picture is physical *and* spiritual. The spiritual can also be referred to as a personal journey, but this does not properly reflect the mental changes a character might undergo. What is experienced and learned on these dual journeys creates a change known as the character arc, that is, what the character was like at the beginning of the journey and how he or she is different at the conclusion of the journey.

In life, adults can look back on the past and see how much they have changed because of relationships, overcoming fears, and the loss of loved ones. In a movie, a character only has two hours to undergo an odyssey to greater self-awareness. This

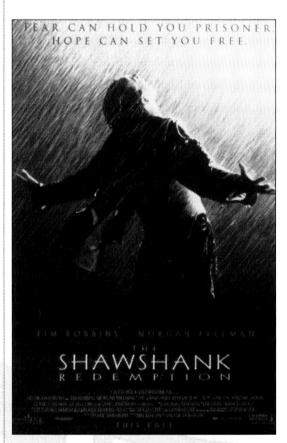

"Get busy living, or get busy dying"; Andy Dufresne (Tim Robbins) in ***The Shawshank Redemption*** (1994) undergoes a spiritual journey while locked away in a tiny prison cell for over twenty years.

journey is perhaps the oldest tradition in writing and storytelling. Ulysses is a very different man when he returns home. Frodo never fully recovers from the scars of his long journey. But journeys do not need to be epics. In a matter of twelve hours, Curt, Richard Dreyfuss' confused character in *American Graffiti,* experiences a taste of life and finally makes up his mind to leave his small community for college.

The effect of a journey on a character's life and the lessons the individual learned, were the "moral conclusion" of plays and literature for hundreds of years. These lessons were sometimes enlightening, as in John Bunyan's *The Pilgrim's Progress* or Charles Dickens's *David Copperfield,* and sometimes tragic, as in Leo Tolstoy's *Anna Karenina* or Henrik Ibsen's *Hedda Gabler.* The journey is a metaphor for a character's personal trip toward maturity and a spiritual awakening. Great characters have undergone great changes. The genesis of many of these tales is rooted in the Bible. They were lessons for the Everyman.

However, the movies have never been in the redemption business. Certainly there are many films that tackle these ancient themes with profound success. But it is doubtful that a screenwriter today will sit down and ponder how to spiritually shake up the main character—especially in an action film when there are things to blow up and bad guys to kill. Nevertheless, spiritual changes happen all the time in movies. Here are just a few motion pictures that have been nominated for Academy Award Best Picture since 1946 that have sent the main character on an obvious spiritual journey:

*It's a Wonderful Life, Miracle on 34th Street, A Place in the Sun, Friendly Persuasion, Ben-Hur, To Kill a Mockingbird, Lilies of the Field, Zorba the Greek, Lawrence of Arabia, A Man for All Seasons, One Flew Over the Cuckoo's Nest, Rocky, Star Wars, Chariots of Fire, E.T. the Extra-Terrestrial, Terms of Endearment, Witness, Rain Man, Dead Poets Society, Field of Dreams, Beauty and the Beast, Schindler's List, Forrest Gump, Babe, Saving Private Ryan, American Beauty, The Sixth Sense, The Lord of the*

*Rings, Million Dollar Baby,* and, of course, *The Shawshank Redemption.*

For a theme in writing that is not openly talked about much nowadays, this internal pilgrimage certainly pops up a lot in the movies. These films have a foundation of religious faith that anchors the story. Because of this, the term *spiritual journey* is immediately seen in a religious context. Though it can be argued otherwise, this is not always the case.

The *American Heritage Dictionary* defines *spirit* as "the part of a human associated with the mind, will, and feelings." In this definition, the journey is anything that forces the mind to think in a wider scope, which in turn creates deeply felt emotions that replace an apathetic view of life. Admittedly, this sounds like a passage out of an eighteenth century medical text. But look at the number of films since 1946 that fit this wider definition of spiritual journey:

*The Best Years of Our Lives, Gentleman's Agreement, The Treasure of the Sierra Madre, All About Eve, Sunset Boulevard, The Quiet Man, Shane, The Searchers, Rear Window, Rebel Without a Cause, Marty, 12 Angry Men, The Defiant Ones, The Apartment, The Hustler, West Side Story, Mary Poppins, Doctor Zhivago, Alfie, The Graduate, In the Heat of the Night, Midnight Cowboy, Five Easy Pieces, The Last Picture Show, The Godfather, Dog Day Afternoon, Chinatown, The Godfather: Part II, Nashville, Jaws, Network, Taxi Driver, Annie Hall, The Deer Hunter, Kramer vs. Kramer, Breaking Away, Ordinary People, Reds, Tootsie, Amadeus, The Big Chill, The Color Purple, Moonstruck, Driving Miss Daisy, Awakenings, Dances with Wolves, Ghosts, The Crying Game, A Few Good Men, Unforgiven, Pulp Fiction, Braveheart, As Good as it Gets, Titanic, Good Will Hunting, Shakespeare in Love, Erin Brockovich, Lost in Translation, Sideways, Batman Begins, Brokeback Mountain,* and the Bond thriller *Casino Royale.*

This does not include foreign classics, especially those of Akira Kurosawa and Ingmar

Bergman, nor the entire Disney film library, nor most science fiction movies. The reason for these long lists is to emphasize that exceptional films—which are also popular films—are about characters who are confronted with a conflict that alters them psychologically and emotionally.

This is the *character arc,* the personal trajectory a character takes during the course of the movie. These are the films that audiences personally connect with because they are about real human problems. Life is not always forthcoming with the opportunities that people fantasize about, but the movies provide a two-hour dose of reassurance. And if the film has characters that overcome changes and endure, these are the films that last because they speak to each new generation of audiences.

***Physical*** The physical journey is created by events outside the control of the main character that causes him or her to take action. This can be a short walk from the character's home to the courthouse to defend a black man falsely accused of a crime. And it can be in a galaxy far, far away—or anywhere in between. The distance is ultimately unimportant; there is no exact measurement for such a journey. Getting a drink from a "Whites Only" water fountain in *The Autobiography of Miss Jane Pittman* can be just as challenging and dramatic as a desert crossing in *Lawrence of Arabia.* Watching a suspicious neighbor with binoculars in *Rear Window* can be as dangerous as crossing a suspended bridge in *The Temple of Doom.*

The long or epic journey that takes the main character far from the comforts of home is the oldest form of storytelling. Most likely, this evolved from an adventurous member of a tribe crossing a distant range of mountains and returning with hair-raising tales of strange creatures and fertile valleys. This extended, perilous quest has become known as the *hero's journey,* and it fits the unlimited expansion of movies perfectly. Over the centuries, every culture has produced such legends. The examination of the epic journey is the topic of many books on screenwriting. Joseph Campbell

Peter O'Toole in ***Lawrence of Arabia*** (1962), crosses hundreds of miles of scorching desert in his journey for adventure and self-enlightenment.

became the reluctant guru of this narrative form after George Lucas talked about the influence of his teachings in *The Hero with a Thousand Faces* and other volumes of mythology.

The epic journey tends to be a series of cliffhangers that befall the main character on the path to the final encounter of revenge, riches, true love, or, usually, all of the above. The journey that stays within a confined location tends to build suspense through character conflict. Both of these journeys are structured for moments of high tension and temporary calms. *Les Misérables* is a sweeping tale set against the backdrop of nineteenth-century revolution. *Casablanca* is set on the eve of America's entry into World War II, but most of the action happens in Rick's Café over a few days. *Les Misérables* has battles, breathtaking escapes, and a chase in the sewers of Paris. *Casablanca* has one quick shootout at the end. One is a grand pageant and the other a subtle chess game of wits, but what ties them both together is marvelous characters.

In the end, it is not how many dire predicaments are thrown at the main character but how the character reacts to each situation, large or small. The reason the line "Round up the usual suspects" has achieved a certain immortality is that when French Captain Renault gives the command, he already knows exactly who shot the Nazi general. It is easy to toss someone into a pit with poisonous snakes, but if it has been established that the otherwise fearless hero has a childlike dread of snakes then his descent is equally humorous and suspenseful.

The best way to experience fully realized characters is not by watching films but by reading biographies and the classic novels. In motion pictures, often characters have been distilled to fit the tight framework of storytelling. Often, only the bare bones of a character is explored. In a novel, the characters can be explored without time constraints or a restricted number of pages. The reason so many screen versions of *The Three Musketeers, A Tale of Two Cities, Pride and Prejudice,* or even Ernest Hemingway's *The Killers* have been made is that these stories have great characters that continue to delight and entertain.

Memorable movie characters are a combination of well-crafted dialogue, casting, music, sets, costumes, the right lens and lighting, and careful editing. In books, a writer can explore the psychology and manners of characters, bringing them to life in rich detail. A successful screenwriter learns to condense time and carve away at a fully realized character until only the prime cut is left. If the screenwriter starts with a lean offering, based solely on stock movie characters, this creates a *generational loss,* the same way a photo image will begin to pale after repeated copies are made. The characters become two-dimensional without benefit of happy writing accidents.

Exceptional novels and biographies are full of scenes and personal encounters that if thoughtfully adapted can become these happy accidents and give screen characters unexpected depth. One of the reasons the characters in *The Shawshank Redemption* are so fascinating is that they are so well developed in Stephen King's novella. A screenplay is ultimately a balance between words and images, but finding the right words and images is an amazingly difficult job. Look at all the films listed in a complete television guide book and then count the number of films that are deemed

outstanding. The single factor that separates four-star movies from all the rest is enduring characters. The more a writer reads, the better the chances of bringing a person to life out of light and shadows.

## 10. Sense of Humor

The quickest way to endear a character to audience members is to make them laugh. Laughter tends to attach moviegoers to a character or gives a villain a suave charm despite an inclination for murder. This is a very old writing trick that works like a charm every time. There is no scientific explanation for the origin of a giggle or a horselaugh; it is just one of these strange phenomena that spontaneously happen because of a few select words or perhaps a silly walk. In *David Copperfield,* a major reason that Mr. Micawber is such a pleasant encounter for readers is that his

Peter Sellers in **Dr. Strangelove** (1994) proves that humor is the best medicine when confronted with the nuclear obliteration of the entire world.

labyrinthine sentences amuse them, while Uriah Heep is despised in large part because he is void of any sense of humor whatsoever.

In a novels there is room to develop characters so the reader gradually gets to know them, but in film characters must be generally established during the first encounter. Movie audiences have been conditioned to respond to characters based on casting, costume, and how they are introduced in the story. Laughter is a great shorthand device in gaining an audience's support or loyalty for a character.

In *Dead Poets Society*, John Keating, played by Robin Williams, might come off as an unfeeling manipulator of students without the ability to weave humor into his lectures. Butch Cassidy would be just another cowboy without his knack for folksy sarcasm. And in *Some Like It Hot*, just seeing Jack Lemmon in a tight dress for the first time tells the audience anything goes from now on.

Humor can be added to the dramatic conflict by giving the main and adverse characters a sense of humor. In *Die Hard*, Bruce Willis pitches out smart-ass remarks to keep his cool and Alan Rickman takes on the persona of a criminal genius because of his cold-hearted one-liners. Humor can defuse a critical situation and make people laugh at the absurdity of politics, like President Merkin Muffley played by Peter Sellers in *Dr. Strangelove*. Or humor can confound an audience's preconceived judgment of horrendous individuals. In *Schindler's List*, Ralph Fiennes infused his character Amon Goeth with touches of humor, which makes this inhuman Nazi officer strangely likable at times.

Comic characters are often called into service to lighten the load for the main character. In Westerns, this is the sidekick. In love stories, it is the best friend. And in the academic world it is usually the geek that supplies the comedy relief. In horror movies, a silly remark relieves the tension before the next ghastly murder. A touch of humor as a release during intense moments in any genre is something for every writer to consider.

A theater full of ticket buyers is a miniature nuclear reactor where at a highly dramatic moment the delivery of an onscreen line or odd expression might evoke a laugh from one person that instantaneously will spread to everyone. For centuries, patrons would boo or throw objects during stage productions to express displeasure, or cheer uproariously for favorite actors. Movies replaced live human targets for flicking images, but a large gathering of people can always result in an unpredictable experience. A few well-placed laughs generated naturally from the characters gives audience members a release and prepares them for the serious stuff that follows.

Charles Chaplin learned early in his career that a few sight gags designed to make people laugh could open the doors to other emotions. In *City Lights*, he balances the melodrama about a blind flower girl with drunken antics and a prize fight loaded with perfectly timed pratfalls. By the end of the movie, the audience is in tears when the girl realizes that the Little Tramp was the one responsible for her regaining her eyesight. However, when Chaplin did *A Woman of Paris*, a tragic love drama without comedy interludes, audiences walked out.

Humor assists in making the impossible possible. If audience members enjoys the journey, they will accept most anything they see, no matter how bigger than life it is. *Field of Dreams* would be preachy and easily perceived as absurd without humor. So would *Rain Man, Forrest Gump, Babe, Fargo,* and *As Good as It Gets*. A touch of comedy sometimes helps make distasteful medicine go down. In *Schindler's List*, when Liam Neeson is reassured by Ben Kingsley that an old one-armed man is an essential factory worker, this is a moment of comic release for the audience. It also shows, despite his warranted fear for safety, that Schindler is becoming compassionate about the fate of the Jewish people around him. This moment of human comedy serves to heighten the tragedy of the old man's sudden murder a few scenes later.

## 11. Sexual Orientation

Starting with the first nickelodeons, the freedom to express sexual activity has come under attack by religious groups, parent organizations, and even individuals representing alternate lifestyles. In American movies rating system, violence is tolerated but sex is suppressed. In 1969, *The Wild Bunch* ended with one of the most violently graphic shootouts ever filmed. The Western received an R-rating but had to cut some of the footage of sex scenes to avoid an X-rating.

This was three years after the demise of the Hollywood Production Code, which had been vehemently enforced since 1934. Under the Code, any display of nudity, extramarital affairs, couples sleeping in the same bed, or overt homosexual behavior were forbidden. Fallen women were acceptable *only* if they met with a violent end or saw the light of Christianity. Because of these puritanical rules, filmmakers became subversive in their depiction of sex. Subtle clues were snuck in movies about sexual behavior or orientation. There things were never referred into in the dialogue but became part of the visual language. When two lovebirds kissed, followed by a blackout, audiences assumed that hanky-panky was afoot.

What evolved from these subversive visual clues was character stereotypes that persist today. In *The Maltese Falcon,* Peter Lorre shows up at Sam Spade's detective office dressed like a high-society dandy and smelling of gardenias. While speaking softly, he runs the curved end of his ivory-handled cane gently over his lips. Astute audience members in 1941 would interpret these telltale signs to mean the character was gay, but the majority of the moviegoers simply saw a very tidy person.

Peppering these suggestive tidbits into a movie was a game with many directors during this era. After all, there was nothing in the Code about a man's personal relationship with his cane. Since homosexuality was one of the best-kept open secrets in Hollywood, the Code ignored these visual clues as long as nothing was overtly said in the dialogue to connect a character to a gay

Peter Lorre in *Maltese Falcon* (1941) coyly chats with Humphrey Bogart while delicately stroking his cane, a cue about his sexual orientation that somehow slipped by the Hollywood Production Code.

lifestyle. Thus through costuming and the manner an actor played a role, audiences over the years were trained to recognize the unspeakable.

In the years since the passing of the Code, these visual clues have created an aggressive guessing game by movie fans and film scholars regarding who was gay and who was playing gay during this era. Robert Walker in Alfred Hitchcock's *Strangers on a Train* plays Bruno with an exasperated little boy's voice. He dresses impeccably and loves his mother maybe a little too much for comfort.

The problem about the years of subversive filmmaking is that these visual clues have become part of everyone's collective cinema knowledge. Even now, any male actor playing a character that dresses or speaks "too well" might be suspected of having an undercurrent of homosexuality. The real dilemma is that these characters were often the deranged villains in movies, suggesting that being gay leads to a life of crime. This came to a boiling point with *Basic Instinct,* for which there were protests about Sharon Stone's wicked character being portrayed as a lesbian.

The difficulty for a writer today is to navigate around these stereotypical characters. A menagerie of them exists, including the hooker with a heart of gold (*Gone with the Wind*), the hooker that falls for the wrong guy (*From Here to Eternity*), the hooker in need of a hero (*Unforgiven*), the hooker who knows too much (*Klute*), the woman that became a hooker because she thought her husband was dead (*Waterloo Bridge*), the hooker that a rich man wants to marry (*Pretty Woman*), the high-priced social climbing hooker (*Breakfast at Tiffany's*), the mother from the wrong side of the tracks (*Stella Dallas*), the no-good daughter (*Mildred Pierce*), the sweet-faced girl who longs for the lights of the big city (*It's a Wonderful Life*), the virgin that does not want to be a virgin but does not trust men (*Pillow Talk*), the gigolo (*The Roman Spring of Mrs. Stone*), the impotent husband (*Rebel Without a Cause*), the two-timing wife (*The Killing*), and the femme fatale (*Out of the Past*).

And then there is the spy that sleeps with the enemy (*Notorious*), the wife that kills her husbands (*Black Widow*), the other woman (*Room at the Top*), the incestuous mother (*The Manchurian Candidate*), the incestuous older brother (*Scarface*), the lecherous old man (*Asphalt Jungle*), the woman who gets turned on by violence (*Bonnie and Clyde*), the drunk gangster moll (*Key Largo*), the wolf in preacher clothing (*Elmer Gantry*), the child bride (*Baby Doll*), the husband that leads an alternative lifestyle (*Far from Heaven*), the evil pedophile (*M*), the nice-guy pedophile (*Lolita*), the pedophile teacher (*A Streetcar Named Desire*), the pedophile murderess (*To Die For*), and the pickup from hell (*Fatal Attraction*).

On the male side, there is the effeminate gay man (*The Bird Cage*), the tragic gay man (*Dog Day Afternoon*), the gay man that denies he is gay (*Advise and Consent*), the gay best friend (*My Best Friend's Wedding*), the beloved gay man (*Four Weddings and a Funeral*), the sophisticated older gay man (*Gods and Monsters*), and the sophisticated younger gay man (*The Picture of Dorian Gray*). And there is a very long list for teenage films. Dying young and lost love are the most popular recurring themes, starting with innocent teenage lovers (*Romeo and Juliet*) and wannabe young lovers who

never had a chance (*Titanic*). As for the normal, happily married couple that enjoys sex and goes to church each Sunday—these characters are usually depicted as dull and behind the times in fashion.

For something that has been censored and is the source of countless protests, sex plays an ever-present role in movies. In most foreign-language films, sex is treated freely and openly as a natural part of life. This has not been true in Hollywood pictures. As the examples indicate, the majority of studio movies with a strong sexual content tend to have stereotypical characters that have gone astray because of forbidden appetites. In large part, this is because of the visual clues that are used to camouflage what is actually happening behind closed doors in movies. With each character type there is an established look about the character that is identifiable to millions around the world because of makeup, costume, and manner of speech.

A writer today needs to be aware of these stock characters for two reasons: to avoid using them as a shorthand approach to storytelling and to use them as red herrings in the plot. This latter employment means playing off the audience's pre-conditioned expectations of a character type but then using this opportunity to craft a complex characterization that is multidimensional. A character can be roughly defined by his or her sexual appetites, but there is always much more to explore. This is the reason that films like *Notorious*, *Pretty Woman*, and *Gods and Monsters* work so effectively.

## 12. Favorite Things

Everyone has something they might run into a fire to save. Usually, this precious item is not a piece of expensive merchandise but rather, a photograph of a loved one or a childhood memento of no value whatsoever. Characters are often defined by personal keepsakes, whether it is a lucky charm or a Dear John letter that has been read a thousand times. This is a shorthand device to establish a character and can easily create a stereotype. But if the character has been given a clear identity, then the use of a personal treasure can add a touch

In **Lord of the Rings,** Frodo's life is interlocked with a ring, which quickly goes from being a favorite thing to an object of great personal sacrifice.

Don Corleone (Marlon Brando) in **The Godfather** (1972) plays with his cat while making an offer that cannot be refused.

of irony or underscore the mental makeup already established.

A favorite thing can be something intangible, like a song that brings back haunting memories or someone's last request. Whatever this thing is, the character is not far away from it, either physically or emotionally. Sometimes they are pure accidents. George Raft, who was in the original *Scarface,* got so nervous that his hands would shake noticeably. Howard Hawks, the director, gave him a silver dollar and told him to focus on flipping the coin during scenes. This became his trademark.

This thing can also be the "MacGuffin." This is a term used by Alfred Hitchcock for an item that everyone in the movie is trying to get or even kill for but the audience "don't care." It is the thing that ignites the action, or establishes the chase, and the skullduggery to possess it is what creates the thrills for the audience. In *Strangers on a Train,* a personally engraved cigarette lighter is used in an attempt to frame an innocent man. In *Winchester '73,* it is a stolen rifle; and in *The Illusionist,* it is the secret to a magic trick. The ultimate favorite thing is the ring from *The Lord of the Rings,* which becomes all consuming for whoever possesses it, thus starting an epic adventure.

## 13. Animals

A way to make an audience like or dislike (sometimes revile) a character is to show how he or she responds to animals. W. C. Fields warns never to act with children or animals, and he is right. A sad-eyed dog or a tabby cat caught in the rain will steal a scene every time. Animal movies have been a genre since motion pictures began. *Rescued by Rover* (1905) was a landmark short wherein the family dog sniffs out a band of gypsy kidnappers. The *Rin Tin Tin* serials are credited with saving Twentieth Century Fox in the early years of the Great Depression, and the *Lassie* series made a fortune for MGM.

An animal becomes part of the visual language of a film, giving the audience instant information about the character it comes in contact with. Sometimes that information is straightforward, establishing that character as a good soul because of a special bond with the animal. This includes almost every Western. In *Lonely Are the Brave,* Kirk Douglas's character risks his own life instead of abandoning his horse during a chase with the law.

At other times, the visual information is conflicting. Bad people are often very kind to animals.

In the opening scene of *The Godfather,* Marlon Brando is quietly petting his cat while considering an act of violent revenge. Blofeld, played by Donald Pleasence with a large scar in *You Only Live Twice,* strokes his spoiled white cat while plotting to blow up half of the world. And sometimes the information is a decoy to the truth. In *As Good as It Gets,* Jack Nicholson starts out by tossing an adorable dog down a trash chute, but later in the movie he cannot part with the little critter.

If a character aims a gun at a dog, the audience recoils in dread anticipation, whereas any number of people can be graphically blown away without raising the mass temperature one iota. However, animals should be used after careful consideration. Animals do not learn lines very well—meaning that to get a good performance out of an animal might take hours of extra time on a set, and often several identical-looking dogs or pigs have to be used to get one coordinated bit of camera blocking. The two turtles in *Rocky* were no problem at all, but Asta in *The Thin Man* used to growl at the leading lady, Myrna Loy, before takes. But if there is justification for a character to have an animal, it can be pure screen gold. For example, the last close-up in *Breakfast at Tiffany's* is of the no-name cat.

## 14. Last Important Thing

A person is lucky to accomplish one important thing in life. Some never do; others are blessed with many. Each set of circumstances affects a character psychologically, sometimes in subtle ways; and sometimes it can be crippling to how characters see the world and themselves in it. This is a quality that a writer uses to underscore the character's private moments. It is literally a state of mind for the character—and might not be mentioned in the entire movie. Perhaps the most important thing is that the knowledge of a character's background can be invaluable inspiration for an actor.

This subtext for the character creates a "look-in-the-mirror" moment in a movie. If the character is young and starting out, there is the look of hope and ambition. If the character is middle-aged

Rocky (Sylvester Stallone) is motivated by the belief that he has never done anything of importance in his life—and now he has been given a golden opportunity.

or older, then the look gradually becomes one of disillusionment. If the character represents evil in some way, then the look is complicated because the pride of accomplishment might be a mask for a dark deed. This is not intended to encourage writing in scenes where the character stares into the mirror, though this happens many times in movies. A visual hint of a character's confidence or lack of confidence is a building block from which a performance can be constructed.

The feeling of achievement is something lasting—whether in a classroom, a small community, or on the world stage—and gives a character a sense of worth. If the writer stores this in the back of his or her mind during the creative process, these feelings of self-worth or failure will seep into the character's actions. As the Wizard of Oz says to the Tin Woodman, "A heart is not judged by how much you love, but, how much you are loved by others." This is more than just Hollywood corn; it is a basic truth of how people think about themselves.

The champion of movies about self-worth and the overwhelming desire to achieve something important is Frank Capra's *It's a Wonderful Life.* The character played by James Stewart feels he has missed out on every opportunity to accomplish something spectacular in life and is about to commit suicide. He is rescued by a not-too-bright angel that shows him how much good he has done over the years for everyone around him. In contrast, there are characters that reach the heights at an early age and then never achieve another moment of glory. In Hollywood lore, this is the tale of Orson Welles or any "wonder kid" that flames out after a big success.

Sports metaphors abound in motion pictures. These are about the single act of doing something remarkable, even if it is only for a few seconds. This world is populated with characters that could have been champions or "contenders," as Marlon Brandon laments in *On the Waterfront,* and characters that are given an unexpected opportunity, like in *Rocky,* who then live up to the challenge. Other characters grow old retelling stories about that one great football catch or the homerun in the ninth inning. Each of these scenarios can easily be applied to other genres, such as gangster films, war movies, the business world, Westerns, fantasy and science fiction, and musicals about the washed-up star and the bright-eyed youngster from the chorus line.

## 15. Is the Character Worth <u>Our</u> Time?

This is an acid test purely for the writer to conduct in private with his or her own conscience. The "our" refers to the audience, which can be millions of people in one night. This audience has seen a lot of two-dimensional characters spouting wooden dialogue ever since sound arrived. Reality television does not require fictional characters, but to see the incredibly shallow ways real people conduct themselves in adverse situations should inspire a writer to spend a little extra time in creating a character on paper that is distinctively unique. Writing is a high-wire act of heightened reality, even if real street life is used as a backdrop, like in a Martin Scorsese film.

The writer should give careful thought to each character to make sure this young Frankenstein monster is not a copycat uttering worn-out dialogue from scores of other movies or television shows. A good character should move the plot forward rather than being pushed by the

Humphrey Bogart and Ingrid Bergman as Rick and Ilsa in ***Casablanca*** (1942) are an example of two characters that audiences consider worthy of watching time and again.

plot. A fully realized character will make decisions to outwit the overused pitfalls of story structure and take the action in a sometimes unexpected direction. A hand-me-down character will continually get kicked in the back end by the standard plot devices and thus bring nothing new to Story Line 101. The effort to create memorable characters is a matter of the writer's personal desire and ambition to write the best story possible.

## 16. Real-Life Experiences

In an interview in *CreativeScreenwriting,* Joe Eszterhas (*Jagged Edge, Basic Instinct, The Music Box*) was asked the following question: "You seem to think too many writers are getting their inspiration from other movies instead of real life." His response is something every screenwriter should think about: "I do, and that's why there are so many bad movies out there. It's not real life that screenwriters seem to be writing about anymore, it's *reel* life. I think that's deadly on two levels.

"One, on a creative level, if you're getting your knowledge of life and what life's about from films, then you're not going to be able to write real people and real characters that people can identify with. Two, in terms of your own life, I really believe in living life passionately and coloring every page, just living life as fully as possible. It seems to me that if you spend most of your time in screening rooms or movie theaters, that's not

Much of the power and nightmarish realism in **Saving Private Ryan** (1998) comes from stories of young GIs that landed on the beach on June 6, 1944.

mation off the Internet. Get involved and interview the people that live in the world being written about, instead of reading or watching documentaries. Do not go to extremes and take unnecessary chances, but seek a better understanding of all lifestyles. Certain genres, such as horror and slasher films, are the stuff of nightmares, which are common experience for everyone.

One of the reasons *To Kill a Mockingbird* works so beautifully is that Harper Lee is pulling from her childhood experiences. On the other side, Thomas Harris did years of research on serial killers before writing *Silence of the Lambs* and *Red Dragon*. Harris's obsession with the subject caused him to identify to a degree with these monsters and then to pull from these personal feelings while writing.

What is referred to as "depth of character" is only found by stirring up the writer's own emotions. And this authentic human touch is missing in far too many films today. The reason that movies like *Platoon, Moonstruck, Awakenings, In the Name of the Father, Schindler's List, Good Will Hunting, The Pianist,* and *Brokeback Mountain* are so effective is that the characters have come alive on screen.

## Three-Act Structure

> " Structure, structure, structure...
> —Billy Wilder on writing for the movies

possible. That's a great loss to the writer, and a diminishment of his own fulfillment and of his own possibilities as a human being."

Though this is listed as the last step for character creation, it is the most essential. Without real human experiences to use as a touchstone, the other steps only add up to a writing exercise. This does not mean going big-game hunting like Ernest Hemingway or drinking yourself to death like F. Scott Fitzgerald and many other American writers. It gets back to "Method writing," in which personal experiences give raw emotions to make-believe characters. All the other steps are intellectual games and tools for piecing together characters, but real experiences generate a human energy that cannot be copycatted.

In doing research on a topic that is unfamiliar, do some legwork instead of pulling all the infor-

Screenplays are traditionally divided into three acts. This has evolved from theater going back to the Golden Age of Greece. Plays can be found ranging from five acts to one act, but the basic storytelling structure remains the same, that is, beginning, middle, and end. The acts are built into the story line of a play to allow the curtain to fall for changes in scenery, makeup, and costumes.

When the curtain rises, the audience is looking at a scene that takes place in a different time period and often on a new set. The fade-out or blackout was used in the early cinema to give audiences that grew up watching plays the same information.

Because plays are broken into acts, the audience is more aware of the dramatic structure of the story. On stage, each scene is punctuated by lighting effects that give visual clues on the time of day, combined with a hint of the emotional conflict because of the choice of color gels. In movies, the audience receives this same information a hundred times or more in two hours. Because there are so many scenes in a motion picture, the exact moment for each "act" change is difficult for viewers to recognize. Because people have grown up watching movies from childhood, starting with seven-minute cartoons, the intuitive understanding of age-old story structure has become blurred in the seamless process of filmmaking.

Alfred Hitchcock defines good stories as "life with all the dull parts removed." A writer borrows from life to establish a sense of reality in characters and dramatic events but then manipulates these elements to fit into a two-hour period. It is an interesting argument to speculate whether stage productions going back two thousand years have conditioned audiences ever since to expect entertainment in two-hour doses. Somehow this has become the standard time to perform a story, no matter whether the action is live or on the screen.

This time factor is what makes the structure in movies critical. Audiences need to be given information quickly to establish a clear knowledge of the characters and at the same time set into motion a series of incidents that create a conflict. The action must then play out until it reaches a dramatic resolution. In film, *action* is the key word and arguably represents the dividing line between theater and motion pictures.

Over the centuries, there have been legendary theatrical productions with chases across ice flows, sinking ships, and chariot races. The technology behind musicals like *The Lion King* and *Beauty and the Beast* has reached the point of almost

re-creating movies live on stage. But no matter how outstanding the production achievements are, the drama is still confined to a stage where characters are forced to confront each other in a clash of words and psychological manipulation in between scene changes.

Chases down dark alleys, airplane dog fights, and police shootouts are examples of a few action montages that do not work convincingly on stage. But they are the essence of movies. Since films grew up in silence, the storytelling approach has been a process to minimize words and distill the drama into action. When sound arrived, films became elaborate stage plays during much of the Studio Era, but lighter cameras and faster lenses gave directors back the freedom of motion.

What has never changed about plays and movies is the time factor: There are two hours to tell a story. This economy of time demands a carefully plotted structure consisting of a Setup (Act I), Turning Point (Act II), and Resolution (Act III). Different terms have been used to describe these act points, but the structural breakdown is essentially the same.

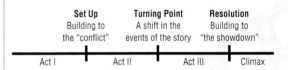

| **Set Up** | **Turning Point** | **Resolution** |
|---|---|---|
| Building to the "conflict" | A shift in the events of the story | Building to "the showdown" |

| Act I | Act II | Act III | Climax |

## Act I: The Setup

> The length of a film should be directly related to the endurance of the human bladder.
> —Alfred Hitchcock

The death of Luke Skywalker's aunt and uncle by the evil Empire in **Star Wars** (1977) is the dramatic conflict that starts the journey and creates the action that follows.

The setup is comprised of a series of events that build to the moment of *conflict* involving the main character. In motion pictures, this traditionally happens during the first thirty minutes or what would be up to page 30 in a screenplay. This is a consistent time factor in film structure that has been an ongoing source of debate among writers and critics. Bringing attention to this time-clock structural device is often credited to Syd Field in his landmark books on screenwriting. There is resistance from many writers about being so confined in the creative progress.

The novel is cited as a literary form that does not have a fixed page number to be hit automatically every time. Thus, the argument is that the novel has greater freedom of personal expression whereas the screenplay is a mere cookie-cutter format that stifles artistic experimentation. In a novel the writer has complete control over the length of story, which can vary from Ernest Hemingway's *The Old Man and the Sea* to a massive undertaking like Leo Tolstoy's *Anna Karenina*.

But this comparison is sidestepping the very nature of a screenplay. To start with, a screenplay is much closer to a short story than a novel. The chief duty of a screenwriter when adapting a novel to the screen is to find ingenious ways to cut down the story to fit snuggly into two hours. Depending on the writer, sometimes this is highly successful,

like *To Kill a Mockingbird,* or an unmitigated disaster, like *The Bonfire of the Vanities*. Usually the difficulties in adapting a novel are condensing the numerous subplots and eliminating the number of characters. On the other hand, a short story is usually about one central character over a finite time period, which is identical to a screenplay.

Over the decades, Syd Field has been criticized for setting forth an assembly-line philosophy about writing for the movies. What is overlooked in this academic finger pointing is that Field's first book on screenwriting came out in 1979, just a few years after *Jaws* and *Stars Wars* turned around Hollywood's financial woes with the blockbuster. Screenplays suddenly were hot properties, and studios were looking for a magic formula to produce runaway hits. Field's book was fortuitous in its timing and an eye-opener to most people because this neglected art form had never been studied in depth.

The great mystery is how thousands of writers for eight decades wrote tens of thousands of screenplays, including hundreds of enduring classics, without benefit of Syd Field's observations. The answer is that the structure of a movie is married to the structure of a play. In 458 BC, Aeschylus wrote the tragedy *Agamemnon*. In the first thirty minutes, clandestine events are set into motion when it is disclosed that Clytemnestra is plotting a bloody revenge upon her husband's return from the Trojan War. This approach to storytelling probably began with the first story ever told.

In all stories, characters are introduced and a way of life is established before destiny steps in. In Hemingway's short novel, an old fisherman sails from his village and catches a giant marlin. In Tolstoy's novel, Anna leaves her husband in St. Petersburg to visit her brother in Moscow and there meets Count Vronsky. In Budd Schulberg's *On the Waterfront,* an exprize fighter, Terry Malloy, is used by a corrupt union boss to lure an informant to his death and then he is asked by the man's sister to help bring the murderers to justice.

## Linear Structure

Setting up the events leading to the conflict is a tradition in storytelling. The main or principal character is established, the secondary characters are introduced, and a chain of events begins. In direct contrast, an adverse character is revealed and the characters associated with this individual are likewise introduced. The description of the adverse character can take on many guises, including outright villain, spurned lover, ruthless criminal mastermind, glory-stealing boss, or deranged killer. At other times, the character causing the problems may simply find himself or herself in an adverse situation. This would include a father who plans to move his family from St. Louis to New York on the eve of the World's Fair or a dashing Confederate blockade runner that falls for a southern belle who is blindly in love with another man.

As often happens in real life, the characters that populate a story find themselves in opposing situations. This sets into motion events that disrupt the normal way of life in this fictional world. These conflicting forces are like musical notes playing in counterpoint with each other. A concerto is defined as one solo instrument accompanied by an orchestra. Within the concerto, there are movements based on a musical theme and each movement can have a variation on this theme or an opposing theme. The structure of a concerto has been well defined over the centuries; thus, the performance fits a traditional length. A composer's challenge is to bring personal innovation to a concerto while working in this highly structured format.

This is the same with a screenplay. The main character (musical theme) is established in the first movement. This movement sets up the conflict

(musical variations) for future movements. Then these variations lead to a resolution or showdown (finale). The opening act of a screenplay is not a newly discovered formula to mass-produce buttered popcorn blockbusters. It represents the same structural puzzle that faced Aeschylus and all the Greek poets: to tell an engaging story in two hours involving a complex character that will entertain a large theater audience.

---

The four things that need to happen in the setup (Act I) during the first thirty minutes (give or take) of a screenplay are:

1. Establish the principal character.
2. Establish the adverse character, or the character put in an adversarial position.
3. Through a series of scenes, introduce the secondary characters and establish the important elements of the world and times the characters inhabit, including customs, technology, and politics.
4. Set into motion events that will lead up to a conflict for the principal character.

---

These are the same rules that most people follow naturally when telling personal tales about friends or past achievements. The main characters are introduced, and the conflict between these characters is established. To introduce an important character in the middle or toward the end of a story upsets an audience; this feels like a "cheat" because it is story information that was deliberately withheld to create a surprise. This is an easy thing to fix by simply referring to the character within the setup. In *The Third Man*, everyone talks about Harry Lime, but the character does not appear until halfway into the film.

*Memento* goes backward in time; nevertheless, all the critical story information is established within the first quarter of the film—not the last quarter. The characters, main story line, subplot, and conflict are all ingeniously laid out in the beginning, the same as any linear script that goes from start to finish. The reason the screenplay works so well is that Christopher Nolan is very familiar with the elements of good storytelling.

After watching *Memento* or any other movie that mixes up the traditional structure like *Pulp Fiction* or *The Eternal Sunshine of the Mind*, there is the temptation to write a screenplay with a non-linear story line. This form of writing is the ultimate sleight of hand and is highly structured—it only appears to be random. It is the difference between pulling a silver dollar from behind someone's ear and making a woman disappear in plain sight. There is an English teacher in John Barth's *The End of the Road* who at one point shouts at his students that they cannot break the rules—until they learn what the rules are. This is excellent advice about screenwriting; write a clockwork script that follows the rules first, and then with this knowledge begin to take calculated chances.

As a thought about introducing all the elements at the beginning of a work, Beethoven composed his Fifth Symphony around four simple notes, which in Morse code are "dot, dot, dot, dash," and they reverberate throughout the music in innovative ways that never become tedious.

## Conflict and Theme

> What we need now is some new, fresh clichés.
>
> —Samuel Goldwyn

Conflict is a situation that befalls the principal character and changes the character's life and behavior. This situation must be of such a nature that the character loses control over what was his or her normal life, whether it was good or bad, sending him or her on an unfamiliar path. Thus, conflict compels the principal character to take action.

Because a film works within a two-hour framework, the focus is always on the main character and how this character confronts this disruption in life.

The conflict cannot be something that the main character has any choice over, meaning the character cannot simply decide to avoid the conflict by running away. Whether or not the character is flawed, it is the realization that the only way to resolve the conflict is to take direct action—thus turning the character into hero, even if it is a blemished hero. The sheriff in *High Noon* starts to run away from the town he has protected for years, only to turn around and return to face the conflict because he could not live with himself otherwise.

There is a big difference between conflict and misfortune. If someone dies or personal fortunes suddenly drop, these are misfortunes that are part of everyone's life and must be dealt with accordingly. A death changes a person, but it is not life changing without special circumstances. To be down and out makes for an unpleasant life, but this is a common situation for a great many people. Life might seem out of control because of unpleasant incidents or extreme poverty, but with time and a will to succeed a person can turn around these circumstances.

Conflict is a device of fiction. Simply stated, conflict takes away control from a make-believe character. Without question, conflict happens in the real world; but most people go through life without the kind of conflict that is found in every work of fiction. If a best friend dies, that is a misfortune. If a best friend is brutally murdered and it looks like the killers are going to get away with it, that is conflict. If someone loses all of his or her money in a poker game, this is a misfortune (combined with an inability to stop before things got out of hand). If the poker game was rigged and it looks like the culprits are going to get away with it, this is conflict because it cries out for revenge.

One of Alfred Hitchcock's best-known story devices is the man-in-the-middle scenario. A man (or woman) is wrongfully accused of murder. The police are trying to arrest him. The man's only hope is to find the murderer himself. He goes on the lam with police after him and the murderer trying to silence him with a bullet. This is a perfect definition of conflict: The principal character is forced into action and through the course of this experience, changes. Conflict creates a basic physics, where every action creates a reaction.

## Act II: The Turning Point

> " I cut my finger.
> That's tragedy.
> A man walks into an
> open sewer and
> dies. That's comedy. "
> —Mel Brooks

From the conflict to the climax or resolution is a vast stretch simply known as *the middle*. The section can be a wasteland for writers that have not created strong characters and good plot points. The middle ranges from ninety minutes to two hours or longer. Within this section, an event or combination of events should occur that begins a gradual reversal of the unfavorable circumstances that have befallen the main character. This turning point creates a window of opportunity for the character and if pursued could lead to a favorable resolution. Thus, the middle is divided into a section in which unfortunate events rain down on the main character (Act II), followed by a section in which the character gains an uneasy footing and starts to turn the table (Act III).

This analysis of how Act II and Act III are divided might differ with other writers' viewpoints. There is a nice symmetry if all three acts are approximately the same length, as they are in a stage play. If the turning point begins Act II, this throws off this symmetry because the turning point is unpredictable. It sometimes occurs exactly in the middle of the film and other times during

the last quarter. This means that Act II can be thirty minutes or it can be sixty minutes long. The difference between the viewpoint that all acts should be the same length and the viewpoint that Act II does not have an exact duration is essentially one of classical music versus jazz.

The amount of story and character information that is loaded into the setup, in combination with the genre of the film, is what ultimately determines where the turning point occurs. The more story points established within the setup equates to a longer time period before the turning point can be reached. This is like jazz, in which the more music themes that are introduced give the solo performer more to play around with. The turning point is a natural part of storytelling, and it is the one freewheeling element that should be left to the writer to play with. The question boils down to how much a writer wants his main character to suffer or be in a state of prolonged doubt before the clouds begin to part.

In most Hitchcock suspense thrillers, the turnabout comes late in the movie. In *North by Northwest*, it is when the Cary Grant character finds out that Eva Marie Saint is actually a double agent and his actions have left her in great peril. In *The Silence of the Lambs*, it is when the Jodie Foster character gets the clue that the serial killer "covets his victims." In dramas, which tend to follow the classic structure, it is often in the middle. In *Awakenings*, it happens when the Robert De Niro character wakes up. *Awakenings* has a single story line that focuses on a doctor and his relationship with a special patient. *North by Northwest* has multiple story lines in which the action cross-cuts between the spies, the CIA, and Cary Grant, who becomes involved with a mysterious woman on the train. The common denominator in all of these films is that the lines of action are on a collision course.

The events leading up to the turning point are a heavy rain falling on the main character and most likely the people he is associated with, like family, friends, even strangers, who get caught up in the downpour of trouble. Act II is Zeus hurling

# BREAKDOWN FOR
# NORTH BY NORTHWEST

▶ Conflict puts a group of characters on a collision course.
▶ This creates action which is the fuel that makes a movie move forward.
▶ Not all the characters make it to the end but each give the story a push.

THE GOOD SIDE:

**Roger Thornhill** (Man on the run — the main character)
**Eve Kendall** (Double agent)
**Clara Thornhill** (Roger's mother)
**The Professor** (CIA agent)
**Lester Townsend** (Murder victim)

SETUP          TURNING POINT          RESOLUTION

ACT I          ACT II          ACT III

CLIMAX

SPIES:

**Phillip Vandamm** (Head of spy ring)
**Leonard** (Second in command)
**Valerian** (Henchman)
**Mrs. Townsend** (Imposter)

---

lightning bolts, and there is no stopping him until he feels the main character's life has been compromised enough. The extent of this personal damage is relevant depending on the genre. In *The Departed*, Leonardo DiCaprio's character endures a living hell that slowly shatters him. In *The Graduate*, Dustin Hoffman has to put up with Mrs. Robinson's nightly sarcasm, but his real problems begin when he falls in love with her daughter.

The turning point is an element that happens in life. Someone goes through a tragedy but gradually gets over it. A person loses a job but luckily finds something better. The human spirit, as William Faulkner says, endures. People spring back. This is why in literature or movies when a turning point happens audiences accept it, because this part of the story they have experienced in some fashion or are hoping will happen soon. Talk shows are full of individuals that have experienced a turning point in life. This is why when an angel visits James Stewart in *It's a Wonderful Life* or when Indiana Jones gets out of the sealed tomb with the poisonous snakes, the audience naturally accepts it.

## Act III: The Resolution, aka The Showdown

> There is no terror in a bang, only the anticipation of it.
> —Alfred Hitchcock

If the screenplay has evolved from Westerns, then there has to be a showdown. The age-old term of *dramatic climax* comes from tragic plays in which the stage is littered with dead bodies. There is a grand finale associated with the term. In movies, the action is usually resolved with a final encounter or showdown. This can be a shootout, like in *Heat* or *Star Wars* or *L.A. Confidential,* or the home town boys winning the bicycle race in *Breaking Away* or whispering a secret in *Lost in Translation.* This is the moment the audience has been waiting for—and hopefully they are not disappointed.

This happens at the end of Act III, which begins when the main character experiences a turn of fortune and aggressively pursues a final encounter, which almost always manifests itself in some type of showdown. This is the part that is usually the most fun to write, because it provides the payoff for all the concentrated thinking and hours of story planning. This section is usually nonstop action or the humorous untangling of a crazy series of misunderstandings. All the plot lines finally merge. Depending on when the turning point occurs this section can be the second half of the movie, like in *Pride and Prejudice,* or the final half hour, as in *Shakespeare in Love.*

The hardest thing to write is also in Act III—the last two pages. If the very last minutes of a movie do not work, then all the ballyhoo that so brilliantly and costly preceded it is lost. This is the final button or coda of a motion picture. A good ending is hard to find. The writer is competing with the hundreds or thousands of movies most people have seen in their lives. Too often, endings are open-ended, meaning that enough of the characters are still alive to have a sequel, or the ending feels safe so no one leaves depressed or overly introspective. A perfect ending, as with *Rocky* or *E.T. the Extraterrestrial* or *Field of Dreams* or *The Sixth Sense,* is like turning lead into gold. Word of mouth about such a film takes over and people honestly get excited to attend.

As long as the ending—those final pages—fit naturally with the arc of the story line bringing all matters to a satisfying conclusion, then audiences will leave content and hopefully happy. If there are story problems that have not been fixed, then the ending most likely will seem tacked on or forced. This causes fizzle. Sometimes endings reveal themselves during the process of writing, or what was the original intention for an ending suddenly changes because the characters take the story in an unexpected direction. And sometimes there are so many story lines, as with *The Return of the King,* that there are several endings. The best thing for a writer to think about is how he or she wants the audience to feel when the final credits roll. Even if the ending has not fully materialized in the writer's mind, there is a sense of direction just knowing if the final movements should leave people laughing, crying with joy, or high on action adrenalin.

## Beats

> I'd hate to take a bite outta you—you're a cookie full of arsenic.
> —J. J. Hunsecker in *The Sweet Smell of Success*

Each act of a screenplay has *dramatic beats* that build to pivotal moments in the story. Every scene is a piece of puzzle that interlocks the plot, or main story line, with the various subplots. A dramatic beat is usually made up of several scenes that are intended to hook the audience's attention to a particular thread of the story line and then must be resolved during the course of the movie. Sometimes these beats happen in quick succession, especially in television, to immediately pull in the viewer.

In *The Usual Suspects* (1995), a seemingly random group of criminals are put in a lineup only to discover later that they were part of a mastermind plot for revenge; this is one of the beats in this complex crime thriller.

Joseph Haydn wrote his "Surprise" Symphony No. 94 to occasionally wake up members of the court audience with a glorious burst of sound. This is what beats are in movies—hopefully not just to wake up people with their heads in the popcorn but to literally raise the blood temperature with a moment of action, humor, romance or an unexpected twist. Each scene is a small beat, because

there should not be a single scene that does not relate to action later in the movie or does not provide information or clues about the characters.

A dramatic beat is an exclamation point in the action, built during several scenes or a sequence. When a writer sits down, he or she usually has several beats of action in mind. A story often materializes with a flash of dramatic action, which then generates several key scenes of the story idea. Sometimes this gift from the Muse is a fully realized opening sequence or a hint of the final encounter.

What the writer needs to do when these ideas hit is start a *beat sheet*. This is like a grocery list of scenes or key moments that begin to form the structure of a story. Each beat should be listed in chronological order and added to as other ideas strike. This process becomes one of connecting the dots: As the beats fall into place, the writer can concentrate on how a series of scenes connects them. Before long, a three-act story is pieced together. Once this happens, the writer can begin to see the movie playing during the writing process. Listening to music that feels like a good underscore for the action helps in this process of internal visualization.

---

## Dramatic Beats for the
## Beginning of *The Usual Suspects*

- A wounded man, Dean Keaton, is seen on a ship late at night. A shadowy figure approaches and after a friendly chat, shoots him. The ship catches fire. We never see the other man's face.
- "Verbal" Kint is brought in as a witness to what happened on the ship. He is a weak character that seems completely out of place in the criminal underworld. Verbal starts to tell his version of the story.
- Flashback: A group of "usual suspects" are in a lineup. They are smart-asses and appear to be fearless. Verbal and Keaton are among them.
- The suspects are interrogated in separate rooms. All deny any involvement in "the trumped up charges" the police are trying to pin on them. They are cool and hard as rocks.
- In a holding cell, the men argue as they try to figure out why they were hauled in. It is revealed that Verbal and Keaton have met before. Keaton tells them all to go to hell; he's going straight from now on. End of flashback.

---

Keeping track of the beats can happen in different ways. Start a computer file; put Act I, Act II, and Act III; and as ideas occur, place them in the area that feels right to the arc of the story. Because they are on a computer, it is easy to rearrange ideas, which will probably happen a lot before the writing begins. Another approach is to get a handful of three-by-five index cards and write the ideas on separate cards. Each card should be a scene. With the cards, information can be added about location, what characters are in the scene, and why the scene is important. There can be drawings to show a few frames of action. These cards can be pinned on a bulletin board as a large, working puzzle.

A modern movie has at least 120 scenes, which is an average of a scene per minute in a full-length screenplay. Many scenes will pop up out of nowhere while writing; but the more the writer can envision in advance, the more control there is over the process. If a writer sits down with only a few ideas, most often scenes will become overly long without a clear focus. This is the literary version of treading water. If a writer knows there are over a hundred scenes and at least half of them have been realized in advance, there is a different tone to the writing. Knowing the story clearly gives the writer energy and a sense of pace, which results in an economy of words—which is essential when working on a screenplay.

## The Format

> **There's action only if there's danger.**
> —Howard Hawks

The following is the screenplay format written as a screenplay. There is one absolute truth: If a screenplay does not look like this, *the format is wrong.*

<u>**The Screenplay Format**</u>

Go down about 1/3 of the page. The title paged is not numbered.




**Title of Screenplay**

Original Screenplay by

Writer's Name


If the screenplay is based on a book, short story or magazine article then it is not an "original" screenplay. The credit would then appear as follows:

Screenplay by

If the screenplay is written with a partner, both names would appear as follows:

Name #1 and Name #2

If the screenplay idea came from someone else, then the credits would appear as follows:

Screenplay by

Writer's Name


Based on a Story Idea by

Name of Person




Name (or individual or company, if applicable)
Address
Phone Number
E-mail Address

"Title of Screenplay"

FADE IN:


EXT. PLACE OF ACTION - LOCATION - TIME OF DAY - TIME PERIOD

The title of the screenplay should be centered at the top of the page.

Information that starts at the left margin (like this) is referred to as "action lines."

Every scene must open with an INT.(Interior) or EXT.(Exterior), regardless if it is ultimately shot in a studio sound stage or actual location.

The scene headings are called "slug lines" and contain the following information: The PLACE OF ACTION is the general location, like PARIS, FRANCE. Next the exact LOCATION, like CAFE ON THE SEINE. The TIME OF DAY is generalized, like MORNING, DAY, EVENING, NIGHT. And the TIME PERIOD establishes if this story takes place in the past, the present, or the future -- once this is stated it does not need to be repeated unless the time period changes.

As long as the action stays in Paris, only the LOCATION and TIME OF DAY need to be stated until the physical action moves to a new location.

The left margin begins 1.5 inches from the left edge of the page.

The right margin is in 1 inch and should be ragged.

The top and bottom margins should be 1 inch.

The title page is not page one. The first page of the actual screenplay is page one, but do not number. The second page of the screenplay begins the numbering process, one inch down on the far right corner, just before the half inch margin.

Use a Times New Roman 12-point font if writing as a computer word document. However, screenwriting software like Final Draft or Movie Magic uses a courier font that resembles an old Underwood typewriter. Since all professional screenplays are now done on software programs, this might be a wise investment to consider.

When a CHARACTER is seen for the first time his or her name is all in caps. The next time the Character's name appears it is in lower case, and this continues throughout the rest of the screenplay. However, the CHARACTER'S NAME is always FULL CAPS over dialogue.

                              FIRST CHARACTER
                        (character's directions
                         are 1 3/4 inches from
                         left margin)
                The Character name is 2 1/4 inches
                from the left margin and *always* in
                full caps.
                        (character's instructions
                         are never more than 3
                         lines and in lower case)
                The dialogue is 1 1/4 inches from
                the left margin.  The dialogue
                should not extend beyond 4 1/2
                inches from the left margin.  A
                line of dialogue should be no wider
                than 3.5 inches.

The spacing and capitalization for slug lines and character
names is automatic in screenplay software programs.

Decide to use either dashes (--) or dots (...) for pauses in
dialogue or cut off sentences, but not both.  Dashes are "in"
right now.


INT.   INSIDE CAFE - EVENING - CONTINUOUS

With a new scene state if the action is CONTINUOUS, or if
time as elapsed then indicate with LATER, THE NEXT DAY, etc.
If there is a jump in time, indicate with TEN YEARS LATER,
etc.

All this information helps the Scenic Designer and the Line-
Producer, who must figure out the budget for all this travel,
which, in turn, effects the actors and crews.

                              FIRST CHARACTER
                        (with passion)
                Character's directions, a.k.a.,
                "asides" in parenthesis give
                suggestions on dramatic mood
                changes or tone of inflection, thus
                should precede the dialogue, not
                afterwards as shown above. But use
                *very sparingly* -- trust the
                actors to understand the emotions
                in the dialogue.

When the First Character sees a SECOND CHARACTER, only the
character appearing for the first time is in all caps.

If the Second Character is suddenly SHOT THREE TIMES (sound
effects), or BLOWN TO ATOMS BY A DEATH RAY (special effects),
these key descriptive words are in full caps.  Do not
capitalize the entire sentence, just the action words
describing the effect.

## 3

> FIRST CHARACTER (V.O.)
> A voiceover -- V.O. -- indicates a
> narrator or a character's inter-
> thoughts.

> THIRD CHARACTER (O.S.)
> The off-screen -- O.S. -- is for a
> character talking but not seen.

Only when the THIRD CHARACTER makes a physical entrance is
the name in full caps in the action line. A mention of the
name should be in lower case until the character appears.

EXT. NAME OF NEW PARIS LOCATION - MORNING

A scene can be a quick, descriptive sentence.

EXT. NEW PARIS LOCATION - CONTINUOUS

For a chase there can be a dozen scenes on one page, each
scene with a slug line and brief action line.

For a chase there can be a dozen scenes on one page, each
scene with a slug line and brief action line.

INT. PLACE OF ACTION - LOCATION - TIME OF DAY - TIME PERIOD

FLASHBACK: If the PLACE OF ACTION and the TIME PERIOD
changes, like to CORSICA during SUMMER, 1804.

The slug line (scene description) gives the location and
times. The action then continues -- perhaps for several
scenes or the majority of the film -- until the following
appears --

END FLASHBACK

INT. FLASHBACK: CORSICA - NAPOLEON'S HOUSE - SUMMER - NIGHT -
1804

A flashback can also be done as indicated above.

Information found on the far right is referred to as
"transitions" and include FADE OUT, END FLASHBACK and
DISSOLVE always in full caps.

> FIRST CHARACTER
> If a character keeps talking until
> the dialogue reaches the end of the
> page, then continue on the next
> page after putting in --
> (MORE)

```
                                                        4.
              FIRST CHARACTER(cont'd)
         -- as shown above -- meaning there
         is more dialogue to follow spoken
         by the same character.

     INT. PLACE OF ACTION - LOCATION - TIME OF DAY - PRESENT

     The slug line must show a return to the original time period
     after a flashback, i.e., PRESENT, or whatever the time before
     the flashback began.

     As a final note, the format of a screenplay is absolute. Any
     attempt to vary from this format could mean that a new script
     will not be read -- which will be an abrupt end to a lot of
     hard work.

                                                    FADE OUT

              THE END
```

## Screenwriting Do's and Do Not's

### Camera Terms

> I'll either become a very rich and famous man, or die like a dog in the gutter.
>
> —Sam Spiegel

Do not use camera terms when writing a screenplay or avoid except when *absolutely* necessary, and then try not to use. There is the great temptation to show off a technical knowledge, but there are two basic, critical problems with doing this: (1) It makes for dull reading, and (2) this is the job of the director. A spec script is meant to be a fast read that, with a few subtle tricks, allows the reader to envision the action of the screenplay. It is a selling tool to make a movie. Camera shots will be done later with storyboards during pre-production. To read a script that constantly has

CLOSE-UP, ZOOM SHOT, and "the CAMERA TRACKS with the couple through the back of the restaurant into the kitchen" makes for an annoying reading experience.

Why annoying? Because no two directors will shoot a scene in the same way. A director reading the script, provided it gets that far, will be thinking, "No, Scorsese used that tracking shot in *GoodFellas*—I'm going to do something different." This is not what a writer wants a director to concentrate on when reading a script for the first time. A director likes to approach a new script with an open mind. If the writing is good, the director will start thinking about camera setups—which is the desired effect. To use camera terms would be like having a composer watch a rough cut of a film with musical cues from other movie soundtracks; it invalidates the first-time experience.

Another reason is to appreciate the potential editing tempos of the film. Studio Era movies might have 250 edits in the entire feature. Today, close to this number of edits can happen during the opening credits. To attempt a description of scene using all the camera directions would be laborious and go something like the following.

```
INT. VICTIM'S BEDROOM - CONTINUOUS

The STEADICAM follows Harry into the bed. ZOOM IN on his face
as he sees the victim for the first time.

HARRY'S POV looking down at the mutilated body - the CAMERA
ROCKS to show Harry uneasiness.

Madeline from CSI steps into HARRY'S POV giving her an
EXTREME CLOSE-UP as she says -

                    MADELINE:
          Whoever did this - must have taken
          hours.

REVERSE ANGLE over Madeline's shoulder as the news hits
Harry. Before he can answer, the CAMERA PULLS BACK as Officer
O'Brien steps in holding a bloody knife in a zip bag.

INSERT of bloody knife.
```

This is not an entertaining read. And there is no guarantee any of these camera shots will be used by the director. Stanley Kubrick might shoot the whole scene with a wide-angle lens in one take. Martin Scorsese might do the scene with a handheld camera following the actors around. And Robert Rodriguez might cover the scene from every angle and add a short flashback of the victim being tortured.

There are a lot of screenplays available online, and some of these scripts might be peppered with camera terms. Be careful. Many scripts are transcriptions done by someone watching the movie and typing furiously away at the same time. Others might be shooting scripts, which will look different from the original spec script that started the project. And directors like Peter Jackson, who also co-authors the screenplay, will capitalize almost everything because he knows what he needs during production. Any writer that has had a successful movie made might personalize the style of his or her screenplays, having earned the right to take liberties.

There are a few terms that can be used sparingly. Associate producer Terrance Donnelly says he likes to see AERIAL SHOTS in a script because he gets to "fly around in a helicopter shooting all day." The other is POV SHOTS because this is part of the visual language of storytelling and is unique to film. POVs allow the audience to see through the eyes of a character on screen. If someone is being followed, all that might be seen is the POV of the person pursuing him or her. The audience will not know who the person actually is, thus creating an uneasy feeling. Or a POV can be used when a character is watching something suspicious, like in *Rear Window*. Hitchcock uses POVs to put the audience in the mind of the potential victim—and the perpetrator.

Starting with the baby boomers, people have grown up watching films and are familiar with most camera terms. This makes it frustrating for a writer not to use them, because shots form naturally in the mind during the writing process. A movie is playing inside the mind, but the writer is blocked from using the technical language of cinema. This is where the innocuous "we" comes in. A writer can put "we see the horror on his face" and immediately the reader is thinking CLOSE-UP, but the term is never used.

```
INT. VICTIM'S BEDROOM - CONTINUOUS

We follow Harry into the bed. By the expression on his face
as he stares down we know it is a ghastly sight.

HARRY'S POV as he rocks uneasily looking at the mutilated
body.

Madeline from CSI approaches with a look of anger and
disgust.

                    MADELINE:
               Whoever did this - must have taken
               hours.

Before he can answer, Officer O'Brien holds up a zip bag.
Inside we see the blurred image of a bloody knife.
```

Here is the same scene using "we" instead of camera terms:

Same scene, and in the reader's mind there are TRACKING SHOTS, CLOSE-UPS, and INSERTS—but none of these terms are used. Another reason to avoid camera directions is to avoid using the wrong terms. For example, a TRACKING SHOT is literally that: The camera has been mounted on a special tripod that moves along small railroadlike tracks. This gives a very smooth movement to the image. There is also a DOLLY SHOT where the tripod is on a platform with thick, balloonlike wheels; skateboards and shopping carts have also been used just as effectively.

However, Harry moves through a doorway from an outer room to the bedroom. The only way to shoot this without building a special set with *wild walls* is to use a Steadicam or handhold the camera. Though the reader will undoubtedly understand what the writer has in mind by TRACKING SHOT, this momentary reflection has taken the reader out of the story's suspense, and it might be pages before they get involved again—if ever.

## The All-Important Slug Line

> I want to give the audience a hint of a scene. No more than that. Give them too much and they won't contribute anything themselves. Give them just a suggestion and you get them working with you. That's . . . when it becomes a social act.
>
> —Orson Welles

The term "slug line" is an old newspaper expression for when a big story has a headline that "slugs" the reader in the face with the news. This is exactly what a slug line is intended to do, serve as a banner headline for the scene that follows. Slug lines are without question the dullest thing for a screenwriter to do, but they are debatably the most important part of the script for many people. A slug line gives the general and exact location for the line producer, casting director, and scenic designer; and it gives the year, season, and time of day for the cinematographer and costume designer.

A slug line effectively becomes the title of a scene, which is an important consideration when using screenwriting software. These programs are designed to pull up certain information so recurring words do not have to be typed over and over. Once MADELINE is typed in for a character's name, the next time this character has a line the writer only has to hit M and (if there are no other Ms) MADELINE'S name will pop up.

The same is true with slug lines. This is why it is important to stay constant when naming a scene location, especially if it is a recurring location. To put BEDROOM one time, then VICTIM'S BEDROOM another time will cause confusion with the reader and the small army of behind-the-scenes people that need to break down the script. Also, to put BEDROOM—

CONTINUOUS and then VICTIM'S BEDROOM—A LITTLE LATER causes confusion. Slug lines are both a concise description of the location *and* a clock. CONTINUOUS means the action immediately follows the scene before. A LITTLE LATER can be several minutes or several hours. If it is several hours, this dramatically affects the lighting for the cinematographer.

If slug lines are not clear about recurring locations and time changes, then a producer will let the line producer—or another writer—fix the problems. As soon as this happens, the original writer loses a little bit of control, which can very quickly escalate. Here are a few tips about slug lines.

The opening slug line is the most important because it establishes the general location and the time period. If all the action stays in NEW YORK and it is PRESENT DAY, then these two bits of information never need to be repeated again in the script. The reader assumes that time stays fixed until told otherwise. If the story remains in NEW YORK but the action switches from SPRING 1973 to PRESENT DAY, then this needs to be stated for each time change.

```
EXT. NEW YORK - CENTRAL PARK - LATE FALL - PRESENT DAY

As DIANE, an attractive middle-aged woman, sits on a bench
looking across the smooth surface of the lake as a dreamy
expression comes over her features.

EXT. CENTRAL PARK - SPRING - 1973

We see YOUNG DIANE touching the surface of the water with her
fingertips as YOUNG TOM gently rows across the lake crowded
with Sunday afternoon boaters.

EXT. CENTRAL PARK - PRESENT DAY

Diane suddenly shakes her head and walks quickly away,
leaving her umbrella behind on the bench.

EXT. OUTSIDE CENTRAL PARK - CONTINUOUS

As Diane hurries out of the park a light rain begins to fall.
She looks back, realizing she left her umbrella.

                        DIANE
                (exasperated; to herself)
             Oh, that's perfect.
```

In the example, NEW YORK is not repeated nor is LATE FALL when the scene returns to PRESENT DAY, because these have already been established and the location and season have not changed. Back in PRESENT DAY the real time is CONTINUOUS since the flashback to 1973 was a momentary memory. If the story stays in the present, then the slug lines do not need to reflect this, but time is still a vital factor.

Once the location of the METROPOLITAN OPERA has been established, this is not repeated. As long as the action stays in or around the opera house, only the exact locations are given, that is, BOX OFFICE, LOBBY, and THEATER. However, if the opera is revisited later in the movie, then the full location is given again.

This shorthand is used with any location where multiple scenes are shot. If the action takes place in a hotel, then the name of the hotel appears in the first slug line, but everything that follows can be ELEVATOR, HALLWAY, ROOM, and so on, with the changes in time next to each one.

The time becomes very important in the opera scene, because the sequence begins at SUNSET before the evening crowd arrives, then cuts to 8 P.M. when the patrons are entering the theater.

THREE HOURS LATER a performance is briefly seen with a theater full of richly dressed opera lovers. Then A FEW MINUTES LATER these people are exiting, but the rain has stopped.

Each of these locations and time changes affects hundreds of crew people and extras. Permission to film in the opera has to be secured. A performance needs to be staged in a grand way. Extras have to be dressed and fed. Because it is extremely difficult to shoot in real rain, the effects team will need to rent and operate special water tanks and hoses.

The time goes from sunset to around midnight, so the interior scenes might be shot on a different day, which the line producer needs to arrange; or if only one day is secured, then things must move like clockwork. The cinematographer must have cameras set outside and covered for the rain, while in the theater another crew is shooting the opera scene and standing ovation.

While this is going on, sound is getting a wild track of audience noises, applause, audience chatter, and rain falling. Meanwhile, costume and makeup are running around touching up people that might be near the camera and hoping the rain effects do not spoil the expensive evening gowns. Most of this

```
EXT. METROPOLITAN OPERA - BOX OFFICE - SUNSET

Diane has managed to change clothes, through her hair is
still damp. She picks up two tickets and walks toward the
lobby, looking for familiar faces in the crowd.

INT. LOBBY - 8 P.M.

The last warning has been given. Downhearted, Diane turns and
enters the theatre.

INT. THEATRE - THREE HOURS LATER

Diane sits next to an empty seat, tears streaming down her
face as the performance of La Boheme finishes. The curtain
falls. During the standing ovation, Diane remains seated.

INT. LOBBY - A FEW MINUTES LATER

The rain has finally stopped. As Diane starts to exit the
lobby a hand touches her shoulder. She turns, gazes up and
sees --
```

information, which gives marching orders to so many people, is found in the slug lines—for a sequence that might last for two minutes.

## Action Lines

Ernest Lehman's classic screenplay for **North by Northwest** (1959) reflects the freedom writers had during the Studio System to describe the visual details in scenes.

> "Always make the audience suffer as much as possible."
> —Alfred Hitchcock

Action lines need to be highly descriptive; paint vivid visual pictures; describe characters—giving a glimpse into the soul of the main characters; provide critical information about sound, costumes, scenic design, and special effects; *and be very short*. The modern screenplay is a streamline read. And it needs to be simple and highly complex all at once. It is a specialized writing style that is more closely akin to Dashiell Hammett and Raymond Chandler than Charles Dickens or William Faulkner, who wrote for the movies briefly.

To show how much the writing in screenplays has changed, following is a passage from Ernest Lehman's *North by Northwest* written for Alfred Hitchcock in 1959.

```
Thornhill looks across at the droning plane with growing
suspicion as the stranger steps out onto the highway and
flags the bus to stop. Thornhill turns toward the stranger as
though to say something to him. But it is too late. The man
has boarded the bus, its doors are closing and it is pulling
away. Thornhill is alone again.

Almost immediately, he HEARS the PLANE ENGINE BEING GUNNED TO
A HIGHER SPEED. He glances off sharply, sees the plane
veering off its parallel course and heading toward him. He
stands there wide-eyed, rooted to the spot. The plane roars
on, a few feet off the ground. There are two men in the twin
cockpits, goggled, unrecognizable, menacing. He yells out to
them, but his voice is lost in the NOSE of the PLANE.

In a moment it will be upon him and decapitate him.
Desperately he drops to the ground and presses himself flat
as the plane zooms over him with a great noise, almost
combing his hair with a landing wheel.
```

This description of the crop duster attack is probably the most famous moment in a Hitchcock film next to the shower scene in *Psycho*. It is also 8½ pages long with very detailed writing—terrific writing, unquestionably, by one of the best screenwriters ever to hang his hat in Hollywood. But today, if this was turned in, it would be thrown back at the head of the writer. Too many words. It reads like a novel. Yet Hitchcock made a few small changes and shot this chase sequence almost entirely as written. And Lehman was nominated for an Oscar (losing out to *Pillow Talk*).

Next is the final scene in *Butch Cassidy and the Sunday Kid*, written by William Goldman in 1969. His screenplay won the Oscar and set a new standard for screenwriting.

William Goldman's fast paced writing style for ***Butch Cassidy and the Sundance Kid*** (1969) changed the screenplay from the lengthy descriptions common during the Studio System to a quick, entertaining read.

> BUTCH
> You don't see Lefors out there?

> SUNDANCE
> Lefors? No.

> BUTCH
> Good. For a minute there I thought
> we were in trouble.

CUT TO

THE SUN, dying

PULL BACK TO REVEAL

THE SOLDIERS, tense and ready and

CUT TO

THE CAPTAIN, moving swiftly about the perimeter, gesturing
his men forward, and as he does

CUT TO

ONE GROUP OF MEN, vaulting over the wall, then

CUT TO

ANOTHER GROUP OF MEN, vaulting over the wall, rifles at the
ready

CUT TO

BUTCH AND SUNDANCE on their, feet. Slowly they move toward
the door as we

CUT TO

MORE AND MORE SOLDIERS, vaulting over the wall.

```
CUT TO

BUTCH AND SUNDANCE, into the last of the sunlight and then
comes the first of a painfully loud burst of rifle fire and
as the sound explodes -

THE CAMERA FREEZES ON BUTCH AND SUNDANCE

Another terrible barrage. Louder. Butch and Sundance remain
frozen. Somehow the sound of the rifles manages to build even
more. Butch and Sundance stay frozen. Then the sound begins
to diminish.

And as the sound diminishes, so does the color, and slowly,
the faces of Butch and Sundance begin to change. The song
from the New York sequence begins. The faces of Butch and
Sundance continue to change, from color to the grainy black
and white that began their story. The rifle fire is popcorn
soft now, as it blows them back into history.
```

Goldman writes in short sentences in a kind of fun film-ese style. There is no doubt this is a screenplay and not something written for the stage. Goldman cuts quickly back and forth, creating a rhythm of editing on the page. By doing this, the reader is unavoidably intercutting images in the mind, causing a mental image of a movie to flicker to life.

Lehman represents the twilight of the old Studio System, in which the writer was encouraged to develop a scene in detail. Goldman's screenplay started what is now known as the spec script, something that is lean and mean for the selling market. There is no question that a screenwriter would love to have the freedom that Lehman did, but those days are gone forever. Goldman's script is fast and enjoyable to read, and, until scripts are submitted in comic book fashion, this will be the standard to work toward.

## Transitions and Capitalizations

```
  I'd hire the devil
himself if he'd write
  me a good story.
         —Samuel Goldwyn
```

Since William Goldman wrote *Butch Cassidy and the Sundance Kid,* one big thing has changed: screenwriting software. In the old day—which has only been about twenty years ago—scripts were typed on manual typewriters. When something got changed, there had to be ways to show what scenes were new and what should be tossed out. New pages were added in a range of different colors, and the numbers on the pages had codes, like 78a, 78b, 78c, and so on.

Traditionally there were transitional words that divided scenes, including

```
                                                        CUT TO

                                                        FADE OUT

                                                        DISSOLVE

     And at the bottom of a page for an unfinished scene:

                                                        CONTINUED
```

If a scene went on for several pages, then CONTINUED would appear at the bottom, always next to the far right-hand margin. Then at the top of the next page would appear

```
CONTINUED

or

CONTINUED (1), etc.
```

CONTINUED was once important because if there were a lot of rewrites, the director or actors sometimes did not know if a scene ended very abruptly or was missing pages. With screenwriting software, all of these terms have become obsolete, except for the occasional DISSOLVE or FADE IN and FADE OUT. One of the many timesaving features of the software is that pages immediately adjust for any changes. Though most software still offers this as a feature, CONTINUED is no longer needed because new changes are integrated with old pages. There is no more worrying about missing pages.

William Goldman uses CUT TO between each scene as a style choice, and because at the time he wrote *Butch Cassidy and the Sundance Kid* there were no books on screenwriting and old screenplays had conflicting styles. For that time period, he felt it was important to make the reader think in terms of a movie. But to write CUT TO is no longer necessary for two basic reasons. The first is that every scene transition is made with a direct cut, so writing CUT TO becomes a redundancy. The reader will always assume a new scene is a CUT TO without having to use the term.

The other reason is that with each CUT TO—and there might be a hundred or more—

three spaces are lost. This might not sound like a lot, but using CUT TO a hundred times amounts to more than four pages. If a writer tells a very complex story, four pages will make a long script look even longer. And long scripts scare readers.

With the other transitional terms, they relate back to old Hollywood features in which almost every scene had a DISSOLVE or FADES. DISSOLVES were inexpensive during the silent era because the cameraman could back-crank the film, adjust the f-stop, and create the effect in the camera. For many years, DISSOLVES had to be processed in the development labs, but with digital editing, they are making a comeback. They have become a director's style choice. Martin Scorsese uses them a lot in his films. And they are sometimes used in period films to give a sense of nostalgia.

With FADES, it is important to remember that when there is a FADE OUT there must be a FADE IN, unless it is the last moment of the movie. FADES are simple to do, but they are dated as a constant interlude between scenes. A FADE is the cinema version of CURTAIN in a play. Now FADES are used when someone gets hit or shot to show the character blacking out or dying. Audiences have now been conditioned to expect something dramatic with FADES.

The other times FULL CAPS are used in a screenplay are when a NEW CHARACTER is introduced, for SPECIAL EFFECTS, and for certain SOUND EFFECTS or MUSIC cues.

When a person, group of people, or animals are introduced for the first time in a screenplay, the name or general descriptions are in FULL CAPS. After this first appearance, the names or descriptions are then written in normal casing.

Jeb Stuart and Steven E. DeSouza's action packed screenplay for *Die Hard* (1988) is a clockwork example of lean structure writing.

Because capitalizations are really to help the line producer put together a shooting schedule, it is important that full caps not be used when someone is mentioned—but when they first physically appear on screen. The reason for doing this is for tradition's sake, because most software programs now generate a list of when characters first appear and what other scenes they are in.

The following is from *Die Hard* by Jeb Stuart and Steven E. DeSouza. The first time McClane is introduced, the name is in full caps; later, it is normal case. The Salesman was introduced early as one of the PASSENGERS.

```
    JOHN MCCLANE mid-thirties, good-looking, athletic and tried
    from his trip. He sits by the window. His relief on landing
    is subtle, but we notice. Suddenly, he hears -

                        SALESMAN'S VOICE
                You don't like flying do you?

    McClane turns, looks at the Babbit clone next to him. Caught,
    he tenses, holds his armrests in exaggerated fear.

                        MCCLANE
            No, no, where'd you get that idea?
```

Many screenwriters are now capitalizing each time a name appears, even after the first introduction. This is usually done by professional writers or is typed up this way once the script goes into production. For a spec screenplay, it is best to stay with the traditional approach.

Anytime there is a LARGE CROWD, NOISY CUSTOMERS, or ONLY A FEW PEOPLE mentioned in a screenplay, they are in full caps. The reason is that the casting director has to find background extras, whether it is three or three thousand. The same is true with animals. An animal wrangler has to round up a TINY DOG or a HERD OF HORSES, even if they only appear for a brief moment.

Sound effects and music are sometimes in full caps. "A woman screams" would not be in caps, because this is something the actor is capable of accomplishing without reinforcement. However, if "the woman's SCREAM echoed through the hall," then this is a sound effect. Actors can provide laughs, yells, sobs, and strange voices. These might be sweetened in postproduction, but the assumption is they are part of a performance.

Action scenes are usually filmed without sound, very much like silent movies. There are microphones to catch the wild sound and general ambiance of a location, but the real sound effects are created in postproduction, often in amazing ways. Gun shots in particular have to have effects, because the blanks used on a set sound like firecrackers. So EXPLO-

SIONS, GUN FIRE, ROCKET BLASTS and a CAR CRASH would be in full caps, along with a T-Rex ROAR and Mummy SCREAM.

These sounds are tied in with visual effects. The believability of movie magic effects comes from the amazing people involved in sound effects editing. Watch an action sequence sometime without sound, and it will be quickly obvious how much the visual senses are influenced by strange noises, crashes, and music. Usually a writer will combine the two effects together, like WHOOSH and LIGHT SABER, WHISTLING and FALLING BOMB, or SCREECHING and PTEROSAUR. Otherwise, just the visual illusion itself should be in full caps, which can range from SPACE SHIP DESCENDS to VOLCANO ERUPTS to GREEN FOG ROLLS IN to SPIDERMAN FLIES from one building to the next.

The only musical cues a writer can suggest are songs and established incidental tunes. The placement of a film's music score is a privilege for the director and composer solely. A writer can say that a Beatle's song is playing on the car's radio. This does not mean the producer will be able to work out a deal, but it gives a nice touch to the mood of the read. In *American Graffiti,* George Lucas uses popular songs of the early 1960s, each song fitting a moment in the film. Do not capitalize the name of the song or the title of a classical work. Put MUSIC followed with "The Name of the Song." Other variations are shown below.

Peter Jackson capitalizes physical objects: STOOL, RING, and PINT OF ALE. Other writers capitalize certain bits of action: We NOTICE, COLLIDING WITH, and airplane LANDS. The rules vary about this, and most examples of different things to capitalize are from scripts by established writers or older scripts in which a new trend was in vogue. If a reader or producer does not believe physical objects should be in caps, then they are going to be constantly distracted while going through the screenplay. Until that big payday, it is best to keep it simple by just capitalizing first appearances, special effects, and music.

## Dialogue

> I'm never going to be shy about anything, what I write about is what I know; it's more about my version of the truth as I know it. That's part of my talent, really—putting the way people really speak into the things I write. My only obligation is to my characters. And they came from where I have been.
>
> —Quentin Tarantino

---

```
He turned up the RADIO and in his best Bruce Springsteen
imitation, belts out: "Born in the U. S. A."

As the couple danced, the BAND was softly playing "Someone to
Watch Over Me."

As the clock radio goes off, George slowly rises into frame;
his head throbbing from the night before. MUSIC: "Thus Spake
Zarathustra."
```

The only way to learn how to write good dialogue is to listen. The way to make good dialogue sound believable is through character. Part of a writer's research is to visit atmospheric locations, find an out-of-the-way table, and eavesdrop on conversations. Everyone has a personal jargon, which somehow fits their looks and public persona. And everyone has certain rhythms and favorite words when talking. Professor Henry Higgins says we are prisoners of our language, and once that was very true.

Now language is becoming homogenized because of the influence of television and films. At one time, a person with a trained ear could tell which block someone came from in New York. Mimicking these accents and slang terms led to ethnic stereotypes in an embarrassing number of vaudeville shows, plays and movies. Writers like Eugene O'Neill, Erskine Caldwell and Marc Connelly wrote characters that spoke in the vernacular of the old South, but to attempt this today would be considered politically incorrect.

Plain old common sense has a lot to do with writing dialogue. If the writer has not grown up in a community with a certain unique vernacular, then trying to capture the essence of this language after a short visit can easily veer into stereotyping. And if the writer is not familiar with the customs of a community but wants to use them in a story, it means there might be a stereotypical impression to begin with. For example, not all Italians are like the characters in *The Sopranos* or *GoodFellas*. It is the writer's duty to get to know the people he or she is writing about.

Dialogue in classic plays ranges from poetry to heightened reality. Movies have taken this heightened reality, or what is sometimes called "street poetry," to extreme realism. Often scenes are improvised to be "in the moment" with a character, which is a by-product of Method acting. Many of Robert Altman's films were made this way, as were *The French Connection* and *Dog Day Afternoon*. Because of this desire to be as realistic as possible, and giving a free hand to actors to make things up during production, the appreciation of carefully crafted dialogue has dwindled—with certain exceptions.

*Out of the Past* (1947) is pure film noir writing with tough, street poetry dialogue that has fun with words: "You can never help anything, can you? You're like a leaf that blows from one gutter to another."

If a screenplay is sold, one thing the writer should be aware of is that the first changes will probably be with the dialogue. This is especially true in comedy. After a few readings, someone is bound to make a few "suggestions" about the way a scene is written. And because the movie process is so long, lines that were once considered sharp and sparkly suddenly seem flat after a few weeks or months. This is why additional writers are called in to doctor a script; it is usually not about the structure but about the way scenes were written, that is, the dialogue.

This does not happen in theater. A director and lead actor cannot sit down and begin sprucing up the dialogue in *The Death of a Salesman*. But it happens all the time in motion pictures because after awhile the originality seems to disappear from the writing. It hasn't—they are the same words that people got excited over in the first place; but reading something over and over breeds apathy. The pace of television does not allow for weeks of rewrites, which might be the reason that many recent shows have dialogue that is refreshingly alive, like *The Wire* and *House.* The television writers are respected for their wordmanship, and the shows benefit from lively, humorous exchanges between characters.

There are still a few genres in motion pictures that are *almost* sacrosanct in terms of language. Film noir demands sharp dialogue, a tradition that goes back to *The Maltese Falcon, Double Indemnity, Out of the Past,* and post-noir movies like *Chinatown, Body Heat,* and *L.A. Confidential.* Film noir is one of the last havens for "street poetry," dialogue that is slightly bigger than life, full of well-turned phrases, and laced with gritty irony.

Crime films, first cousins to noir, are also steeped in dark city language, stretching back to *White Heat, Asphalt Jungle, The Killing,* and continuing with *The Usual Suspects, Sin City,* and *Pulp Fiction*—anything by Quentin Tarantino. The plots of these films follow a similar trajectory in which the characters get involved in a crime that goes terribly wrong and in the end takes many of them down a long, dark alley to nowhere. The characters and dialogue make these films tick and enjoyable to watch.

A writer needs to become a sponge, soaking in different styles of language and the usages of slang terms. From the novels and plays of past centuries, there is a good impression of what the language of the common people was like. But because writing in olden times tends to be rich and romantic, there is no real key to the past. Starting in 1927, when sound came in, almost every group of people has been recorded and the events of their lives dramatized. The oral traditions of these people has been caught on film; but just as important, so have their expressions and mannerisms, giving an invaluable visual record of gestures and body language that punctuates a string of words. The

movies over these eighty-some years, from Hollywood and especially foreign cinema, are mirrors to the times in which they were shot. These films contain a wealth of language for a writer with a good ear.

Production designers, cinematographers, and costume designers study old films constantly for creative ideas. So should any ambitious writer. A familiarity with these vintage movies in terms of plot structure and the delightful variety of dialogue will prove useful every time a writer sits down to start a new story. This is a writer's perpetual homework. The *business* of a writer is to listen, observe, and live life— with a practical eye that every person walking past has a story.

One of the best training grounds to learn the craft of dramatic writing and develop a knack for dialogue was the theater. As film schools have sprouted up since the 1970s, there has been a separation of theater and film. In some colleges there is still a lingering antifilm mentality, believing it is not a true art form. This is unfortunate, since by now film has proven, if nothing else, that it is not a passing fad.

In the decades leading up to film schools, the only way to get acting, directing, or writing experience was by doing stage productions. This is how writer David Mamet got started. When this breach began between film and theater, hopeful young writers turned to spec scripts for film and television and went directly into sitcoms or series without ever attempting an original stage play.

The boundaries of theater force a concentration on character and dialogue. Here a writer can explore personal or universal themes and experiment with language. The writer can learn the craft of storytelling and the invaluable lessons of how to hold an audience's attention with carefully chosen words. With these skills in place, then there is the likelihood of multifaceted characters when the writer journeys into film and television. But at the moment, this training ground is not being used to its real potential.

## Write, Write, Write

> Film your murders
> like love scenes, and
> film your love scenes
> like murders.
> —Alfred Hitchcock

The only way to learn how to write is to write. And when starting out, *finish everything!* The worst habit a writer can get into is to give up on a screenplay because he or she has lost interest, hit a snag, thought of something better, or thinks it sucks. This is psychological game playing—the id out of control. What a writer loses when a story is abandoned, locked in a zip file never to be opened again, are the most valuable lessons about writing. These are lessons no one can teach. And they are the lessons that determine if the person has the soul of a writer or not.

Writing is constant problem solving. There is the problem of how to make a slightly used story sound brand new and the problem of making characters come alive on the page. When a story seems boring, or the plot pieces do not fit together, or whatever the other multitude of excuses are, it is literally the subconscious (or the Muse assigned to the struggling writer) saying something is not working. This does not mean the story is bad, but it is an indication that something is off track and the writer needs to review the situation by reexamining the pieces of the puzzle again and again; and suddenly a light will click on. Solving a nagging story problem is the greatest feeling in the world for a writer.

The sheer process of finishing a screenplay is daunting. The number of would-be screenwriters who never finish a script is gigantic. They give in to the mind games and toss in the towel, probably after starting three or four other scripts that never get finished. To finish one script and solve critical problems the first time out, are worth more than all the books, magazines, and seminars on screenwriting put together. Writing starts out as fun, but it will eventually become difficult when a story stalls. To keep writing—and break through these difficulties—is the ultimate test and the greatest lesson for a writer.

# Screenwriting in a Nutshell

American motion pictures uses *linear storytelling* with very few exceptions, for example, *Citizen Kane* and *Pulp Fiction,* which tell stories from different points of view in a series of flashbacks or flash-forwards. *Linear storytelling* follows the simple formula known as melodrama. Like a three-act play, the story starts with a life-altering situation or *conflict* befalling the principal character. This conflict ends Act I, which is known as the *setup.* The situation grows more complicated until events reach a *turning point* for the principal character, ending Act II. The events ultimately move toward a *resolution* at the end of Act III, resulting in a *dramatic climax,* or *showdown,* where everyone is happy, dead, or somewhere in between.

| **Setup** building to "conflict" | **Turning Point** | **Resolution** |
|---|---|---|
| Act I        Act II | Act III | Climax |

The *principal character* (*major character, hero,* or *"star"*) drives the action. In a linear structure, there is *only one person* at the center of the action. The story is about the principal character's adventures or misadventures and how the conflict affects him or her.

The *secondary character* (*antagonist* or *villain*) creates the *setup* for the *principal character.* The *secondary character* does not need to be evil like Dr. No; he or she can be very charming like Rhett Butler or sexy and funny like Marilyn Monroe in *Some Like It Hot.* But without the involvement of the *secondary character,* life—at least, movie life—would go on as normal and nothing extremely unusual or conflicting would happen to our *"star."*

The *setup* is an adverse situation, or *personal conflict,* that drives the *action,* that is, "something must happen to the principal character to change the course of his or her life." The *setup* usually occurs roughly thirty minutes into a movie after establishing all the main characters in a "normal situation," at least normal for them. The *setup* or *conflict* is a life-changing problem that the *principal character* cannot simply walk away from but must confront head-on, that is, take action.

The *turning point* occurs when the *principal character* gets a clue or inspiration on how to change the tide of events. For example, Will Smith in *Enemy of the State* finds the Gene Hackman character, or Scarlett O'Hara swears she will do anything before she goes hungry again. All this leads to a final *resolution* and *dramatic climax,* or final "showdown" to borrow a western term, like finding the Lost Ark or realizing your best friend is not going to marry you after all.

A screenplay *must be written in an exact way* or no one in the industry will read it; thus, it will never get produced. The screenplay is a blueprint for a movie and the tool for "studio bean counters" to establish the number of actors, locations, night shots (always very expensive), chases, and special effects. Some of the rules are as follows: Each scene must begin with EXT. (exterior) or INT. (interior), the location, and the time. The first time a character appears, that is, the actor playing that character, THE CHARACTER'S NAME must be in caps. Each time there is a SPECIAL EFFECT, SOUND EFFECT, or CAMERA term, it must be in CAPS.

# CHAPTER FIVE

# STORYBOARDS AND PREVISIONALIZATION

> I don't understand why we have to experiment with film. I think everything should be done on paper. A musician has to do it, a composer. He puts a lot of dots down and beautiful music comes out. And I think that students should be taught to visualize. That's the one thing missing in all this. The one thing that the student has got to do is to learn that there is a rectangle up there—a white rectangle in a theater—and it has to be filled.
>
> —Alfred Hitchcock

Other directors had sketched scene ideas before Alfred Hitchcock, but the Master of Suspense made the term *storyboards* known to the public. For Hitchcock, storyboards represented pre-planning, economy, and control. His first job in motion pictures was as a title artist for silent films. He was a very skilled cartoonist, sketching the little profile of himself that is recognized around the world. He was also an organization freak and liked to minimize the potential for chaos. After all, as a child

Alfred Hitchcock would spend months in pre-production creating storyboards that visualized every shot in the movie, which is why he drolly claimed to like the development process more than shooting—because had already seen the movie.

he memorized railroad schedules and the street names in New York. Thinking out his films in minute detail came naturally to him. As he became more involved in thrillers, the genre he is identified with, pre-planning the suspense leading up to the fright moments took dozens of perfectly organized drawings. Almost all of Hitchcock memorable sequences are essentially silent movies done as montage.

The British film industry was very poor in the early Sound Era compared to that of neighboring countries of France, Germany, and Russia. To save money on production, Hitchcock thought through his movies and eliminated the need for the full coverage that the Hollywood studios did. Full coverage meant shooting every scene with a master shot, medium shots, reversal angles, and a variety of close-ups. One short scene could have as many as a dozen shots, most of which were tossed out in the editing room—not a very economical way to make a movie. Hitchcock thought like a camera. As he read the screenplay, he was able to envision each scene in his head, something most filmmakers still cannot do. He saw in terms of edits and began drawing little pictures for every camera setup, with each frame representing a cut. By doing this, he covered scenes with just a few shots.

With 70 different camera angles in the notorious shower scene in *Psycho* (1960), these rapidly edited shots go by in less than a minute; an approach to creating storyboards is to use a camera to shoot possible setups.

His ambition early in his career was to go to Hollywood, where there were better toys to play with. He knew that producers like David O. Selznick (whom he eventually made four movies with) would take the full scene coverage and spend months editing the movie together—with no interference from the director. This was standard for all the studios during this era. Hitchcock knew the art of editing well and despised the idea that someone would play around with his picture in his absence. Shooting from storyboards gave him the control he wanted; whether he was in the editing room or not, there was only one way to piece the picture—his way. Selznick referred to it as "that damn jigsaw cutting."

Hitchcock said that he hated shooting a film, because he had already shot it in his mind. His style was unique during the Studio System, when seamless filmmaking was insisted upon by the moguls. Hitchcock made the camera the star. He even had it in his contracts that a movie star could not object to where he placed the camera. Each shot in his movies is full of visual information for the audience. He deliberately conditions his audiences with standard, low-angle shots, but suddenly he will move the camera so it is aimed down on the actor. This abrupt change in angle subconsciously tells the audience something dreadful is about to happen. These are carefully thought-out booby traps meant to play with the emotions of the audience. "To me, *Psycho* was a big comedy," he would say with a smile. "Had to be."

Storyboards began to be used more often as films returned to location shooting in the 1960s,

The artwork for **Star Wars** (1977) brought George Lucas's futuristic world alive, a process that is impossible with a screenplay; this is one approach to previsionalization for large-scale movies.

when planning an action sequence was vitally important because hundreds of people were involved. It got down to money. The irony is that with storyboards producers could now control directors, within reason, that might be three thousand miles away. The responsibility to check off the story shots usually fell to the assistant director or line producer. In the heyday of disaster films, like *The Towering Inferno* and T*he Poseidon Adventure,* storyboards were a necessity to keep track of special-effect shots.

Special effects are what made storyboards an important part of pre-production. It is one thing to say, "And then all hell broke loose," in a screenplay. But then someone has to go out and create this epic battle. In the 1970s, movies like *Nashville, One Flew Over the Cuckoo's Nest,* and *Dog Day Afternoon* did not need storyboards; but *Close Encounters of the Third Kind, Star Wars,* and *Raiders of the Lost Ark* most certainly did. With these mega popcorn blockbusters, storyboards were essential because part of a scene would be shot but the remainder of the scene might be done months later in postproduction. Every detail had to tracked, or else images would not match up or certain shots might be missing.

Flash-forward thirty years and the average budget for a small film is now thirty to sixty million dollars. *One Flew Over the Cuckoo's Nest* cost $4.4 million. And big budget features like *King Kong, Superman Returns,* and several of the *Harry Potter* movies cost over two hundred million dol-

lars. Now so much is riding on these blockbusters that two-dimensional storyboards are inadequate to show the complexity of key action scenes. Storyboards are used regularly on the small films, but the special-effect juggernauts needed something else.

Starting with *The Empire Strikes Back,* battle scenes were shot with toy miniatures and hand-sketched animation. From this evolved a process the wonder kids at Industrial Light and Magic call *previsionalization.* This is computer-generated three-dimensional animation showing all the shots and edits in a special action sequence—an animated storyboard to make a movie. This process begins sometimes a year before principal photography. The animations can be used on the set for actors to respond to visual images while acting on green screens for weeks at a time.

## Creating Storyboards

> A special effect is a tool, a means to telling a story. A special effect without a story is a pretty boring thing.
> —George Lucas

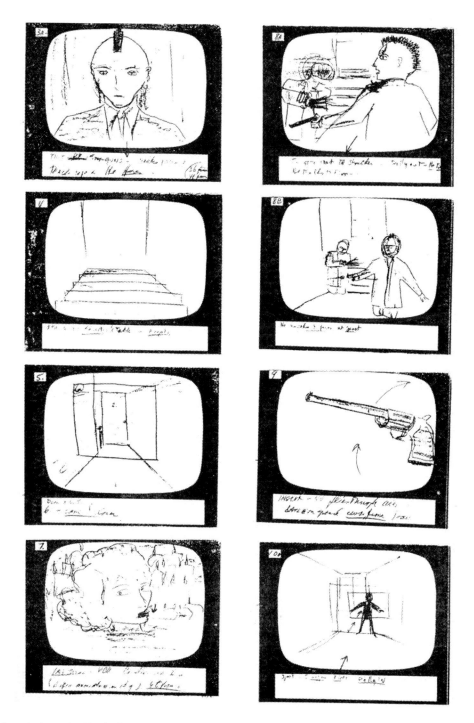

These storyboards drawn by Martin Scorsese for the climatic sequence in *Taxi Driver* (1976) show that someone does not need to be a trained artist to get a visual concept across; sometimes, pure enthusiasm is all that is needed.

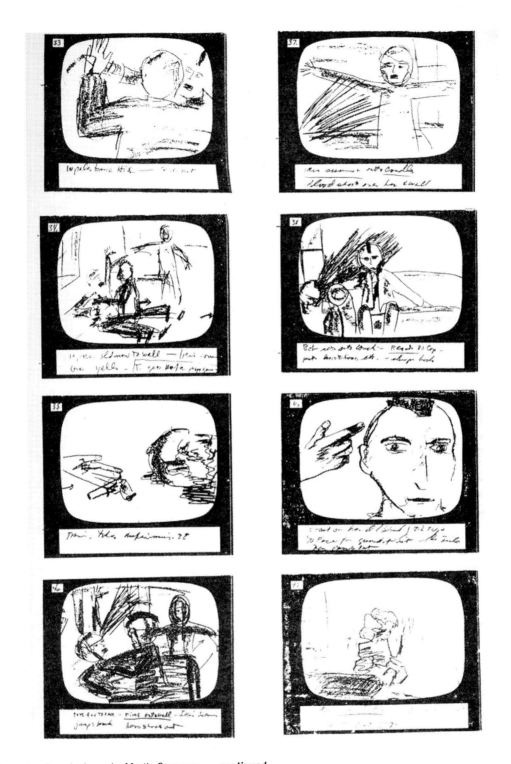

These storyboards drawn by Martin Scorsese . . . *continued.*

Storyboards are a shot-by-shot breakdown of an entire film or a major sequence that demands a lot of camera coverage. The purpose of each frame of a storyboard is to create what the director wants to see through the lens of the camera. This is when all the technical terms are put to use. Long shots, two-shots, low angle, tracking, POV, close-ups, and extreme close-ups are all drawn depending on the dramatic demands of a scene. One scene might be just one shot, or there could be a dozen or more. Every director will have a personal take on where to place the camera, and most likely no two directors will shoot a scene the same way.

In a perfect world, everyone would have the natural ability to sketch, just like walking, but this is not the case. Most directors are not fortunate like Hitchcock or Terry Gilliam, who can spend a few minutes and come up with a clever caricature. Martin Scorsese, like most, uses stick figures and then scribbles in red pencil the violent moments. The ideal storyboard is not only to illustrate the camera's perspective but also gives a hint of the lighting, scenic design, costumes, and the mood of the dramatic action.

This is when a true artist is required. Storyboard art is a special field that takes special talents. It is not simply a matter of creating a life-like picture; there needs to be a sense of cinema art. The images should appear to be moving, following one another with a sense of pure visual storytelling. Each frame must have a logical connection with the next, like a film being edited. Sometimes the images should be cartoonish to show a light mood; other times, they need to be dark and realistic to capture the drama.

This phase of production is critical because it will probably be the only time a small group of people can spend hours discussing and "creatively arguing" about the look and mood of a movie. These drawings will then be the literal blueprint for the film. If done with style, these tiny pictures will influence every phase of production and be referred back to constantly. Most important, they will announce the director's vision of the film so there is not a backlash of second guessing during the shoot.

It is commonly reported that student filmmakers check out every bit of equipment for a weekend—except a tripod. This usually implies that the film will be shot as cinema verité, giving a documentary expression to the film. If there is not a match cut, or the reverse angle breaks the 180-degree line, the filmmaker will simply claim this is what documentaries look like. What this probably precludes is time spent in pre-production thinking through the film one carefully calculated take after another.

The cinema verité technique only works because it is used so frequently, especially in television, that it has a numbing effect on the audiences. Where is the line drawn between sloppy filmmaking and carefully crafted style? That is a question only the filmmaker can answer. In *Children of Men*, Emmanuel Lubezki moves the camera in amazing ways, but it is all thought out and planned in advance. And certainly Hitchcock did not go in and start randomly shooting different angles for the shower scene in *Psycho*.

Working on storyboards alone and then, if possible, with an artist makes a director think about style, and this begins the process of discovering how he or she personally interprets the visual language of a film. Each frame, representing a single take in a movie, is a small problem to solve on how it will connect visually with the next frame and what information can be compacted into it. Tilting the camera an extra three degrees will have a subtle psychological effect on the audience. Going in for an extreme close-up on one line of dialogue will cause moviegoers to store that bit of information.

Storyboards release the inner child in directors, making it perfectly all right to sit around all day doodling. Taking a course or buying a book on simple drawing techniques and perspective is a wise and, after some practice, satisfying investment. But until the spirit of Rembrandt visits, stick drawing will have to do. With minimalist art, to use a diplomatic term, it is best to work with small rectangular frames; thus, stick figures do not look so overwhelmed or lost in a lot of white space.

An aspect ratio (the displayed width of an image divided by its height) of 1¼ by 2½ inches will create a workable dimension for simple drawings. This will give eight rectangles per page, side by side, with space for notes or dialogue underneath. Do not be intimidated with making large circles or lines. The rectangle needs to be filled the same way a close-up on screen dominates the space. Even in a simple form, this will give the cinematographer a clear idea where the camera needs to be placed and how to frame the actors in the shot.

Medium shot with character dominating screen

Close-up showing character's inner thoughts

In a two-shot or reverse angle, one figure is diminished by the other, creating a triangular effect on screen. The eye goes to the dominant figure. This shot is then repeated over the shoulder of the second figure, which will then be edited back and forth during the dialogue.

The placement of the figures on screen tells the audience who is in control for that moment. The eye automatically goes to the upper right part of the screen, so this is the most powerful position for a figure. The figure on the left side of screen is deemed weaker by this placement. In action sequences, the events usually move house left (audience's left) to house right (audience's right). This positioning and movement of action has been part of cinema language since the beginning. It probably evolved because most people are trained to read left to right, but now people everywhere are conditioned to the dynamics of movies.

In the reverse-angle shot, the left figure is smaller on the screen; but because the eye naturally strays to the left, there is still the sensation of domination. This is why reverse angles are customarily shot over the right shoulder of one figure (actor) and the left shoulder of the other figure. This allows for one figure to be slightly turned away from the camera when listening, thus not upstaging the other figure.

Two-shot with head of left figure larger than right figure (over the shoulder)

Reverse angle two-shot with left figure smaller than right figure (over the shoulder)

Even by using simple stick figures, a few easy-to-draw tricks can supply a lot of information about what is happening in a scene. Missing are the environmental touches that would be provided by the scenic design, costumes, and expressions on the characters. However, the real purpose of storyboards is to show what the camera sees. Arrows can demonstrate the movement of a walking or running figure.

In a close-up, the eyes should be above the imaginary center line of the screen. An egg-shaped circle with a curved line over the area for the figure's eyes can convey which direction the figure is looking. And a curved line going from top to bottom (head to chin) can show the direction the figure is facing.

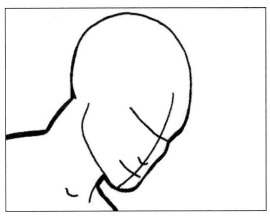

Example of "egg-head" facing right and looking down

Balloon arrow showing figure turning away

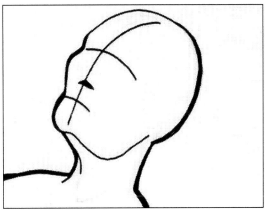

Example of "egg-head" facing left and looking up

The following are easy-to-draw methods to create buildings, streets, trees, mountains, and other background objects, plus ways to draw figures walking; running; and, with slight accent lines, exhibiting emotions. Study movie scenes for different ways to open and close the action. Every scene is a minidrama. Most scenes open with an establishing or wide shot; but when the dialogue starts, the coverage goes to medium shots and close-ups, especially in television.

Simple perspective drawing for buildings

A good learning experience is to watch two minutes of a favorite movie scene and then draw shot-by-shot storyboards. When making up storyboards from an original screenplay, draw the basic figures in a scene first, going quickly from one frame to the next, and then return to put in a few simple details. This helps prevent the process from becoming too tedious.

Simple perspective drawings for mountains and different landscapes

Stick figures walking and running

Examples of ways to show fear (flying sweat bead), laughter (action accents), and other basic emotions

If the film does not have ongoing sequences of action, then drawing storyboards might become laborious because of a lack of variety in camera setups. This can be deceptive, because some of the hardest scenes to shoot are people eating at a table or sitting on a bus or plane talking. These seemingly simple setups create camera blocking problems: An actor is cut off, the lighting is uneven, or the sound has an echo.

Then there is the choice of lens. A short lens will have the actors in the background out of focus, and a long lens can make the actors seem slightly alienated. In *12 Angry Men,* Sidney Lumet constantly changed lenses, depending on the dialogue or the character that was speaking. This gave a remarkable sense of movement, despite the fact that all the action takes place in one small room.

An alternative is doing "the poor man's" storyboards. This is a slightly misleading expression, because it involves a camera and developing photographs. Of course, a digital camera eliminates the second problem. This process begins by going through the screenplay and making a list of camera shots for each scene. Then go to the locations, or locations that can temporarily cheat for the desired look, and take stills of each shot on the list.

If done digitally, it is an easy matter of arranging the shots in order and playing with the framing and angles. The only drawback to this approach is that the director is not spending as much time with each shot about subtle changes in composition and edit points. But for short films, it makes sense. The important step, as it is with drawing storyboards, is to carefully consider each shot and determine how it advances the visual story.

The method that is becoming increasingly popular is shooting a scene by "editing in the camera." This means shooting each shot on the list in continuality with a video or digital camera. The process is constant starting and stopping, capturing every shot, while trying to judge how long each take should last. This can be done weeks in advance by using friends or volunteer actors to walk through the action.

Editing in the camera is a process that dates back to John Ford and other old-time directors that learned to shoot quickly and effectively during the Silent Era. Steven Spielberg talks about editing in the camera on films like *Schindler's List* and *Saving Private Ryan.* It is an excellent way to make sure everything has been covered and there are no holes in the continuity. When shown, it is literally a rough cut of a scene. With cameras becoming less expensive and of higher quality, this is becoming a quick form of previsionalization.

The following is an example of working through a screenplay, taking notes on camera setups, and roughly sketching pictures to help form a visual conception of the film.

*Handwritten: TITLE w/ PHASES OF MOON?*

*Handwritten: ANIMATED* *CLOUDS?*

"FULL MOON LOVER"   **FULL MOON LOVER**

*Handwritten: SCOUT CANADA - NEW ZEALAND?*

FADE IN:

EXT. TRANSYLVANIA ALPS IN ROMANIA - SHORTLY BEFORE SUNSET
LATE SEPTEMBER - NEXT YEAR

*Handwritten: MUSIC: UPBEAT, TOUCH OF GYPSY OR FOLK - DISSONANT BASS UNDERSCORE...*

*Handwritten: CGI "LOOK" - DARK BLUES*

*Handwritten: AERIAL TRACKING SHOT? VW CGI?*

Mandy Applegate's yellow Volkswagon Beetle convertible is
winding up a mountain road. A heavy FOG entwines the valley
below.

*Handwritten: CGI - LIKE OLD UNIVERSAL HORROR EFFECT...*

GRAPHICS:  Transylvania Alps in Romania

EXT. APPROACHING THE PASS - CONTINUOUS

*Handwritten: CGI MIST - MAKE CASTLE LOOK LIKE IT'S SMOLDERING*

As the Beetle zips past, the sinister remains of a medieval
castle shrouded in MIST, revealed on a distant hill.

CREDITS begin.

EXT. MOUNTAIN PASS - CONTINUOUS

*Handwritten: HEAD-ON TRACKING SHOT*

MANDY APPLEGATE and her dog, CHARLEMAGNE, are seen briefly as
the Beetle slows down for the steep stretch of road leading
into an ancient village.

*Handwritten: DOG WATCHING ROAD LIKE A PASSENGER...*

Mandy peeks over her shoulder at the castle as the evening
sun disappears. The vibrant image of a red harvest MOON peeks
over the top of the decayed citadel.

*Handwritten: CGI - BLOOD RED, CRATERS...*

*Handwritten: DUAL BLOCKING AS THEY LOOK BACK @ CASTLE*

From deep in the brooding darkness of the dense forest, a
chilling HOWL OF A WOLF is heard.

*Handwritten: PENETRATING, LONELY...*

EXT. MANDY'S BEETLE - MOUNTAIN ROAD - CONTINUOUS

Mandy and Charlemagne share a momentary look of uneasy
disbelief.

                    MANDY
              (chatting with her best
               friend)
          And this is a perfect example of
          why we should've left earlier. Next
          time just say shut up, Mandy, and
          let's go. No time for trivial
          shopping -- nope, Mandy, it's
          getting too damn late, let's go.
          Hit the trail. Got that? Okay?

Charlemagne gives a short BARK of agreement, which --
incredibly -- almost sounds like an "okay."

*Handwritten: BARK - SLIGHT JAW MOVEMENT*

Mandy Applegate is very attractive in a no-fuss, scholarly
way. Her plain-Jane appearance camouflages the fact she is a
passionate romantic who constantly charges into new
adventures without hesitation.

Her travel companion, Charlemagne, is a dashing All-American
mutt with extremely expressive features, a street-wise savvy,
and a die-hard loyalty to Mandy.

ANGRY-
REVENGEFUL

FOGGY

2.

Another HOWL is heard -- closer this time. Mandy accelerates
down the dark road and is quickly engulfed in the FOG.

CGI- ROLLING,
SWALLOWS UP CAR

EXT. TRANSYLVANIA ALPS - NEW LOCATION - CONTINUOUS

UNIVERSAL GOTHIC LOOK

The Beetle descends into the storybook village. Except for
the sagging network of telephone lines, and a few cars parked
on the cobblestone streets, the village is virtually
unchanged since the Sixteenth Century.

SHOOT
GARGOYLE
CLOSE UPS
FOR INSERS

EXT. ROMANIAN VILLAGE - TOWN SQUARE - CONTINUOUS

LOWER, NEARBY...

The HOWL OF THE WOLF grows more intense. Mandy stops the
Beetle beside a stone angel in the center of town and checks
her map.

HEADLIGHTS GIVE MOVEMENT TO FACE...

COBBLESTONE
ROAD...

EXT. MANDY'S BEETLE - CONTINUOUS

PASSING SHADOW OUTSIDE REAR WINDOW?

Mandy nervously studies a hurriedly drawn map, then searches
the deserted square for a potential landmark.

                    MANDY
          Well, old buddy, not only don't I
          think we're in Kansas, anymore -- I
          don't think we're in the Twenty-
          First Century, anymore. Or the
          Twentieth, or the Nineteenth, or
          the -- Actually I think we took a
          wrong turn somewhere near
          Hieronymus Bosch.

CGI- SLIGHT
MOVEMENT-DON'T
GIVE IT AWAY.

Charlemagne cuts in with a low BARK to indicate he gets the
general idea.

MUSIC FADES

BARK!

                  MANDY (CONT'D)
              (figures out the map)
          All right, Mr. Impatient. This
          looks like the way. At least, I
          sincerely hope it is. Yep, I most
          sincerely hope -- I hope -- I hope--

SUDDEN LOUD
BURST IN REAR
SPEAKERS- SCARE!!

The HOWLING suddenly reverberates from a shadowy side street,
sending a shiver of fright through both of them. Mandy drops
into gear and pops the clutch.

LOUD ENGINE NOISE /SQUEALING

EXT. ROMANIAN VILLAGE - TOWN SQUARE - CONTINUOUS

The Beetle spurts across the square and disappears down a
narrow, dimly lit street.

For an instant, the phantom form of beast-like CREATURE
lunges  from the FOG and disappears behind the stone angel.

EXT. MANDY'S BEETLE - CONTINUOUS

CGI-TALL SHADOWS

Mandy navigates through the rolling FOG. Charlemagne turns
around in the passenger seat, pensively surveying the road
behind them.

TOAD'S WILD RIDE...

CGI- GLIMPSES OF BUILDINGS
COMING HEAD ON...

MANDY
(looking over)
You see something?

Charlemagne gives a short BARK and a medium BARK, which
sounds a lot like, "No people."

*CGI- SLIGHTLY BIGGER MOVEMENT...*

MANDY (CONT'D)
Exactly. First thing I noticed --
No people.
(on a talking jag to cover
her fear)
I wonder if they get the "Sopranos"
in Romania? That's probably where
everybody is, don't you think?
Glued to their primitive little TV
sets watching Italian-American
stereotypes brutally bump each
other off. That would explain it,
Hun?
(catches her breath)
You know, maybe, just maybe, this
authentic gypsy cookbook idea isn't
such a clever idea after all. I
mean, who's gonna know if it's a
real gypsy from Romania or a real
gypsy from let's say, ah -- New
Jersey?

Charlemagne GROWLS viciously at a flash of movement in the
fog behind them. This really puts Mandy on edge.

*FEARLESS / PROTECTIVE*

MANDY (CONT'D)
Oh, I really wish you hadn't done
that -- I mean, seriously --
(glancing behind her)
What is it, old boy -- what -- ?
(turns back around)
Never mind. Don't tell me, I don't
want to know.

Charlemagne turns to Mandy and BARKS once, which sounds
distinctly like, "Faster!"

*A LITTLE MORE MOVEMENT*

*SCREECH*

MANDY (CONT'D)
Good idea!

Mandy pushes hard on the accelerator and the Beetle springs
out of view.

A long ANGUISHED HOWL is heard, overlapped by a distant
rumble of THUNDER and an incandescent flash of LIGHTNING.

*• ROLL FROM FRONT TO BACK SPEAKERS*
*• MUSIC REINFORCES SOUND EFFECTS*
*RAPID UNDERSCORE.*

*BACKLIGHTING GIANT, OVERHANGING TREES*

EXT. ROMANIAN VILLAGE - SKYLINE - CONTINUOUS

A FULL MOON has risen over the ghostly village. Storm CLOUDS
cascade across the enormous image of the moon, as the HOWLING
ebbs away into the forest.

CREDITS end.

*CGI- BURNT AMBER - ROMANTIC COUNTER-POINT TO SCENE*

*SWIRLING, GODS GONE CRAZY...*

4.

*[Handwritten annotation, left margin:]* HARD TO SEE ON ALL FOURS, SLOWLY RISING

EXT. TRANSYLVANIA ALPS - ROADSIDE - A FEW MINUTES LATER

Mandy hurriedly pulls up the Beetle top. A flash of LIGHTNING turns night into day, revealing for an instant the advancing silhouette of the Creature behind her in the forest.

A prolonged roll of THUNDER sends her scurrying back inside the car just as the RAIN pours down.

INT. MANDY'S BEETLE - CONTINUOUS

*[Handwritten:]* SUDDENLY - DROPS RICOCHETING OFF VW...

Mandy steers wildly with one hand, forcing the top latches closed with the other. Charlemagne has his paws over the passenger seat staring out the back window.

*[Handwritten:]* PAWS ON SEAT: EYES WITH A HUMAN CURIOSITY...

*[Handwritten, left margin:]* VERY DARK, SHADOWY, GLOWING EYES

EXT. TRANSYLVANIA ALPS - ROADSIDE - CONTINUOUS

In the eerie strobe effect created by the CLOUDS flowing past the MOON, the beastly form of the Creature is seen weaving through the trees, racing after the taillights of the Beetle.

INT. MANDY'S BEETLE - CONTINUOUS

CHARLEMAGNE'S POV: Out of the RAIN-STREAKED rear window the Creature is seen momentarily in a burst of LIGHTNING.

Charlemagne leaps into the back seat, GROWLING at "the thing" behind them -- which suddenly disappears.

*[Handwritten, left margin:]* SLOW ZOOM OUT BACK WINDOW..

Mandy looks wide-eyed into the rear view mirror, but only sees the deserted road behind her. She speeds up, having difficulty keeping the Beetle from fishtailing in the rain.

> MANDY
> We gotta be close -- we just gotta be --
>      (to Charlemagne)
> I would venture to say that whatever you're growling at cannot hear you from inside this car -- but, on the other hand, it is indisputably scaring the crap out me. Calm down, old boy -- calm down. It's probably only a cuddly little creature of the forest that's just as frightened as we are -- well, me anyhow.

*[Handwritten:]* GYPSY CAMP

A flash of LIGHTNING reveals a circle of trailers in a clearing about a half mile up the road. There is a curious, Brigadoon atmosphere about the trailers, as if they just appeared out of the mysterious MIST.

*[Handwritten:]* CUT - (2) FLASHES, FIRST TRAILERS APPEAR GHOSTLY... SECOND THEY LOOK LIKE A LOST CIRCUS

EXT. TRANSYLVANIA ALPS - IN THE FOREST - CONTINUOUS

EXTREME CLOSE-UP of glowing red eyes watching the Beetle drive away in the rain -- giving the impression that the chase is over.

*[Handwritten:]* FILL SCREEN REVENGEFUL - INTELLIGENT CUT IN (2) FRAMES OF BLACK WHEN CREATURE BLINKS

# PART THREE

# PRODUCTION

" It is kind of fun to do
the impossible. "

—Walt Disney

# CHAPTER SIX

# THE MANY ROLES OF THE PRODUCER

> I'd rather direct than produce. Any day. And twice on Sunday.
>
> —Steven Spielberg

The first producer was Thomas Edison. He oversaw the invention of the motion picture camera; built the first studio, the Black Maria; and made the first movie, *Fred Ott's Sneeze*. This means the producer has been around longer than the director, cinematographer or even movie stars. However, even with this advance in time and place, the general public has little idea what a producer does—except write checks.

There are probably not more than a half dozen producers that are familiar to the average moviegoer, and most of these are associated with a particular film or their names are forever linked with a moment in film history. People know David O. Selznick because of *Gone with the Wind* and perhaps because he brought Alfred Hitchcock to America. A few might know Samuel Goldwyn for *The Best Years of Our Lives*. The Irving Thalberg Award is given at the Oscars; but as a producer, he is best remembered for dying young and making important films at MGM, though most people today would be hard put to name even one.

Hal B. Wallis left his mark on more than 350 movies during the Golden Years at Warner Bros., but his name usually gets a blank stare when mentioned. Sam Spiegel produced four films that are on the AFI's Greatest Motion Pictures list. The films are immediately recognizable to anyone, but Sam is not. Robert Evans is known because of *The Godfather* and *Chinatown,* but most people do not realize he saved Paramount Pictures from being auctioned off.

Then there are Jerry Bruckheimer and Steven Spielberg. Bruckheimer is known for big, noisy, slick blockbusters and stylish televisions shows. He has made small films like *Flashdance* and *Glory Road*. His name will probably be around for a long time because he has the knack for entertaining mass audiences. So does Spielberg, who, despite the fact that he says he does not like it, has produced over a hundred projects and has also found time to direct more than thirty films.

Bruckheimer is the man behind the curtain to moviegoers. His public persona is very low profile. Everyone feels like they know Spielberg, because he makes such neat movies that have been part of people's childhood for two generations. Spielberg's name has come to represent a certain kind of filmmaking, like Fellini, Hitchcock, and Disney.

A producer with a golden touch in motion pictures and television. Like many of the old moguls, Jerry Bruckheimer, on the set of *King Arthur* (2004) with Clive Owens, is involved in all phases of production, with credits ranging from *Top Gun* to *Pirates of the Caribbean* to the hit *Crime Scene Investigation* television programs.

Walt Disney is without question the best-known producer, with thirty-two Academy Awards to show for it. But most folks do not think of Uncle Walt as a producer type. He was a nice guy that made great cartoons and fantastic amusement parks. In fact, while Walt was doing all these marvelous things, his brother Roy was running around like crazy raising money and putting deals together. But his name does not appear on one film, and he did not get his star on the Walk of Fame until 1998.

Then there are the studio moguls, Louis B. Mayer, Darryl F. Zanuck, Harry Cohn, Jack Warner, and Adolph Zuckor, some who produced and others did not. Mayer, Warner, and Zuckor ran the studios and let others be heads of production, while Zanuck and Cohn were closely involved in production, but each in different ways. Zanuck, who was a very good writer, oversaw the development of the screenplay, while Cohn was more involved in the details of production.

To study each one of these producers and what they did on movies results in utter confusion about the duties of a producer. The only common factor is that most did not write the checks. Some producers are on the set all the time; others rarely show up and are more involved in development and marketing. There is an angry debate over the actions of the Motion Picture Academy of limiting the number of producers potentially eligible for Best Picture honors to three.

This was after five producers strolled up on stage to grab Oscars for *Shakespeare in Love*. The repercussions of this ruling came to a head when the "producer" who developed and put the financial deal together for *Crash* was then told by the Academy he was not eligible to be nominated as one of the three producers. The following year, *Little Miss Sunshine* had five producers who worked equally hard sharing all the duties and responsibilities, but only three were allowed to be nominated.

So, if the person who raises the millions for production is not a producer and the people that do all the work putting a film together and marketing it are not considered producers, then there is no wonder there is confusion in the public's mind. From 1933 to 1937, Oscars were given to Assistant Directors, who were usually the people who did all the action, crowd, and special-effects scenes. This award disappeared over controversy about sharing credits.

However, the one producer that never receives credit is the line producer, who puts the budget together; oversees every day of producing; works closely with each department, including the second unit; and is responsible to the front office if the film goes over budget or schedule. There has never been a big award for this producer—who actually *produces*.

This identity crisis gets more exasperating when compared to theater and television. In each of these professions, the role of the producer is clear-cut—most of the time. A play can take a year to get on its feet and travel to Broadway, and during this time the producer is out raising money, attending auditions, booking theaters, meeting with the writer and director and costume and set designer, and planning the press campaign. In television, the executive producer is often the head writer and oversees each of the scripts, works with the many different directors, and plans scads of schedules out for weeks in advance.

The common thread between these two worlds is that the producers have a single golden egg to hatch. There are exceptions, and there are always the good and the bad to contend with, sometimes notoriously. But when a theatrical producer takes on a play, the investors are uneasy to hear this same person is involved in a dozen other productions. And in television, a hit show is six days a week for years. In this world, there is an omnipotent presence that comes up with the money or has the power to put a show into production with one tactful phone call. But after this happens, the role of the producer is clearly defined by the daily demands of the production—one production, one set of duties that are part of an established tradition in this field.

In film, a producer might spend years getting one film green-lighted. As a safety net this producer has a dozen other projects in various stages of production, from recently secured rights, to development, to pre-production, to postproduction and marketing. This is considered smart business, because to spend five years on something that never happens is the road to prolonged sorrow. There is also a pedigree issue with this antigravity definition of a movie producer. The lineup of usual suspects ranges from Jerry Bruckheimer to some self-inflated huckster with a ten-thousand-dollar line of credit on a MasterCard. Since there are no clearly defined duties and a secret hand to becoming a producer, anyone can say he or she is a producer because he or she has optioned his or her grandmother's memoirs for one dollar—and some poor fool is ready to invest in it.

When an actor, director, cinematographer, designer, or animal wrangler is hired, the duties and expectations are spelled out in the contract. There is equal respect for each area; and though sometimes actors try to tell the director where to place the camera, for the most part there is a long tradition of established responsibilities for each profession. Producers also at one time had clear marching orders.

## Producers in the Studio System

> The sign of a clever auteur is to achieve the illusion that there is a sole individual responsible for magnificent creations that require thousands of people to accomplish.
> —Louis B. Mayer

During the Studio System, the role of the producer was far less fragmented. A producer was a hired hand, just like stars and directors. Some were involved in the script development; most were not. Most important, the producer did not have to worry about finding funding for a new musical or Western. Once the script was rubber-stamped as being completed, it was given to the front office, which ran a budget and schedule. If the script had class, stars were assigned, the budget would be revised, and it would go on the A-list assembly line. If the script was good but not star material, it was handed over to the B department, which often had more freedom to experiment because there was less day-to-day supervision.

A top producer like Hal B. Wallis would be involved in this process, but most producers were given the script, the stars, the budget, the designers, the crews, and the technicians in a big brown paper package. The job was to use this army of talented people and bring the movie in on time and up to the standards of the studio. If the movie had more gloss than expected with star-making performances and did a tidy business at the box office, the producer had a chance to climb up the ladder and perhaps be assigned to a more prestigious unit or even become the head of a special unit.

MGM Studio was called a dream factory with the motto "more stars than there are in heaven"; on these sound stages, the studio turned out a film each week during the glory years of the 1930s and 1940s.

Units in the studio were little fiefdoms that revolved around special groups of actors, directors, designers, and, in the case of MGM, musical geniuses. MGM in its heyday had three musical units. Some of the fiefdoms were at the top of the hill, others in the rocky valley below. Each unit had a specialty, ranging from Westerns to mysteries, musicals, comedies, and costume dramas. This is almost exactly like theater and television. The reason for the similarities is the proximity effect, in which everything is within a short walk.

In theater, rehearsals are in one location and the performances are in the same theater until the end of the run. A producer can walk across the street from his office to see how the new musical number is progressing. The same is true with television. All the reoccurring sets are built on sound stages, whether it is the CTU Headquarters in *24* or Seinfeld's living room. If Jack Bauer goes out to save the world once again, the action, whether it is supposed to be Washington, D.C., or the desert in Mexico, is all filmed within driving distance of the studio. Because the producer has one production to oversee, he or she is involved with shooting problems on that production six days a week. Hollywood studios were exactly like this, with sound stages, back lots, and ranches to shoot on. And because the producer, unlike Max Bialystock,

did not have to seduce little old ladies for the next day's shooting money, it was a cozy, well-defined world.

## The Independent Producer

> " How could this happen? I was so careful. I picked the wrong play, the wrong director, the wrong cast. Where did I go right? "
> —Max Bialystock in *The Producers*

When the old studios lumbered into the sunset, the independent producer was born—big time. There have been independent producers since the beginning of time. Certainly all the plays during the Golden Age of Greece were not masterpieces. Somebody probably walked into the Athens play-reading committee and proclaimed he or she had a hot new tragedy. Because there are no records of these early independent producers it probably means they and their families were exiled for life.

The same is true with the early years of silent movies. Up until the arrival of sound, new studios were popping up everywhere, back east and up the coastline of California. Sound forced all film production into studios; and because soundproof stages with thick walls were very expensive, only eleven studios survived. The only two notable independent producers part of this tightly controlled landscape were David O. Selznick and Samuel Goldwyn. Both made prestige pictures that were highly successful and because of this were able to bankroll future productions from box office revenue. *The Best Years of Our Lives* grossed almost as much as *Gone with the Wind*.

They worked out deals to distribute films into theater chains controlled by the major studios.

When the studios had to sell off the theaters they had owned for decades, the end was in sight. Television with free shows was the nail in the coffin. From this emerged the independent producer who had two giant tasks the Studio Era producer never had to face: raising money and finding distribution. At this same time, the star system was going through a complete overhaul. Clark Gable's name on a marquee would no longer guarantee a big opening.

The producer now had to woo investors; get into bed with distribution companies; find new talent; work out of a rented office; oversee production; negotiate with the unions; and, of course, write the checks and hope they didn't bounce. For awhile, these producers acted as satellites outside the chipped walls of the studios. It was a good-old-boy system in every sense of the phrase. These producers were privy to inside connections and made inside deals. A true outsider could not get his foot in the door. But this changed in the blink of an eye with a series of low-budget horror films, shot quickly by complete outsiders. *The Night of the Living Dead* and *The Texas Chainsaw Massacre,* bankrolled by a group of dentists, turned the film industry on its head. From this point on, a producer could be the person next door in any town and in any country of the world. The only rules were to find the money and make the movie.

## Will the Real Producer Please Stand Up?

> 66 I don't care if my pictures never make a dime, so long as everyone keeps coming to see them. 99
>
> —Samuel Goldwyn

It is physically impossible for one person to raise money, find distribution, land an A-list director, cast stars, develop a screenplay, book locations, oversee the intimate details of production, and keep everybody happy. But it happens all the time.

However, what *does not* occur is that all of these hats get equal attention. With this many self-imposed obligations, the two sides of the brain are working overtime and at some point something has to give. The perfect producer is a Renaissance person that knows the arts, business, diplomacy, science, and military strategy and is a forward thinker. Most producers are working with one or two flat tires in these disciplines. This in itself is still remarkable, because a vast majority of people are working with additional flat tires.

This has nothing to do with the lack of little gray cells Hercule Poirot talks about but, rather, has to do with the lack of education that balances the arts with business. To learn about producing, someone has to jump into the pot of boiling water. There are precious few courses offered regarding the basic business of film production, especially compared to screenwriting, directing, acting, and cinematography. This makes no logical sense considering that for all these other artistic endeavors to happen, someone has to form a corporation, raise money, and distribute the final cut, just to name a few things.

Over time, a producer will gather people to help in a project, many of which have special knowledge or experience in certain areas of production. These handpicked individuals had assigned responsibilities that demanded respect during the long production process. Because no one wants to be called Producer 2, Producer 3, or Almost-the-Producer, prestigious titles evolved over the decades.

### Producer

This title from the very beginning of motion pictures, as in theater, is given to the person that is most involved in the production. A film can be in development, languishing for years, and a producer will pick up the project and carry it through all stages of production. In most situations, it is the producer that options the property that begins the process.

The Producers Guild of America (PGA) gives the following conditions for receiving this credit: The "Produced by" credit is given to the person(s) most completely responsible for a film production. Subject to the control of the Owner, the "Produced by" would have significant decision-making authority over a majority of the producing functions across the four phases of a motion picture's production. Those phases are Development, Pre-Production, Production, and Postproduction and Marketing.

## Executive Producer

In a studio-produced motion picture, this is the CEO or the representative that oversees the production on behalf of the studio. The screen credit for this producer's involvement has gone through changes since the Studio System. Irving Thalberg refused screen credit, which is probably why people do not associate him with *Grand Hotel, Mutiny on the Bounty, The Good Earth,* and other MGM classics. However, David O. Selznick's credit was always above the title, even before he turned independent. Max Youngstein, one of the five men that took over management of United Artists in 1951, said that everyone agreed up-front not to take credit—a decision he later regretted when he went independent.

The title of Executive Producer can be given as an honorarium to a major investor or someone that brought a package deal to the studio, like a star, director, and screenplay. Powerful agencies like William Morris and International Creative Management are able to put package deals together from clients they represent. For years, there has been a push to give agents that jumpstart a production a special Oscar. The duties of the Executive Producer vary greatly. Some receive credit for getting a movie out of development and into production. Others oversee the financial, administrative, and some creative aspects of pro-

duction, though are not involved in the technical side of shooting.

In television, the Executive Producer is usually the creator of a series and the head writer. In this case, the individual is very involved in all aspects of a series. The title is not an honorary one but an acknowledgment of the guiding force behind the show. Because this title is sometimes fancy window dressing and on other occasions given as recognition of someone intimately involved in every step of production, it is often confusing to audiences—and sometimes to people within the industry as well.

## Co-Producer

This person is involved in the day-to-day production and reporting back to the producer, that is, the major that sees the orders from the general are carried out. Traditionally, the co-producer is there to release money as needed and keep a running account of how the production is proceeding. A producer's presence on a set can disrupt activities or create nervous tensions; because of this, the co-producer often becomes the trusted eyes and ears for the producer, warning of storms brewing and recommending good days to visit the set for morale purposes or to witness special effects. This person can also be the Production Manager.

## Associate Producer

This is an individual who might share financial, creative, or administrative responsibilities along with the producer or is someone given an honorary producer's title in recognition for financial backing or creative contributions to a production. Because there is no clearly defined set of duties, this can be a catch-all title. Sometimes a person will take an associate producer's credit instead of co-producer because he or she feel it has a nicer sound to it.

## Line Producer

This is the busiest person on the set. The line producer is usually the first to arrive and the last to leave. He or she will know the budget chapter and verse for every area of production. The line producer creates the shooting schedule and uses charm and dogged persistence to keep the director on course and within budget. During the course of a day, the line producer has to keep track of union breaks, warn of any potential violations of rules, talk to fire and police about road closures or safety issues, and coordinate with stunts and special effects before a dangerous take. If weather or crowd conditions get out of hand, the line producer has the authority to shut down all activities.

## Budget and Scheduling

> " An executive cannot expect love—ever!
> —Darryl F. Zanuck "

A screenplay has to go through a series of hurdles during the development process. An agent will submit a script to a studio executive or production company. The agent will probably have made inquiries about the kind of stories producers or stars are currently searching for, so that a submission will hopefully be a good match. Depending on the agent's reputation and past track record with the company, the screenplay will either be given to a reader, who will write up a coverage of the script along with a recommendation, or be given the fast track and go directly to the personal assistant of the producer or star. Many A-list stars refuse to look at a new script unless there is a financial offer in place.

If a screenplay attracts attention with a studio or production company, the next step is to create a budget and schedule to determine the production costs. This is a process that can take a week or two, depending on the expertise of the person doing the research. This is a very specialized field because there are hidden expenses in putting together a motion picture budget that only someone with years of experience will be aware of or catch. The

Co-founder of DreamWorks, no one has been as successful as Steven Spielberg as director and producer in Hollywood history, with diversified producing credits that include *Back to the Future, Who Framed Roger Rabbit*, and *Letters from Iwo Jima;* seen here on the set of ***Schindler's List*** (1993) with Liam Neeson.

budget and schedule is the selling tool for the producer. Each line item needs to be accurate with current rates. Any mistakes will reflect badly on the producer and might end a potential deal.

There are software programs and rate books that make this process much easier today. For decades, the budgets were handwritten and schedules were put together in large black books with long, thin color strips to indicate the shooting schedule for a particular day. There were constant revisions, and unless attention is paid to details, confusion could quickly erupt.

For someone new at putting together a budget and schedule, especially if there are expectations of union or guild participation, it is wise to find a professional, usually a veteran line producer, to do the original work. Once everything is finished, go through it one item at a time with the professional to have a clear understanding that all the figures are correct and that there is built-in overage for safeguard. There is a big difference between a studio budget with union crews and an independent budget with nonunion or mixed crews.

A screenplay is usually written with a vision of being a Hollywood blockbuster or a low-budget independent feature. The trick is to find the right professional or line producer to put the figures together. This is a good time to watch the credits of movies similar to the screenplay and do research on the production team. Most line producers will be happy to do a little freelancing.

## The Screenplay

The first step in creating a budget and schedule is to break down the screenplay. This process should not begin until everyone who has a say in the production is convinced the script is as tight and polished as possible. Every time a scene is changed or a new scene is added, it will affect the budget in some way. Once a screenplay generates excitement, then put on a penny-pinching producer's hat and read through it looking for sequences that might be expensive to shoot.

Many times a writer will give into temptation and add action scenes that dramatically escalate the budget. Before a budget is put together, a decision needs to be made whether these scenes are critical to the overall story line or not. Sometimes simple changes can be made to keep budget figures down. A high-speed car chase that ends in explosions can be rewritten to a foot chase through deserted streets, which can be equally as exciting depending on how the sequence is shot.

There are three major steps in breaking down a screenplay: (1) Group the scenes together shot in a single location; (2) List the principal actors and extras, including animals, that appear in each scene; and (3) Break these scenes into one-eighths. Location and cast breakdown are now standard features on screenwriting and budget and scheduling software; but if the information in the screenplay is contradictory then the readout will reflect multiple locations for what is actually a single location.

## Locations

This is when uniformly written slug lines are important. Movies are shot out of sequence, because it is economically unfeasible to jump back and forth as the action is indicated in a linear screenplay. One location or set is covered at a time. The slug lines should clearly state where the action takes place. This saves time grouping all the locations together. Sometimes a location will have to be revisited if the action calls for changes in weather, like Central Park in the summer and again in the winter. However, this production problem is quickly being eliminated because locations can be altered with CGI, sometimes without the actors present.

Next, it has to be determined how much time separates each scene in the location, which can be a few seconds or ten years. This is vital information for the cinematographer to set the right lighting mood, the costume designer to alter garments, props to clean up or distress a set depending on the preceding action, and for makeup to age the character appropriately. Even two hours between scenes will demand a different intensity in lighting and subtle changes created by the character's movement. Not to have this information consistently stated in the slug lines will make the job of breaking down the screenplay tedious and long.

---

Slug lines written without consistency.

Each of these slug lines read as different locations, when in fact it is one location:

```
INT. OFFICE OF PHILIP MARLOWE, PRIVATE EYE - RECEPTION ROOM -
DAY

INT. RECEPTION MARLOWE'S OFFICE - NIGHT

INT. PRIVATE EYE RECEPTION ROOM - AROUND MIDNIGHT
```

## Actors and Extras

When a character first appears in a screenplay the name should appear in FULL CAPS to make it easy to catch during the budget and schedule breakdown. In the action lines, characters appearing in a scene should be mentioned, along with extras. Software programs will not catch characters or crowds if they are not written into the scene, which can result in hours of double-checking. This might seem redundant to the writer if scenes involving the same characters are close together, but this goes back to one of the basic purposes of a screenplay: to provide production information.

This process is always a little difficult because for casting extras, assumptions have to be made based on the information in the screenplay regarding time and location. If the characters eat at the same coffee house each morning, then the same cook and waitresses might be there. If so, this creates reoccurring roles in the movie for characters that are part of the background action. Then there might be regular customers that show up. And if the coffee house is a popular place, it will probably be crowded and noisy. This situation can lead to improvisation while shooting, thus creating new dialogue and speaking roles that were not in the original script.

The following location description has only barebones information about characters. From this, assumptions must be made about the number of extras.

```
INT. COFFEE HOUSE - EARLY THE FOLLOWING MORNING

Marlowe stumbles in, sits at the counter, and nods to the
HEFTY WAITRESS for a cup of coffee.
```

With a little more description, the scene comes to life.

```
INT. RED EYE COFFEE HOUSE - THE FOLLOWING MORNING - 7:30 A.M.

The place is packed with NOISY CUSTOMERS grousing about work.
Marlowe stumbles in. The only seat left is at the counter. He
slumps down and nods to EDNA, the hefty waitress, for a cup
of coffee.
```

The line producer, or whoever is putting the budget and schedule together, must fill in the gaps for every scene. A screenplay that describes the dishes and signs on the wall makes for a dull read, and this kind of detail is not needed. A few general brush strokes provide information for casting, lighting, props, costumes, makeup, and sound. The name of the coffee house makes it sound like a rundown joint. The time is a half hour before work begins. If the customers are loudly complaining about their jobs, then this is probably a blue-collar crowd. If there is only one seat left, it is implied the place is small. And by giving the hefty waitress a name, presents the idea of casting someone who is very un-Edna-like.

A producer uses a screenplay like the bible of production facts. Whether the words are on the page or not, every scene presents a stack of problems that must be solved. The first problem to address is if the scene is important or not. If the scene is an atmosphere moment showing a haggard private eye at the end of a long night, then the time can be changed to 6 a.m. with no customers in the place yet. This gives a lonely feel to the main character; but, more important, it eliminates thirty or more extras that must be auditioned, costumed, fed, and paid. And if the scene is to simply set a mood, then this can be done on a deserted street, avoiding the rental of a space and hours of scenic makeover.

However, if the scene is important because the private eye sees someone suspicious in the corner of the coffee shop, then the next problem is to either find a location or build a set on a sound stage. There is a touch of realism about a location that is hard to duplicate. To find the right location is not an easy task. A location scout must touch base with the local film commission and then search neighborhoods for hours taking photographs. If the location is an active business, then a deal with the owners must be negotiated to compensate for any lost income. Often the shoot will have to be scheduled for an off time or day, like midafternoon or Sunday morning.

Next the production designer will decide how much the space must be altered to have the right look for the scene. This involves set dressing and props and could result in the removal of signs, posters, and other wall items, plus replacing the cash register and dishes for a different look. The top of the counter or the seats might not be the right color or style, which could involve finding replacements or temporary covers. All this will need to happen in a few hours.

In conjunction with this makeover, an area for costumes and makeup must be found nearby or created by blocking off a side street and bringing in tents or trucks. Lights and sound will need extra power, so generators and yards of cable must be arranged. The placement of light instruments and microphones will have to be coordinated with the director, cinematographer, production designer, and wardrobe. On the day of the shoot, the street outside the front windows will be closed to location traffic, which requires permits and arranging an alternate route with the city. Vehicles and stunt drivers might be brought in after rehearsing off site.

Prior to all this activity, a casting call will go out for extras, with the hope of finding individuals that live nearby to cut down on potential travel per diem. The casting director then scours hundreds of résumés and head shots for the right faces and body shapes. The actors that are selected will be issued short-term contracts and tax forms. On the day of the shoot, extras go through an assembly line to put on costumes and makeup. The first assistant director or acting coach might give brief, individual direction to each extra to create a character background and what to talk about or pretend to talk about during the scene. And if the shoot lasts for several hours, snacks and a meal will be served.

If it is decided to build a set instead of going through the bureaucracy of shutting down roads and hiring crews to gut and restore a space in a short time period, the trade-off is hours of construction while paying rent on a sound stage. Casting and the coordination with the other departments remain the same. The benefits are avoiding possible unfavorable weather conditions, curious onlookers, security, outside noises, transportation expenses, and a rushed time schedule—all of this to shoot what might be only two minutes on screen.

## Eighths

The next step is to break each page of the screenplay into one-eighths. This is a system to determine the length of shooting time for each location. There is a mystery about who began this process, but it evolved during the early years of the Studio System to become common practice. Every page of a screenplay is divided into eight-eighths, which during an action sequence can actually be eight different scenes. For a scene that goes on for two pages, this would be 16/8 ($2 \times 8$). A three-and-one-half-page scene equals 28/8 ($3 \times 8$, plus 4 for the half page), which can be written as 3 4/8. An average day of filming is three-and-one-half pages of a screenplay. For a 120-page screenplay, this amounts to a thirty-seven-day shooting schedule.

To determine anything less than half a page is an educated guess done purely by eyeball, but knowing that one-half of a page is 4/8, this process soon becomes second nature. After each scene is assigned eighths, then the scenes in a single location are grouped together. Adding all the eighths for a single location gives the number of days' shooting in that location. If the Red Eye Coffee House appears four times in the script, with each scene roughly 12/8, or 1 4/8 (always keep the total in eighths and not 1 1/2), this would be 24/8, or 3, which would be one full day of shooting. The following day in the schedule would be in a new location.

This next location needs to be the one closest to the preceding day. If the sets are on a sound stage, then the sets need to be ready according to the master schedule. However, if the scenes are on location, then the schedule needs to reflect the shortest move to the next location. This location will be prepared in advance, either the night before or weeks in advance depending on the amount of action and scenic changes required. Like a ripple effect, a production moves forward in the line of least resistance. If there is going to be shooting on locations and sound stages in a city for several weeks, it is wise to schedule one or more sets to be completed early in case weather forces a location crew to close down for a day.

Eighths are measured from the beginning of one slug line to the top of the next one, the complete duration of a scene. The total for the number of eighths in a scene is written next to the slug line for that scene. If a scene goes on for two pages, the total next to the slug line immediately tells the reader how long the scene is. Every page is 8/8, so if a scene is the last 2/8 of the page and continues for the next page for 3/8, the total next to the slug line for the scene is 5/8. A scene with only one slug line and one line of action is still an eighth; there are no half-eights or one-sixteenths. Besides, if the scene is part of a chase, then it could take a full day to shoot it. This is when experience is a valuable factor.

## The Use of 1/8s to Break Down a Screenplay

---

EXT. SPACE MUSEUM - FRONT STEPS - CONTINUOUS

Big Sam stops at the top of the steps and surveys the
view.  The snow-lined streets are heavy with traffic.  A
large CROWD mills around outside.  Eddie stands next to
Sam, not happy with the deal, but resigned to the
situation.

The LITTLE BOY in the astronaut suit passes Eddie and
drops one of his souvenirs.  Eddie bends over to pick it
up.

Two BULLETS hit BIG SAM squarely in the chest tossing him
violently backward on the steps.

In an instant Eddie pulls out his gun, pushes the Boy out
of the way, and FIRES at the black limousine stopped at
the base of the steps.  He hits a MAN hanging out of the
back door, sending him flying inside.

Several more SHOTS are exchanged. Eddie hits a SECOND MAN
in the front seat.  The limo swerves away into the
traffic.

PEOPLE AROUND THE MUSEUM are SCREAMING, lying flat on the
ground, or running in confusion.

Eddie turns toward Big Sam -- his concern for this man is
evident.

Big Sam is struggling to his feet.  Eddie grabs him.

                    EDDIE
          Put your weight on me -- we're getting
          out of here --

Suddenly TWO MORE BULLETS are FIRED.  One nicks Eddie's
left arm, the other hits Sam in the shoulder.

The Quiet Man from the space museum is at the top of the
steps, firing wildly at Sam and Eddie.

The Quiet Man turns and rushes into the panicky crowd.
Eddie stands up and waits for the Man to become visible
for an instant.  It is an impossible angle.  Eddie FIRES.
The Man tumbles down into the cluster of people.

Big Sam has a hard time moving now, his eyes half-closed.
Eddie holds onto him, looking for help.

                    EDDIE (CONT'D)
          It's going to be okay, Sam -- It's going
          to be okay.

Eddie grabs a male BYSTANDER and pulls him over to Sam.

4.

>                    EDDIE (CONT'D)
>          Watch him -- watch him!  I'll be right
>          back -- just don't leave him.

The Bystander nods, afraid to move and afraid of being so
close to a dying man.

Eddie is in a lot of pain as he runs toward the street.
When the traffic slows down for a moment, Eddie steps in
front of a car and yells to the DRIVER.

>                    EDDIE (CONT'D)
>          We got an injured man over here.  I need
>          your car -- I got to get him to the
>          hospital.

Eddie opens the door for the Driver to get out.  The
Driver sees Eddie's gun and is scared.  He nods that he
will wait.

People move around Sam, whispering, pointing.  The
Bystander lets Sam rest against his arm.  Sam looks
around, smiles, embarrassed by the attention.

Eddie breaks through the people and lifts Sam up with the
Bystander's help.  The two men assist Big Sam into the
front seat of the car.

Eddie hurries around to the driver's side and gets in.

>                    EDDIE (CONT'D)
>               (to the driver)
>          Thanks.

Eddie slams the door and tears into traffic.

The Bystander watches the car leave.  His coat covered
with blood.

---

EXT. CITY STREET                                    1/8

Eddie's car is weaving in and out of the noon traffic,
picking up speed.

---

INT. EDDIE'S CAR

Eddie is concentrating on openings in the traffic.  He
looks quickly over to see how Sam is doing.

Sam is calm, staring out the window but seeing nothing.   3/8
He has difficulty breathing.

>                    SAM
>          Did you see who it was?

Eddie doesn't answer, keeping his attention on the traffic.

EXT. CITY STREET - NEW LOCATION - CONTINUOUS

Eddie zigzags around the slower traffic. Cars turn out of the way, HONKING.

INT. EDDIE'S CAR - CONTINUOUS

Eddie looks down at his wound; his shirt and pants are soaked in blood. He presses down on the accelerator.

Eddie takes a sharp turn, then aims for a clearing. He is clipping 90 miles per hour but is in total control, his eyes calculating every object on the street.

EXT. CITY STREET - NEW LOCATION - CONTINUOUS

Eddie's car narrowly avoids a truck at an intersection. The car swerves, headed toward the on-coming traffic. After a moment Eddie manages to cut back into the right lane.

INT. EDDIE'S CAR

This last action revives Sam for a moment. He gives Eddie a crazy look.

> SAM
> What are you trying to do -- kill us
> both?

Sam tries to laugh at this bit of irony, but the pain cuts him short.

> EDDIE
> We're almost there, Sam -- hang on.
> Goddamn you, hang on.

Eddie hits the HORN to clear away the traffic.

EXT. CITY STREET (NEW LOCATION)

Eddie continues to swerve through the cars.

EXT. HOSPITAL - EMERGENCY ENTRANCE - CONTINUOUS

Eddie's car races up to the entrance and comes to an abrupt stop. Eddie gets out of the car. There is no one around.

INT. EMERGENCY WAITING ROOM - CONTINUOUS

TWO ORDERLIES are involved in a playful conversation with the RECEPTIONIST. Eddie crashes into the waiting groom, his rage continuing to build.

                    EDDIE
          I need some help out here.

The orderlies leap up and make a dash outside.

EXT. EMERGENCY ENTRANCE - CONTINUOUS

Eddie opens Sam's door, catching the limp body of the wounded man. The orderlies pull a stretcher over.

INT. EMERGENCY WAITING ROOM - CONTINUOUS

The orderlies rush the stretcher with Big Sam into the Emergency Room. The Receptionist starts paging for the house doctor.

INT. EMERGENCY OPERATING ROOM - CONTINUOUS

The orderlies park Sam's stretcher next to the operating table and quickly transfer the man to the table with Eddie's help.

The orderlies prepare the room for the doctor. Big Sam grabs Eddie's coat with a firm grip, and pulls Eddie toward him. His words come with great effort.

                    SAM
          Get him.

Eddie nods that he will.

                    SAM (CONT'D)
               (his words barely a whisper)
          I should have listened --

                    EDDIE
               (with deep affection)
          Not you, Sam --

## Hidden Expenses

There are a multitude of things in a screenplay that are not *and should not* be written about. They become boring and tedious, with all the excitement of reading a shopping list. But when it comes to creating an accurate budget, they have to be perceived and accounted for. Every scene will have hidden expenses. They are not a critical part of the dramatic action of the script but are essential to creating a believable visual picture for the action to take place in. This is a knowledge born out of making movies.

To describe a character walking down a street late at night might seem simple and straightforward, but there are all sorts of hidden expenses lurking beneath the surface. Most cinematographers like to water down a scene, especially for a night scene, because it gives an added quality to the image with the reflections. Streets are not deserted for long periods of time. To shoot a lone figure walking, hands in pocket, and then have someone enter at the upper right corner of the screen will immediately kill the mood.

Crowd security has to be posted and permits applied for that grant street closures. Everyone that lives in the neighborhood or runs a shop has to be contacted and their approval secured. Some people will be paid to turn lights on. And if there are any signs or posters with real names, they will have to be temporarily removed, which is additional work for props. Suddenly one person on a street will generate into twenty or more people working off camera.

If a scene takes place in a coffee house, shot on location, then the establishment might have all the dishes and silverware needed for the scene. However, if the action takes place in the 1940s, then special dishes and items will have to be ordered or made. And if the scene is shot on a sound stage, everything will have to be purchased to make it look authentic. James Cameron talks about how hundreds of thousands of dollars were spent on recreating all the elaborate dishes and crystal glasses for the dining scene in *Titanic*—and then the flood gates were opened and every piece was destroyed.

Most of the time, a line will automatically be put into a budget for props and set decoration that covers the expenses for these incidental items. But to troubleshoot a script means to be able to previsionalize the scene and make educated guesses. This means understanding the characters and then making a mental picture of the physical space these characters live in.

People like to personalize their living environments. A film buff will certainly have classic movie posters on the wall. An eccentric lady might live in a house full of priceless antiques from a sentimental era. Someone who loves to prepare food will own the finest knives and skillets. In a film, these items if cheaply duplicated will read as fake or theatrical to an audience. They are hidden expenses because the rental and insurance of such expensive items will exceed an average budget estimate. They are items that probably will not be mentioned in a screenplay but are anticipated based on the budget planner's insights into the characters and practical experience.

## The Producer as Writer

> An audience is never wrong. An individual member of it may be an imbecile, but a thousand imbeciles together in the dark—that's critical genius.
> —Billy Wilder

Every scene in a screenplay must be analyzed for each area of production, have an individual budget line created for it, and then fit into a master schedule. A scene might be one of several shot in a single day. Through this process, the producer becomes a writer on the screenplay—not in terms of writing dialogue but by adjusting critical elements found in the script. Scenes that do not move the action forward are eliminated, times are changed, and effects are canceled or abridged to fit the budget demands.

What happens during this process becomes writing by checkbook. A screenplay comes in with a higher budget than anticipated. Because of the genre, audience expectations, potential competition, and a dozen other factors that may or may not be relevant, it is determined that the only way to go forward is to cut the budget. The first response is to say the screenplay works *but* some of the scenes can be cut back or simplified. At this point, every scene is put under the microscope and thus begins a gradual whittling-down ritual.

Crowd scenes are reduced, locations are found that can cheat for a variety of places, action sequences are rethought for a lower number of effects and stunts, and dialogue-heavy scenes (a term that gives screenwriters hellish nightmares) are examined word by word. Stars like great dialogue, but audiences like action—and audiences buy tickets. It is the oldest Hollywood formula for success.

At the end of this celluloid bloodbath is often a pint-size version of the writer's original vision—a vision that originally got a lot of people very excited. The scope of the project has been mortified because of budget cuts, and part of the sparkle is now gone. In a well-structured screenplay, every scene is important to the story line; thus, when scenes are cut, story problems surface. The solution is not to reinsert the scenes, because they were trimmed for budget reasons. The obvious fix is to play with the script.

The producer by doing his or her job has altered the screenplay. However, the project would have been dead on the launch pad if these alterations, which had gone from a few to many, had not been made. In some ways the problem can be blamed on the writer for not thinking like a pro-

ducer during the creative process. Fixes are always difficult. A writer will have spent countless hours perfecting the story line, and any change will seem like a step backward.

What happens next is a sad tune that is familiar to a great many productions. The producer will try personally to fix the problems or bring in another writer to assist in this operation without anesthesia. A new writer will have new ideas that seem golden because they get the story back on track—a story that was derailed during the budget process. Soon the original story is like George Washington's axe: A museum had the axe, but the handle rotted and was replaced. Eventually the blade rusted and was replaced. But the museum sign still proclaimed it was Washington's axe.

As a result of this mad dance with the screenplay and budget, the producer is cast as the villain. However, plays and novels do not cost a hundred million dollars, and most often an enjoyable film comes out of this process. What is finally seen on the screen is because of the tireless efforts of the producer. Sometimes a director will take over the problems of fixing a script, but the producer is the one that holds the wings on and lands the plane.

No producer really wants to change writers. This is partly because it can become very expensive but ultimately because there is a certainly loyalty to the writer that came up with the story in the first place. There will probably never be a solution to this turnabout in which the producer becomes an involuntary writer during the budget process. Sooner or later, the 120 pages of a screenplay that costs fifteen bucks to copy must be turned into a multimillion-dollar feature. The compromise is for the writer to indeed learn more about budgets and schedules (keeping this stored in the back of the mind while creating), and for the producer to become aware of the great stories with great themes and what makes them work. The ideal movie person is a writer that can direct and produce. This way the three major hats in the filmmaking process are worn by one dynamic individual.

## Building the Perfect Producer

The Perfect Producer is the smartest kid on the block, who knows everything there is to know about every area of production. On a typical day, the Perfect Producer is a psychiatrist, penny-pinching accountant, the drill sergeant from *Full Metal Jacket,* spiritual leader, cinema historian, corporate shark, best friend, child of Satan, Earth mother, asylum guard, enlightened philosopher, a teller of bawdy tales, a Nobel-Prize-winning economist, the basketball player from hell, Mary Poppins, a master chef, chemical engineer, sketch artist extraordinaire, life of the party, a wet puppy who needs a hug, and someone who can describe in detail a sequence from any movie made since *The Great Train Robbery* in 1903. If the director, cinematographer, costumer, and animal wrangler all get food poisoning from the salmon dip, the Perfect Producer can take over without losing a minute on the schedule. And then there is that whole walking-on-water thing.

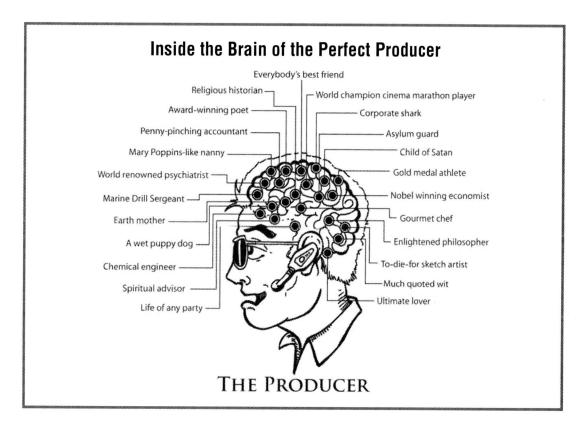

### Inside the Brain of the Perfect Producer

Everybody's best friend

Religious historian — — World champion cinema marathon player

Award-winning poet — — Corporate shark

Penny-pinching accountant — — Asylum guard

Mary Poppins-like nanny — — Child of Satan

World renowned psychiatrist — — Gold medal athlete

Marine Drill Sergeant — — Nobel winning economist

Earth mother — — Gourmet chef

A wet puppy dog — — Enlightened philosopher

Chemical engineer — — To-die-for sketch artist

Spiritual advisor — — Much quoted wit

Life of any party — — Ultimate lover

THE PRODUCER

Many of these human traits are a gift of genetics or an obsession stemming from wounded childhood memories about being the last kid to be picked for a baseball game. Whether it comes natural or through sheer tenacity, a producer needs to be the ultimate people person. There are many producers that are not and, consequently, make a working experience miserable for everyone. Putting personality aside, the one indispensable requirement to becoming the Perfect Producer is to know as much as humanly possible about every area of production.

A producer needs to know *motion pictures* in the same way as a director, writer, cinematographer, production designer, or any other key personnel on a set—not just from an operational standpoint but from the perspective of each of the artistic professionals involved. This goes beyond a comprehensive understanding of the filmmaking process; it is an appreciation of the aesthetic values of each art discipline found in film extending from the Silent Era to the present.

A motion picture is a large ensemble of artists brought together by a producer to tell a story. Ideally, a producer needs to communicate with each of these artists in their own professional language as a sign of respect and to explore all the values possible for a film. A producer should know how light has been used by great cinematographers going back to German expressionism, or the influence of Cedric Gibbons on production design. At one time, this knowledge was learned by working in a studio for years, literally growing up in the business.

After the Studio System ended, there was no place for producers to learn the trade. The actors, writers, cinematographers, costumers, and the other artists found freelance work or went into television. Film school became the new training ground for these artists—except producers. A film producer became an outsider in this circle of artists, where once the producer was the center of influence. Most film schools grew up in theater departments, which traditionally have had a prejudice against emphasizing business practices.

During the 1960s and 1970s when studios were bought by Gulf-Western, Coca-Cola, and TransAmerica, the studio executives were brought in from Ivy League universities because the film schools at this time did not have programs for basic business procedures.

Somewhere along the line, schools decided that learning to sketch like Albrecht Durer had nothing in common with the principles of business strategy. This might unhappily be true for most professions, but the combination of these diverse disciplines is essential in the education of a producer. Film production is about creating art, a basic fundamental that often gets overlooked, and this is true now more than ever in the past. Being the watchdog to an eighty-million-dollar budget and having no background in costume or scenic design will eventually lead to conflicts over purchasing or result in wrong creative decisions based purely on bottomline considerations. This also sets up the potential for the producer to be easily bamboozled.

The role of the producer has debatably gone full circle since the glory days of the Studio System. During the late 1960s, many directors acted as producer, because the studio or production company would green-light a movie and get out of the way. The difference between then and now is that films like *Easy Rider, The Rain People,* and *American Graffiti* cost less than a million dollars, as opposed to $8 million to $16 million for modern independent features like *Little Miss Sunshine* and *Sideways.* With an average studio budget of $80 million to $120 million, the producer is no longer someone who waves blissfully from the bleachers when shooting starts. CGI-dominated features like *Sin City* and *300* have brought film production back to the sound stages, making the twenty-first-century producer look more like a healthy, tanned Irving Thalberg all the time.

Only recently have major film schools begun to offer courses in business and accounting. However, a degree in the business of film production and marketing is still a rarity in business col-

## Proposal for Film Business Courses

Almost every major business today has some involvement with the motion picture and entertainment industry. This would not have been true ten years ago. International marketing, merchandising, product placement, endorsements, the Internet, computer games, cable and satellite television, publishing, iPods, management training, public relations, music, and other spin-offs have become part of the progress to tap into an ever-expanding consumer marketplace.

Giant corporations like Sony, AOL Time Warner, Viacom, and News Corp own studios, television stations, publishing houses, cable companies, theme parks, sports teams, newspapers, magazines, and computer games, which in the last five years have become more profitable than motion pictures. The average American spends at least 3.5 hours per day watching the news, television shows, or a DVD from Netflix; searching the Internet; or playing an interactive game.

The motion picture and entertainment industry touches almost every level of business, including management, accounting, law, international trade, investment, rights, and especially marketing. And while most practices are similar in all these areas, there are also factors that are completely unique to this high-profile industry.

Twenty-five years ago, motion picture companies produced movies—and they were the sole product. Now studios like Disney, Paramount, Fox, Universal, and Warner Bros. are part of a vertical integration structure that includes cable television, theme parks, travel, best sellers, music concerts, Broadway musicals, restaurants, clothing, merchandise, software, furniture, and an increasing number of other items and activities.

Students have grown up in this multimedia world and are curious about how to "break" into it. In surveys conducted with over five thousand students since 2001, 62 percent said they would like to take courses in motion picture business or pursue a minor or major in this diversified field. In film study courses offer for humanities or global awareness requirements, over 27 percent of the students enrolled were from the business college.

An overwhelming number of students around the world have a desire to get into motion pictures. Unfortunately, this industry has a high failure rate—not from lack of personal effort but from a lack of understanding of how the BUSINESS works. Whether a student wants to be a director, writer, actor, or some other glamorous occupation, most likely he or she will need to create a project to showcase his or her talents. This means raising money, budgeting, scheduling, and marketing. Students are not being educated in these areas. Nor are they being made aware of the hundreds of other job possibilities in motion pictures and entertainment.

leges around the world. This is oddly out of date, because a convincing argument can be put forth that every large corporation is in the film business. This would include television advertising, training videos, product placement, celebrity spokespeople, and the Internet. The reason directors often make good producers is that they know both sides of filmmaking, that is, the artistic product and the business. The only way to build the Perfect Producer is through a change in education that finally reflects the daily influence of film on everyone's life.

# Sample Introductory Courses

## The Motion Picture Business: An Introduction

This course is designed as a comprehensive overview of the many aspects of filmmaking, from Hollywood to the independents. The Motion Picture Business will look at the evolution of the movie studios and how the business of filmmaking has changed over the decades. The course will examine the different areas of a motion picture, including all stages of development, production, and marketing. The roles and duties of the various positions in a motion picture will be examined, from producer to director to the crews and designers. The students will learn how these different positions interact and what equipment or materials are required in each area. From this information, the student will gain an understanding of the budget demands for all stages of a motion picture, including the differences between an independent film and a union production. The contractual demands of each union or guild within the motion picture industry will be explored, for example, the Directors Guild of America (DGA), the Writers Guild of America (WGA), and all the trade unions. Students will be taught to break down a screenplay to create a budget and schedule. They will then learn the steps of turning a screenplay into storyboards, production designs, and creating a previsualization program. During the semester, professionals from the film industry will visit the class to share their experiences with the students and give evaluations on projects.

## Entertainment Business and Law

This course will explore the similarities and differences in the many fields of public entertainment, including theater, television, film, music, computer games, and Sports. Each of these fields will be examined in regard to management, personnel, product, special activities, evolving technology, and marketing, with a special focus on the legal and contractual demands. Students will learn about intellectual properties, copyrights, creative partnerships, merchandising, coventures, and the legal requirements related to the formation of a for-profit corporation versus a not-for-profit organization. From this, students will gain a practical understanding of the laws and contracts peculiar to these diversified entertainment fields, plus gain insights to how most businesses today are in some way involved in entertainment, thus requiring a special understanding of these legal and contractual demands.

## Producing for Hollywood

This course will give students a thorough understanding of the many roles of a producer by providing a working knowledge of motion picture production and financing. The history of film financing will be explored, from the early days of Hollywood to the present. A special focus will be placed on the problems and travails that face the producer in the technological age of the twenty-first century. Producing for Hollywood will explore the available conduits for film financing on both independent and full-union productions. To achieve this, the students will break down a feature film screenplay to create a comprehensive schedule and budget. The student will then apply this information to create a business plan and proposal to attract potential investors. This proposal will include a marketing and advertising campaign for the final product. As part of the course, students will learn the art of contract and legal negotiations.

# Unspoken Rules for the Producer

> " Credit you give yourself is not worth having.
> —Irving Thalberg "

Everyone involved in a film is there to tell a story. The main responsibility of a producer is to create a working environment that allows this army of talent to create without distracting interruptions and to keep the production on track. The producer plays God in the sense that everyone in the middle of a production is not seeing the overly used term "the big picture." The producer needs to stay above the control mayhem of a motion picture production. After weeks of little sleep and thirty-some setups a day, everyone on the set begins to lose perspective about the pace and quality of each scene. The greatest contribution a producer can make, without fury or accusations, is to give cool, relaxed advice that helps solve problems instead of manufacturing new ones. The trick is that this advice must be right on target each time.

## Storyteller

A producer must know the *art* of storytelling, which is more important than an army of accountants. A well-constructed story has the potential of going through development quickly, attracting the attention of major talent, and doing well at the box office. A badly constructed story can have millions thrown at it to make it work, like *Sahara* and *The Island*. Storytelling is an art, which by definition means it is comprised of elements that if mixed together with skill can affect the emotions of an audience on many different levels. A producer needs to be familiar with these elements the way a doctor, lawyer, or mechanic is familiar with the tools of their profession.

There are convenient but true analogies—a producer that does not know what makes a good

story tick is going to be an outsider on important decisions that affect all the hard work it took to raise money and get a production started. The solution is to read. This is a lifetime of homework assignments. Read the classics; read the modern novels that have made an impact; read books on how to write; and, in a symbolic sense, read great movies—look at them for story structure and economy of character development.

## Organization

A producer must be extraordinarily organized all the time, which, of course, is not always the case. There are legendary tales of producers who could not make a definitive decision on casting or the color of a costume, or who called meetings at 3 a.m. because they suddenly had a breakthrough idea. And there have been producers that kept everyone in a state of suspended animation about what happens next because they liked playing puppet master in mass confusion.

Though it cannot be said that this breed of producer is extinct, he or she is probably not working in television or on big-budget productions today. A producer must know how to put a business plan together, pitch an idea, raise capital, hire a staff, put together the creative team, and keep track of every heartbeat through the three stages of production. Each of these steps takes concentration and organization. To do all these things successfully is an adrenaline rush for some people and a tedious nightmare for others. Sit down sometime with an airtight budget for a project, and then try to figure out how to cut back 20 percent and still achieve the same results. If this proves to be hours of excitement, then this is the road to becoming a producer.

## Image

A good producer commands respect. Some get respect through fear; others are given respect because of organization and dedication; and many get respect through a combination of these methods. Like the old metaphor, a producer is a general given an army to complete an impossible task.

Without respect from everyone involved, this army is not motivated to the fullest. Look at what happened to Patton when he slapped the soldier and how long it took him to get back into the fight after this one incident.

A producer needs to be slightly elevated above everyone else—not in a pretentious manner but as that mythical figure on the hill that everyone works hard for and is eager to please by excelling at an assigned task. This can be lonely at times, because it means giving up a lot of recreational madness during the course of a production. The producer has to be in control at all times; and sometimes, on a bad day, this is a matter of giving an Oscar-worthy performance to mask the inner conflicts. It is wise to always plan some decadent pleasure as a reward when the production wraps.

## Decisions

A producer's decision is final. The trick to not abusing this power is to always be right with each decision. This is tantamount to being King Solomon during production. A producer that knows the business and has hands on the pulse of the production should hopefully have an objective wisdom that makes decision making insightful and for the best interest of the production. Trust the people involved in a situation that requires a firm decision and listen to them carefully. Often, the right decision evolves out of a brief meeting at which the obvious solution pops up during the course of trading ideas.

A producer can take satisfaction in reaching an agreeable compromise in a controlled situation. At other times, a producer will have to make those dreaded hard decisions. When this happens, give careful thought, and make sure the decisions are right. Producing a movie is a seemingly endless series of problems, and a good producer will troubleshoot every possible scenario with the hope of being prepared for half of the things that will befall a production. The other decisions are made from personal experience and a "damn the torpedoes" determination.

## The Director

A producer's relationship with the director seems to fall into two categories: idyllic or highly volatile. Brian Grazer and Ron Howard have worked without any public clashes for years. Sam Spiegel and David Lean argued constantly. Both teams have made terrific films. The producer and director have come to represent the two extremes of production—the money and creative freedom. If approached this way, then there will certainly be land mines every two feet of the journey.

The producer's main contribution to a film is in development and pre-production. This is the time when every proposed action has to fit snugly into a budget and schedule. And this is when lights, equipment, sets, costumes, crews, and all the other production components are talked about and talked about and finally agreed upon. This is the producer's domain. Production is the director's domain. It becomes like Eisenhower and Patton; the director is on the front lines during a time of extreme concentration. To besiege the director with matters that should have been addressed in pre-production is like walking up on stage during a Broadway show and giving critical notes with no thought to the timing of the situation. It destroys the focus of the director. This does not mean that if the unforeseen happens the producer should let the director drown. Getting things quickly back on track is what the producer is there for, usually to the great appreciation of the director.

## The Actors and Crew

Learn everyone's name. Always say "hello" with a sincere smile. If someone is asked how they are doing, wait for an answer. And give a great party when it is all over. Genuine courtesy and respect will add a quality to the production that money literally cannot buy.

# CHAPTER SEVEN

# THE DIRECTOR

> There are a thousand ways to point a camera, but really only one.
>
> —Ernst Lubitsch

Mention the word *director* and most likely Alfred Hitchcock, Martin Scorsese, Steven Spielberg, or Quentin Tarantino come to mind. Each of these directors has made remarkable films that will probably be watched a hundred years from now. And each, as Ernst Lubitsch humorously observed, certainly knows how to point the camera. Yet each is distinctly different in his personal approach to directing.

Martin Scorsese with Robert De Niro on the set of *GoodFellas* (1990), a partnership that has resulted in some of the most compelling and complex characters in American film.

Hitchcock is remembered for suspense thrillers and storyboarding every detail of a motion picture in advance. Scorsese is identified with the gangster genre (although he has made everything from musicals to period dramas) and improvising on the set with his cast. Spielberg is known for high-action special effects movies that he plans out meticulously and groundbreaking films about war, which he shoots from the gut without storyboards. And Tarantino is associated with highly stylized crime films with long passages of rich, tough dialogue.

Hitchcock's favorite director was Luis Bunuel, and he was also heavily influenced by F. W. Murnau during his formative years in Germany. Scorsese talks about the personal impact by the directors of the Italian Neorealism movement and the French New Wave and gritty American auteurs like Samuel Fuller and Nicholas Ray. Spielberg traditionally watches four movies when planning a new production: John Ford's *The Searchers*, David Lean's *Lawrence of Arabia*, Frank Capra's *It's a Wonderful Life*, and Akira Kurosawa's *Seven Samurai*. Each of these directors has very different visual styles and approaches to moviemaking. And Tarantino, the only writer-director of the four, is unabashed about the homage his films pay to spaghetti Westerns by Sergio Leone and B-genre drive-in features.

Hitchcock's thrillers move in a linear story line, usually with a time clock connected to the actions of his main character and an occasional dream sequence or flashback. When Scorsese won his Academy Award for *The Departed*, it was for the first film he made with a structured story line. His movies are character driven and episodic, like the foreign cinema of Jean-Luc Godard and Roberto Rossellini. The majority of Spielberg's movies reflect his love of plot-driven Old Hollywood adventures, serials, and Saturday matinee Westerns in the style of Howard Hawks, George Stevens, and Michael Curtiz. And many of Tarantino's films play with time in a jigsaw structure, with scenes out of sequence.

The technical style, recurring themes, and the storytelling approach of these popular directors are different. To create a clear definition of what a motion picture director does based on these four men would be difficult and often contradictory. Even the directors that had the strongest influence on them are varied with individualistic approaches to moviemaking. Hitchcock, Scorsese, Spielberg, and Tarantino use the same tools for filmmaking. However, returning to Lubitsch's comment, each points the camera differently—but this difference is exactly right for their personal vision of the shot.

The common thread between these directors is character. Each has brought shadows on the screen to life. The list of great characters is long and includes Roger O. Thornhill, Norman Bates, Travis Bickle, Bill "The Butcher" Cutting, Qunit, Indiana Jones, Vincent Vega, and Bill, who The Bride is trying to kill. Somehow through the infinite variation of casting, camera setups, lighting, lenses, costumes, scenery, props, sound, special effects, music, and—of course—good writing— full-blown characters are born. This association between directors and realistic characters is arguably what separates film from theater and literature.

A novelist will spend eight hundred pages elaborating on a character's multifaceted personality, but the vision of that character will ultimately be defined by the reader's imagination. In this way, the character is slightly changed by everyone who picks up the book. Charles Dickens and Jules Verne had illustrators capture moments in their novels, and these sketches still influence how Ebenezer Scrooge and Captain Nemo are portrayed over a hundred years later. A playwright uses dialogue to structure a character. This character will be different in every production because of the actor's personality and the scenic environment of the production. From Hamlet to Willy Loman, the audience will retain a vision of the actor playing the role on a given evening.

Film freezes one actor's performance forever. This performance is captured the way the mind remembers, from quick bits of action and a variety of angles. The mind recalls flashes of a particular person or a large event, from long shots to close-ups, the way a film is edited. As a result, a motion picture becomes the collective memory of everyone who sees it—and everyone has the *same* memory. A character on screen is remembered as a real experience, and the more depth that character is given the more lifelike that experience becomes. The director traditionally receives credit for these small miracles.

## The Auteur Theory

> I've come to the point where I like Pauline Kael's reviews of Godard more than Godard's films.
> —Quentin Tarantino

Every director will have a different approach to the same story. Give Hitchcock, Scorsese, Spielberg, and Tarantino the identical scene to direct and each will cast and shoot it in a different

Jean-Luc Godard shot **Breathless** (1960) on locations in and around Paris with a lightweight camera and the actors improving their dialogue; the radical style of this little movie brought worldwide attention to the French New Wave movement.

way, more than likely changing the script in the process. This *viva la difference* gave rise to the auteur theory in the 1950s by Francois Truffaut, Jean-Luc Godard, and other critics for *Cahiers du cinéma*. Many of these young men later became the rebellious directors of the French New Wave.

The auteur theory maintains that a film reflects the personal creative vision of the director and the camera replaces the pen, making the director the *auteur* or author. The members of *Cahiers du cinéma.* acknowledged that movies were the product of an industrial assembly line but declared that great directors put an indelible mark on their films. This was achieved through a process called *mise en scène*, and this is where the theory becomes a free-for-all.

There is no clear definition of *mise en scène*, which is translated as "putting into the scene" or "setting in scene." In general, this means how sets, props, costumes, lights, and actors are arranged before the camera, which includes *blocking*, a theatrical term given to the movement of actors within a scene. Some critics maintain this refers to all the visual elements, while others argue that it is an almost mystical aspect related to the emotional tone of the motion picture. The reason this

becomes so difficult is the collaborative nature of filmmaking.

The members of the French New Wave championed certain directors and ignored others. Hitchcock, Howard Hawks, Jean Renior, and Sam Fuller were praised, but Michael Curtiz was overlooked. Curtiz has an unmistakable visual style, which Spielberg says influenced him. He directed classics in almost every genre, including *Angels with Dirty Faces, The Adventures of Robin Hood, Casablanca,* and *Yankee Doodle Dandy.* Confusion arises when only a select few are nominated by a select few to be part of the auteur club. The simple fact is that every director qualifies because the tools and process are the same, but only a select few become legendary.

The reason for this is based on not simply the bigger-than-life personality of the director but how the director interacts with a small army of highly creative artists. What is often missed in the critical efforts to elevate a director to a near mythical status is the director's choice of talent he or she uses on a recurring basis.

Billy Wilder wrote most of his films with Charles Brackett and I. A. L. Diamond; used cinematographer John F. Seitz on *Lost Weekend, Sunset Boulevard,* and other films; and worked with Edith Head many times. Hitchcock also had a long association with Edith Head; used cinematographer Robert Burks on a dozen movies, including *Rear Window* and *North by Northwest;* and had Bernard Herrmann score eight of his films, including *Vertigo* and *Psycho.* Spielberg has used composer John Williams and editor Michael Kahn for over thirty years and cinematographer Janusz Kaminski since *Schindler's List.*

The director, for better or worse, is the sum total of the people working on a production. A director is often given blanket credit for the style of a film, when the end result is actually a close collaboration with someone else. Spielberg made three of the *Indiana Jones* movies with cinematographer Douglas Slocombe, and they have a different look than his other films. Francis Ford Coppola shot the three *Godfather* movies with

Gordon Willis. George Roy Hill let the great cinematographer Conrad Hall do all the camera setups on *Butch Cassidy and the Sundance Kid,* a duty normally considered the director's sacred domain. On a production, the role of the director might change several times simply because of the diverse ways films are put together.

## The Roles of a Director

> For a director there are commercial rules that are necessary to obey. In our profession, an artistic failure is nothing; a commercial failure is a sentence. The secret is to make films that please the public and also allow the director to reveal his personality.
>
> —John Ford

Someone has always assumed the role of a director. In prehistoric times it might have been a caveman that told the storyteller to stand closer to the fire so everyone could see. In Ancient Rome, someone had to coordinate the gladiator battles with feeding the Christians to the lions. For centuries, the duty of staging a new play was assumed by the playwright or the lead actor of a company. Whether for small events or spectacles, a delegated individual has been responsible for well-timed entrances and exists.

In the early years of motion pictures, the director also operated the camera. When narrative films came in, the duties of director and cinematographer were separated. Then as movies became more complicated, they were shot out of sequence. This process is unique to motion pictures and is probably the best definition of this liveliest art form. Plays, novels, dance, sculpture, and painting represent a finalized performance or exhibition. Film is a thousand different performances, done weeks or months apart, out of chronological order, manipulated by many different departments, and eventually edited together.

An actor might not see who he or she is performing opposite until a year later. Music, which reinforces live action on stage, is added as the last thing in postproduction. Unlike the continuous presentation of an opera or stage play, following weeks of rehearsals, movies usually roll without a day of rehearsal, often with the last scene first, and end up with a million feet of exposed film that must be edited down to 120 minutes or less. If a scene is shot thirty different times, from a half dozen angles, the final cut might be comprised of a few frames from each take.

Sound effects and CGI are usually started months prior to the first day of principal photography and completed days before the premiere. Planning and scheduling are different for every film, dictated by the availability of actors and technical talent, time of year, budget constraints, location openings, release dates, and dozens of other critical factors. This is tantamount to building a skyscraper from the top down, with everyone coming in on different days to work.

The director is responsible for keeping all this together and on time.

The difference between a producer and director is that a producer *should* have in-depth knowledge of all aspects of filmmaking but a director *must* have this knowledge. An observation was made by Professor Daniel Witt that "sometimes a director directs, and sometimes the lead actor directs, *and* sometimes the cinematographer directs, and so on." One person has to be in control. The days of the megaphone and riding crop are long gone. Today a director rules by ability and organization. The word "rules" applies because a movie set is not a democracy.

How different directors rule is the stuff of legends. Cecil B. DeMille did use a megaphone and often gave inspirational speeches before a scene. John Ford berated his actors, bringing stars like John Wayne to tears. William Wyler retook scenes sometimes fifty times without giving a single note to the actors—except to do something different. Alfred Hitchcock wore a suit and used his storyboards like the Bible. Elia Kazan would whisper a quick character idea in the ear of an actor right before the camera rolled. David Lean would study a scene for hours, while hundreds waited, until he got the right opening shot. John Cassavetes often handed the camera to an actor with the abrupt instruction to start shooting. Steven Spielberg never rehearses a scene and sometimes accomplishes sixty setups in a single day. And Quentin Tarantino likes to act out a scene for the actors.

Though directors can be tough, demanding, and sometimes cryptic with performance notes, the real horror stories from movie sets are about directors who are not organized and ready to shoot. No one sets out to make a bad film. That is not a bankable concept. Bad movies are made because the script is not right and the director does not know how to fix the problems. The

auteur theory might give too much credit to the director as being solely responsible for a film's style, but without question the director must guide a wild assortment of egos and personalities into a single vision. If this does not happen early in the production process, then someone else will assert an alternative vision. This conflict is known by the old war horse term: *creative differences.* To walk on a set unprepared is akin to being blindfolded in a jungle full of poisonous snakes and wild beasts. The end result is not an attractive sight.

In no other art form does it take a hundred or more highly skilled people to photograph an insert of a hand. To achieve this takes a screenwriter, producer, cinematographer, grips, makeup artist, costume designer, prop master, sound engineer, composer, maybe a special effects creator, and an actor or double. And all these people want to know what the hand is doing, how it is lit, what age it should be, if part of a garment is seen, if the hand is holding anything, if it touches anything, if it is slightly deformed, what mood the audience should sense, and what the motivation is of the character whose hand will be seen? Only the director can answer all these questions.

The most confusing aspect of filmmaking is that 98 percent of the time only parts of the human anatomy are being shot. Everything in this massive creative process comes down to a lens two inches in diameter and where to point it. From this, everything else evolves. The director must learn how to "think" like a camera. Every time a lens is moved, changed, or adjusted in a small way, it creates a different psychological impression. The placement of a lens will show if someone is depressed (down angle), normal (slight tilt up), powerful (low angle), or demonic (extreme low angle). A 28-mm, 50-mm, 70-mm and 210-mm lens will give very different looks to each of these angles. And an ultraviolet, diffused, or polarized filter will further alter the appearance of the image. For a play, the director is looking at full figures; in film, the director is constantly searching for variations on medium and close-up shots.

# Inside the Mind of a Modern Director

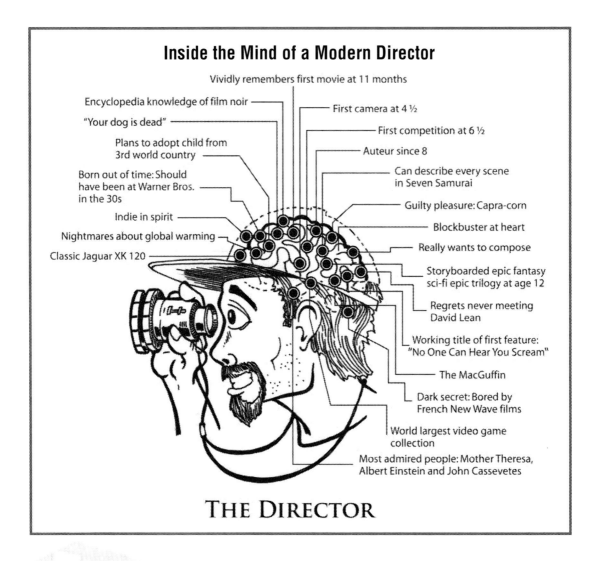

- Vividly remembers first movie at 11 months
- Encyclopedia knowledge of film noir
- "Your dog is dead"
- Plans to adopt child from 3rd world country
- Born out of time: Should have been at Warner Bros. in the 30s
- Indie in spirit
- Nightmares about global warming
- Classic Jaguar XK 120
- First camera at 4 ½
- First competition at 6 ½
- Auteur since 8
- Can describe every scene in Seven Samurai
- Guilty pleasure: Capra-corn
- Blockbuster at heart
- Really wants to compose
- Storyboarded epic fantasy sci-fi epic trilogy at age 12
- Regrets never meeting David Lean
- Working title of first feature: "No One Can Hear You Scream"
- The MacGuffin
- Dark secret: Bored by French New Wave films
- World largest video game collection
- Most admired people: Mother Theresa, Albert Einstein and John Cassevetes

## THE DIRECTOR

## Working with the Producer

> I don't think either one of them could have created it without the other. They were a great team.
>
> —David O. Selznick on Irving Thalberg and Louis B. Mayer

A rocky relationship with a producer is a ticket to a highly unpleasant shooting condition. Two bigger-than-life personalities are at work, which can quickly degenerate into unpleasant turf wars. Because there are so many different kinds of producers, most of whom have never had the benefit of a structured educational program, there are no absolutes on how these two forces interact. The one attitude that quickly ignites hard feelings is to treat the producer as the enemy or outsider—just someone to write checks with no artistic abilities.

The role of the director is well defined, and during the course of a production it is easy to take the perspective that the producer is interfering with creative decisions. The wisest choice a director can make is to find time to keep the producer updated on how the creative aspects of the production are coming together and to request help with potential problems.

The director and the producer are problem solvers. The producer's job is to make sure that everything is ready for each day of shooting and to take care of any obstacles that could delay the production rollercoaster from reaching its destination. The director is responsible for the inner workings of the production, making sure that everyone from actors to grips has a clear, unified focus on the creative aspects of the film.

The producer has spent months or years finding the money, possible distribution, and bringing together the creative team to make a motion picture. The last thing the producer should feel when the process goes from pre-production into production is that he or she is the kid that brought the baseball to the game but is not allowed to play. The producer's mark is on the film as soon as it goes into production. By this point, the screenplay is prepared, the people are in place, and the goal of the production is set.

If any of these components are weak, that is if the screenplay is not ready or if the scheduling is not properly prepared, then the production will likely be in disarray because the producer's work is incomplete. If the producer does not have an artistic vision or a desire to make an original film, then this can perpetrate the kind of conflict that is most common on a set: the director trying against all odds to fix problems that should have been taken care of in pre-production. This is a mammoth task for a director, which can be exasperated by the interference of a producer who is responsible for the production problems to begin with but does not have a clue regarding the real source of the confusion.

A director must learn to be a wise *manipulator* of people. This is not the manipulation of ego-driven game playing or pitting people against each other. This benign manipulation is making judg-ments on the abilities of key personnel and bringing out individual strengths during production. The director needs to be able to observe how each individual works and the kind of pressures that individual can take during the stressful course of a production.

The key to this manipulation is simple. The director should sit down with each individual in a comfortable atmosphere and ask what he or she believes his or her strengths are and what might grate on him or her during a production. This is not a chat about personal problems and should not veer in that direction. This is about finding out what the individual considers ideal working conditions to give his or her best possible effort.

This equates into a surprise attack because most people are not asked these questions directly. Usually shooting begins and everyone has to keep up with a pace and attitude that is established by the director and line producer. There is no time to share ideas about maximum effort or individual contributions during this stage. To actually talk about what it takes for individuals to give their utmost during a production is the kind of conversation that people love to have but rarely get.

These individual meetings can create a sense of dedication. Not all of the ideas will be possible. Many of them will probably be impossible. But a surprising number of these ideas will be a natural part of the process. Most of them boil down to simple respect for hard work and personal effort. An individual knowing he or she had a voice in preparing for a well-organized shoot can result in a close connection with the production from the beginning.

The director and producer especially need to have this conversation. The director should sit down, compliment the producer on getting the production started, and then present how he or she would like to run the shoot and how the producer can help in this venture. If the conversation goes smoothly and a mutual understanding is established, then this is a good time for the director to diplomatically assign the producer some special duties.

Having met with the key personnel, the director can ask for the producer's assistance in giving each individual as much support as possible, such as by implementing some of the little things that might have come out of the one-on-one meetings. This must not be a conversation about personalities but about working conditions. Recruiting the producer into the creative side of the production ensures that each individual potentially receives more attention, which can build a greater sense of dedication in all departments.

## Production Meetings: Troubleshooting

> The sound and music are 50 percent of the entertainment in a movie.
> —George Lucas

Production meetings should be a daily part of a shoot. The meetings before the production begins are always the most pleasant. Everyone has a chance to talk about what they have created and show examples of costumes, props, and scenic design. During production, these meetings are more nuts-and-bolts, because the focus shifts to troubleshooting, staying on schedule, and examining problem areas. The first meetings are about the potential. Subsequent meetings are about the reality of how things are pulling together.

The director and producer should work out a method for running meetings. The director needs to be in charge but always allowing time for the producer to give critical updates or share good news. This kind of teamwork is a talent unto itself. When a meeting runs smoothly, it energizes everybody involved and bypasses any potential hard feelings.

After the initial planning sessions, once the shoot is in process, production meetings need to be well organized *and quick*. Once it is established

that the meetings follow a lively pace but still give everyone an opportunity to speak, people will organize their thoughts and comments concisely. The following are suggestions for running a productive meeting:

1. **Start on time.** Once in production, people will start showing signs of weariness from the maddening pace of daily shooting. The last thing anyone wants is to have critical time taken away from future preparations. If meetings get into a routine of starting late by waiting for someone, people will always show up late. If meetings begin on time, then people will quickly adjust and arrive as scheduled.

2. **Agenda.** Before the meeting, everyone should be sent an agenda listing the topics to be covered, along with a request for any new business. A critical reason for meetings during production is to ensure that all departments are talking to each other. Everyone has to feel equal in the production process. If an agenda is sent, then it is important to stay on course with the topics or after awhile it will become a free-for-all. Peter Bart with *Daily Variety* recently wrote: "'It's even worse in television than movies,' one friend told me recently. 'I had a meeting last week whose sole purpose was to evaluate previous meetings.'" This antiproductive approach should be absolutely avoided.

3. **Troubleshooting.** Ask each individual to focus on three issues (or fewer) he or she would like to troubleshoot. If a list with no restrictions is requested, then most likely everyone will pencil in ten items or more. By asking for just three, people will evaluate what are real problems and what are minor stumbling blocks that can be taken care of without unnecessary discussion.

4. **Starting the meeting.** The director needs to come into the meeting without displaying too many battle scars. Be upbeat and set a quick pace for the meeting. Start with positive updates about the how production is going. Then go around the table, following the order of the agenda, and give everybody at least five

minutes to talk about their issues. This should not be an exact time, because some topics will generate more discussions; but if people know they have a limited time, they are more concise.

5. **Do not waste people's time.** If people talk succinctly about their areas and, hopefully do not bring up any surprises, then after going around the table people can be dismissed. If possible, never keep someone in a meeting whose attendance is really not really necessary. To have someone sit for an hour when the discussion does not involve his or her area is a waste of time and creates resentment.

6. **Meeting supplies.** Have a blackboard or a large drawing pad for people to write information on or make quick drawings. Have copies of the agenda to scribble notes on, plus a few writing pads and extra pens and pencils. Sometimes it takes five minutes for everyone to run around getting something to write with, which always results in a useless discussion. If the budget allows, have water, juices, soft drinks, and coffee to wet whistles and cool nerves. But avoid alcoholic beverages; this rapidly creates a party atmosphere and if done meeting after meeting will set up a pattern in which things will ramble and people will stay just to be friendly, when in reality there is work to do.

7. **A sense of order.** To have one person dominate a meeting and go on and on about his or her area and to have this happen over several meetings will quickly irritate everybody in the room. If things are not proceeding on track, there is a tendency to have meetings deteriorate into finger pointing. A meeting should not become a public execution, even if it is verbal. If someone has made a mistake or caused delays, then meet the person one on one. To humiliate someone in front of peers invites further mistakes to be made because suddenly the individual's focus has been split and a bit of dignity has been lost. If an individual becomes an ongoing problem, then this should be dealt with quickly and in private. A

production can become a beehive of rumors, and there is no reason to add extra fuel to the buzz with public displays of disharmony.

8. **The producer to the rescue.** It is wise to establish with the producer a method of playing good cop and bad cop. The strength of the producer is the illusion of being the final word. If someone is being constantly argumentative during meetings, then it is up to the director to step back and let the producer intervene. This should be coordinated with the producer before the production begins. However, if a frontal charge by the producer becomes necessary, it should be done with the intention of restoring peace to the proceedings. It is important to divorce the director from personal conflict and rancor with an individual who is an intricate part of the daily production.

9. **A little praise.** Use meetings to compliment individuals that have done exceptional work. Do not adlib something on the spur of the moment because it will seem hollow and artificial. But if someone has done exceptional work, compliment him or her. This is a reward that people remember, and it is an incentive for others.

10. **Finish on time.** Try to finish on time or early. If this is done consistently, people will come in with energy and present their topics clearly. The reward for being organized is to get home a few minutes early. And after a couple weeks of production, a few minutes is a big reward.

## Script to Screen

> We didn't need dialogue. We had faces!
>
> —Norman Desmond in *Sunset Boulevard*

The director's relationship with the writer is the most unique of any position on a production. The writer is the first to be a part of the process by creating a screenplay that gets everything rolling. But once production begins, the writer will probably no longer be involved until the premiere. Nevertheless, the weeks, months, and sometimes years of a director and writer working on a screenplay can be dentistry without Novocaine or the most rewarding experience of the entire production.

Academy Award screenwriter Sterling Silliphant tells the story of when he went to the Polo Lounge to meet with director Norman Jewison about the screenplay for *In the Heat of the Night*. Silliphant recalls that as he sat down he noticed the screenplay was thick with paperclips. When he asked what the clips were for, Norman Jewison quickly replied, "Oh don't worry, there's only a couple things here for you." Then for the next three hours, Jewison went through the script paperclip by paperclip.

To have told Silliphant that all the clips were about his screenplay would have a put him on the defense immediately. Instead, Norman Jewison pretended there were only a few things to talk about, which clearly changed as each clip was removed and each page discussed. By the end, Silliphant remembers, it was the most satisfying experience of his career, because the whole conversation was about making the script better.

Every writer has certain buttons that can be pushed to get maximum effort. Some writers can be given a few notes and return the next morning with two different versions. Others need to go away for a week because their process of thinking through problems requires time alone to figure out how to fit in the new pieces of the puzzle. Charles Chaplin was notorious for closing down productions and disappearing for days and even months at a time until he thought through a story problem.

It is essential for the director to understand the working style of a writer. This involves discovering what the writer's work habits and other interests are. The director must understand that in the writer's mind, after months of solitary hard work, there is a sense of accomplishment and the feeling that the screenplay is ready for production. But ultimately, the director must push the writer to explore changes that might feel uncomfortable.

A director will have visions of the movie that are only suggested in a screenplay. With a screenplay, the writer does not have room for long descriptive passages or character psychology. It must be roughly 120 pages and a quick, enjoyable read. What the writer sees in these pages may be very different from what the director envisions. This happens constantly. If the writer could turn in a graphic novel, then there would be less discussion about the look and style of the movie because it would be there in glorious black and white. The writer is trying to create images with a handful of words, and the director is seeing more images than could possibly fit on a page.

The common ground between the writer and director should be questions about the basic story elements. What is the film about? What is the theme? What should the audience feel during pivotal scenes? And how original are the characters? The answers to these questions should be evident when reading the script. But sometimes the writer weaves in hidden meanings intended to underscore the major theme of a movie.

This is clever craftsmanship on the writer's behalf, an affective part of storytelling in a narrative form, but these subtle touches can be lost in a movie if not given a visual reinforcement. For example, the way cinematographer Roger Deakins lights Tim Robbins as the character of Andy Dufresne tells volumes about the spiritual journey of the character, but the audience is only subconsciously aware of these visual clues.

The first step in a director's working relationship with a writer should be the search for a common vision. A writer is restricted to how much can fit on a page. So what else was on the writer's mind when creating the story? This can become a treasure chest of visual ideas. Like Norman Jewison, without using the same surprise tactic,

# Questions for the Director to Ask

**Is it a movie?**
Does it tell a visual story?

**What is the point of view?**
Entirely on the main character?
Multiple stories cross-cut together?

**What's the genre?**
How has the genre been reinvented over the years?

**Who is the main character?**
What are the strengths of the character?
What are the weaknesses of the character?

**Who is the adverse character?**
Why is he or she (or it) the adverse character?
How do your two principal characters cross paths?

**What is the conflict?**
How does the conflict change the main character?
What are classic conflicts in this genre?

**What unique touches has the writer brought to the story?**
What is the underlining theme?
What symbols, hidden meanings, or metaphors are used?
Does the dialogue help define each character?
What visual language has the writer used?

**What "level of reality" does the story exist in?**
Realistic (*Traffic* or *Crash*)?
Larger-than-life or mock reality (*Old School* or *Wedding Crashers*)?
Exaggerated reality (*The Eternal Sunshine of the Spotless Mind*)?
Fantasy (*Lord of the Rings* or *Pirates of the Caribbean*)?

**What is the intended mood of the story?**
Is it upbeat, dramatic, humorous, suspenseful, scary?
What kind of journey is the audience intended to take?
Is the mood established during the first minutes?

**What causes the showdown ("climax")?**
How does the showdown resolve the conflict?
Does the showdown fit the mood of the story?
Is the showdown final or open-ended?
And will the showdown be a *pleasant surprise* to the audience?

the director should go through every scene and let the writer talk about each one.

To go through a script and analyze it from the writer's point of view can be an eye opening process for a director. First, it shows how carefully the writer crafted the screenplay, with every scene having a purpose. Talking about each scene separately can get the camera rolling inside the director's head, opening up thoughts about setups, lighting moods, and scenic or costume design only hinted about in the screenplay. This process can reveal whether all the dramatic ingredients are in place and whether each scene is a stepping stone to another moment in the story.

If there are *story problems* (that infamous term used when there is something wrong with a screenplay but no one can quite put a finger on what it is), this scene-by-scene inspection will often locate the smoking gun. Usually there is a scene or sequence that sends the story down a side path and away from its original direction, often the result of a writer's indecision about whom to consecrate on as the main character.

If a story problem arises, the director can use a Method-acting exercise with the writer: Ask what certain character would do in situations not in the screenplay. What would a character do after winning a lot of money or how would a character react if someone suddenly started shooting? Putting characters into different scenarios can galvanize the inner personality of a character that is only marginally developed. This exercise can help strengthen the image of a character in the director's mind.

A question a director can ask that will immediately form beads of sweat on a writer's forehead is, What can be eliminated from the screenplay and still have the story work? This is a scrutinizing looking at the very basics of a story—like, for example, the movies during the 1930s that ran for ninety minutes and everyone talked at a machine-gun pace. If there is any fat on the story, this is a good way to find it.

The director has to feel an ownership of the screenplay at a certain point, and quite often this becomes a situation in which the writer feels that changes are being made to please the director—and to keep the paychecks coming. This is not a self-satisfying way to write but it is the reality of the assembly-line system in Hollywood that goes back to the early days of silent comedies when twenty gag writers were hired for a Keystone Kop two-reeler.

Unfortunately, a difficult thing for a director is to recognize when a writer has given everything possible and is now treading in deep waters. Replacing the original writer should be avoided if possible, not just for economical reasons but for creative reasons as well. A writer will feel burned out because the process has become an endless spiral. This usually results when a writer is constantly sent home to work in private and not communicated with by the director.

A new writer must begin by questioning every scene to find a fresh spin. Thus, many times a screenplay will detour in a completely different direction. This is most likely the result of the new writer and director having fun reshaping the make-believe world in the original screenplay. As other writers are brought in, the screenplay suddenly becomes a public utility vehicle that everyone can ride around in, and take turns at writing scenes. This usually leads to a troubled script that never pulls together.

## Acting for the Camera

> " Acting on stage is surgery with a scalpel. Acting in film is surgery with a laser. "
>
> —Michael Caine

Performance arts are intended for a large audience. Ever since the first person stood in front of a group of people and passionately told a tale of heroism, audiences have accepted the theatricality of a dramatic presentation. Over the centuries, actors have been trained in voice projection and body movement, because every part of their physical being had to project emotions to people seated hundreds of feet away.

Soliloquies or asides were created by authors for actors to explore the internal emotions of characters. Later, when electricity transformed theaters, a follow spot could be iris downed to show an actor's face delivering lines—the closest theater can come to a close-up. To be an actor meant training in dance, singing, character movement, period styles, sword play, makeup, and sometimes the not-so-subtle art of mimicking the vernacular of minority cultures.

An actor's life was typically a hard life. It was not considered a noble profession even though royalty turned out for the plays of Shakespeare and Molière. Actors were looked upon as a source of amusement and entertainment but considered part of the rebel mass. Some actors became the superstars of their era achieving fame because of performances in certain plays, like William Gillette with *Sherlock Holmes*. Others became infamous because of notorious circumstances, like John Wilkes Booth, who was noted for his portrayal of *Richard III*. At the turn of the twentieth century, Sarah Bernhardt achieved international fame and was one of the first "legitimate actresses" to try the new medium of motion pictures.

The actors that achieved success were usually clever business people that knew how to watch the box office and counted the revenue immediately after a performance. They knew the art of promotion. In a new community, many would give teaser performances for the privileged class. They understood the public was fascinated by the acting world, even seduced by it, and they would use all their charms and influence to create a respectable name for themselves.

However, most actors lived a very humble life, performing sometimes a dozen shows a week and traveling long hours on trains to perform the next

Laurence Olivier in *Hamlet* (1948) represents the classic approach to acting in which a character evolves from the outside in through an interpretation of the dialogue and the use of costumes and makeup.

day in a new theater. There is the old saying that acting gets into the blood, and there is a certain amount of truth in this. Performing in front of a large audience and receiving applause or hearing people weep after a heartfelt monologue is an intoxicating feeling for a performer.

For centuries, the art of acting was a hand-down tradition. Usually a young actor would be accepted into a company, then tour with that company for years learning to play a variety of specialty roles, going up the ladder from character parts to villains to leads. The head of a company would often be the mentor to these young aspiring actors and would teach them by practical stage experience the abilities to move in costume and pause for a laugh and other tricks of the trade.

Performances were constructed from the outside in. The author would write expertly crafted dialogue that carefully explained the character motivations. The actor would find the right costume, determine the appropriate movement, and complete the transformation with makeup and perhaps putty across the nose to give a defining appearance. Lord Laurence Olivier is credited with saying that once he found the nose he found the character.

Starting with the Greeks, plays were written about bigger-than-life characters, such as revengeful gods, kings, queens, and other nobles that had fallen from grace or were wrestling with inner demons. These parts were written in poetry and expressed great themes. Classic characters were defined by a traditional image on stage, and for centuries there was a particular look for heroic figures, villains, and comic characters. Audiences could identify a favorite character actor quickly by a costume they were associated with, like sidekicks in old Western movies.

All an actor needed to know about a character was on the written page. Richard III confides to the audience about his evil plots and cunning manipulation of people. Shakespeare's plays have inspired many interpretations over the centuries, but each performance is anchored to the exquisite language that clearly states the conflict and foreshadows future events.

Because it can be argued that theater is the oldest of all art forms, actors that took to the stage over the centuries were proud of this grand and sometimes notorious tradition. An arrogance attitude developed about the stage performance being a pure art form, which manifested itself when motion pictures suddenly arrived. No one foresaw that a million people could see a performance in one evening in theaters around the world; to theater people, it appeared excessively commercial.

Unquestionably, motion pictures changed the art of acting—but not immediately. It took several years for early pioneers to understand the power of the camera. Most early movies were done "full-figured," much like a stage play with the camera positioned at a low angle, giving the audience the sensation of being in center seats near the stage. Audiences were able to look at the silver screen and effectively see a theatrical performance unfold before their eyes. Of course, there was no dialogue; pantomime expressed

emotions without words. Gradually directors began experimenting with the camera and the power of the close-up was discovered.

The close-up was perfected by D. W. Griffith and his longtime cinematographer Billy Bitzer in a series of short films. Griffith would cut to a character's face and through the expressions in the eyes reveal the character's inner feelings. Dramatically, this expression was often contrary to what the scene was about. In *Birth of a Nation*, actress Lillian Gish says good-bye to two of her beloved friends that are leaving with great enthusiasm to fight for the South in the Civil War. In a full shot, her body language shows how thrilled and proud she is for them. But her close-up shows the audience she is fighting back tears and hiding the fear that she may never see them again.

The close-up is what separates motion pictures from theater. A close-up projects an actor's eyes to be three feet tall on a screen. With the slightest movement, these eyes can portray fear, anxiety, love, or passion and invoke an instant reaction from the moviegoer. Even standing a few feet from an actor during filming, the expression in the eyes might seem small and insignificant until projected on the screen. There is a story that writer-director Philip Dunne came up to Gary Cooper after a scene and said he did not see the emotions he had asked for. Cooper politely suggested Dunne should look at the scene and then he would re-shoot it if necessary. It was not necessary; everything was there, and Dunne had been sitting next to the camera during the take.

Charlie Chaplin became a master of the close-up, and many critics credit him with being the first great motion picture actor. Along with Buster Keaton and other silent comics, Chaplin played full figure in most of his routines, like dancing in *City Lights* or turning into a chicken in *The Gold Rush*. But Chaplin would bring the camera in close to show his love for a blind flower girl who had regained her sight, or to show his heart breaking for being stood up on New Year's Eve. These strong emotional feelings are what partly endeared his Little Tramp character to people around the world. Audiences could relate to his human reactions, unlike Keaton who played all his scenes with a "deadpan" expression.

Motion pictures came in at a time when theater was going through a cultural revolution. Playwrights were turning toward more realistic themes—themes that examined social ills and the complications of the human psyche. This was stimulated by the writings of Sigmund Freud and emerged as *expressionism* in Germany. The dramas of Henrik Ibsen, Anton Chekhov, Sean O'Casey, and Eugene O'Neill became lightning rods for change and breaking from the literary traditions of the past.

A new kind of acting needed to be found. In part to avoid censorship and scandals, these new playwrights hid meanings between the lines. After a thousand years, plays were no longer a clear explanation of the characters' behavior. The playwright gave his or her characters deep secrets, and this demanded that actors convey emotions that skirted the meaning of words. Suddenly acting became about finding different layers of a character expressed through body language and subtle reactions.

From this theatrical revolution in playwriting, a new style of theatrical performance was born that became popularly known as the Method. This springs from the "Stanislavski System" that was pioneered by the Moscow Art Theater at the turn of the century. It was popularized by Stella Adler and Lee Strasberg with The Actors Studio in New York in the late 1940s and 50s. The central idea of Method acting is to find the "theatrical truth" of a moment. The Method—or the "torn T-shirt school of acting," as it was nicknamed—exploded on the American scene in the late 1940s with powerful new plays directed by Elia Kazan of *All My Sons, Death of a Salesman,* and the groundbreaking production of *A Streetcar Named Desire* with Marlon Brando.

When Brando left Broadway—never to return—for Hollywood, he made six films in five years that changed movie acting forever. The films were *The Men, A Streetcar Named Desire, Viva Zapata!, Julius Caesar, The Wild One,* and *On the Waterfront.* These movies became acting lessons

Marlon Brando in ***A Streetcar Named Desire*** (1951) is forever associated with the Method school of acting in which the character evolves from the inside out, through a series of exercises that release real emotions and allow the actor to be "in the moment."

for disciples of the Method, including James Dean, Paul Newman, Al Pacino, Dustin Hoffman, and Robert De Niro.

Each actor would spend long periods of time finding the core of a character, not through makeup or costumes but by psychologically connecting with the character and digging deep inside to find kindred emotions. Robert De Niro drove around in a taxi late at night in New York for weeks to *become* Travis in *Taxi Driver.* He wanted to understand the loneliness and the isolation of the character—so that the truth would be in the eyes—an understanding about movie acting that goes back the silent era with Gish and Chaplin.

The defining difference between classic acting and Method acting are the words "as" and "is." Olivier would be billed "as" Hamlet, whereas

Brando "is" Stanley Kowalski. This distinction began with the marketing for *Hud,* when posters exclaimed that "Paul Newman is Hud." Whatever approach, what the audience sees on the screen must be real, and the only way to achieve this is through relaxation and reacting.

> The difference between good acting and bad acting is the difference between acting and reacting. In a bad picture, you can see 'em acting all over the place. In a good picture, they react in a logical way to the situations they're in.
>
> —John Wayne

Listening and reacting are the essence of all acting. If done with a sense of spontaneity, i.e., hearing the words for the first time, this creates a believability of character for the camera. If the actor is tense or insincere in the delivery of lines, the camera will not *like* him or her. This an old chestnut term that is very true; the camera *likes* some actors and not others, and no amount of acting lessons will significantly alter this.

What can change is that the more experience an actor has before a camera, the more relaxed he or she becomes. Overcoming the fear or intimidation of the camera allows the actor to be "in the moment" when reacting to lines. Because there is usually no rehearsing for a scene, pretending to hear the lines for the first time is sometimes the reality of acting in film or television.

To bring out the subtleties of performance, theater actors rely on the director. In film, actors must

rely on themselves. There are two general kinds of film directors that have become clichés in the public's imagination. One would be the Cecil B. DeMille or Otto Preminger type, yelling instructions at the crews and giving pep talks to the stars. The other is the actor's director, like George Cukor, Elia Kazan, or Martin Scorsese, who works with actors to bring out subtle, complex performances.

The reality is that the first category of director, the "glorified traffic cop" as some have referred to themselves, is most common in motion pictures. There is simply little or no time for rehearsals. On a stage play, the director is able to spend three or four weeks working with actors to create a sustained performance over a three-hour period. The film director is under constant pressure to decide on camera placement, what lens to use, and a dozen other technical decisions. Each line of dialogue might be shot from a different camera angle, and each angle will change the nuances of an actor's performance.

A good screen actor must understand what each lens and camera placement does to a performance and then make appropriate adjustments in his or her delivery. These are technical aspects that a director does not have time to explain to an actor while a hundred people impatiently wait.

With the limitations now placed on movies being shot so quickly, there is little time for rehearsals once production begins. Steven Spielberg says he never rehearses, because he wants that nervous energy in an actor's performance. Francis Ford Coppola or Mike Nichols, directors that come from theater, will often demand a short rehearsal period of a week or two before a production starts. Most directors will at least have a roundtable reading before the camera rolls. It all depends on the screenplay.

If the script is *12 Angry Men,* then rehearsals make sense, but if it is *Pirates of the Caribbean,* with a hundred speaking parts and actors that only appear in one scene, then a rehearsal would probably be mass confusion. For a television program, a lead or recurring role has the opportunity to explore the depth of a character and for the writers to lean from this. With film, an actor is expected to arrive with a fully realized performance.

Auditioning is an arduous process for actors. It is something that most people could not endure, which is the process of beginning rejection over and over again. The reward is obtaining the occasional speaking part or landing a series. The problem with actors is that the competition is so enormous that there is usually no time to tell someone why he or she did not get the part. Quite often it is something the actor has no control over. It can literally get down to the eyes being the wrong color or the height being too tall or too short. Often it has nothing to do with the actual reading. The production company is looking for a certain type to fill a role, with fifty people auditioning, so the actor leaves not knowing if it was a bad line reading or purely physical.

Once cast, there are many instances in which an actor stepping in front of a camera for the first time freezes up. Someone who has been trained on the stage is used to a rehearsal before walking out on opening night. In film and television, the pace is so rapid that suddenly staring at a camera can feel like facing a gun. A movie set can be a hostile environment to a new actor. In theater, once the play begins, all the technicians and the stage manager are one hundred feet away. In film, a small army is within an arm's length. To overcome these anxieties, an actor must prepare *before stepping in front of the camera.*

> When an actor comes to me and wants to discuss his character, I say, "It's in the script." If he says, "But what's my motivation?," I say, "Your salary."
> —Alfred Hitchcock

When a production starts, there are many things that can happen between an actor and director. There is no predictability about it. The primary thing is for the actor to arrive ready to perform. There is no time to find the motivation. Like Hitchcock says, motivation is a paycheck. An actor must to be relaxed, disciplined, and aware of what is happening on a movie set. The good news is, after leaping through the flaming hoops of auditions and callbacks, an actor has been chosen because he or she is endowed with the right looks and reads well. The only thing left is for the actor to live up to everyone's expectations. Some ways to prepare follow.

## Act

Find every opportunity to get in front of an audience. Take classes; this applies to everyone interested in motion picture and television. For a director, this gives an appreciation for what actors go through. It is important to understand the process of memorizing lines, learning blockings, memorizing new dialogue, and maintaining a relaxed exterior. Also, acting is a part of daily life in the movie business. Pitching an idea is acting. Convincing investors to come into a project is acting. The project is a giant organization based around acting, so find an opportunity to learn the basics.

## Don't Give in to Temptation

There are a few wolf-in-sheep-clothing opportunities to avoid. Though it might be tempting to be in a feature by showing a "little flesh," all in the cause of breaking into serious filmmaking, nothing is sacred on the Internet. This is an era in which one foolish act can haunt someone forever.

## Acting Workshop

Anyone serious about screen acting will probably journey to Los Angeles or other film capitals. There will be many acting workshops available at film schools, through the Screen Actors Guild, and privately. They will vary from cold reading auditions to voice training to developing a character. Take as many as time and money will allow. Probably no single professional works as hard to prepare as an actor does. An actor needs to constantly be in shape—mentally and physically. A writer can take a year off and still be able to sit down and knock out a clever page of dialogue. A director sometimes does not make a movie for two or three years. For an actor, a long period of idleness usually results in forgotten lines and renewed nervousness in front of the camera. The only way to control these little demons is to constantly find ways to perform and talk about the craft.

## Acting Coaches

A good acting coach will help a film actor in a way that directors do not have time for. A coach will help an actor prepare for an audition, give character insights, and talk about how to move and how to dress—in short, all the things that are impossible to do on a set once production begins. In film and television, acting coaches are invaluable in preparing new actors and stars to appear before the camera with a rehearsed, well-thought-out performance. Like everything in this topsy-turvy business, it is wise to do some research to find an acting coach with good recommendations.

## Blocking a Scene

The blocking of a scene is usually a mystery until the actors arrive on the set and see where the director has set up the camera. This can be a simple two-shot at a table or a complicated series of movements for a single camera shot. If the scene is on location, the blocking could change several times. The important duty of the actor is to know the lines. Moving and timing dialogue to hit marks take a lot of concentration. If an actor is fighting for lines, this can create costly delays and be the start of a bad reputation.

## Concentration on the Set

Concentration is a big part for preparing of a role. A busy set offers a lot of temptations. It is always a temptation, especially early in a film

starting with student productions, to be around friends and new acquaintances for a good time. That is not why the actor is there, even if the gig is on a volunteer basis. An actor has a responsibility to stay focused and concentrate on the character. This comes in many varieties. Some actors stay in character through the entire day of shooting, which sometimes unnerves fellow actors. Other actors play video games, read books, knit, take naps, or review lines. To be disruptive on a set is probably the greatest sin an actor can commit. It is also exceedingly unwise to give acting advice to fellow actors during a shooting day. Something like this can be easily overheard and can quickly create an unfavorable image. Especially early in a career, be pleasant and be prepared.

## Hitting the Mark

A mark is usually a white piece of tape put on the floor for an actor to hit or stand right behind in a scene with movement. If the actor goes beyond the mark, focus will be broken. The trick is not to look down for the mark while giving lines. To avoid this nervous glance, stand at the mark and then step backward, counting each step, to the starting point of the scene. Then rehearse the scene with the lines while mentally counting.

## Character Background

While learning lines for a scene, think about where the character has just come from. This is a "back story" that is fun to devise. Has the character left a situation that has put him or her in a good or bad mood? Is the character pensive or frightened about something? What has happened to the character immediately before can establish a motivation for how the scene is played. There is a sense of personal history, instead of popping in cold like a bubble out of nowhere. At some point, sit down and invent a biography of the character. It does not need to be shared with the writer or the director; this is a private insight to the character. If an actor truly knows the character, this can lead to some inspired business or line deliveries.

### Blinking

People blink a thousand times a day, but on camera it shows a sign of character weakness. Run lines in front of a mirror and concentrate on keeping the eyes wide open. But sometimes this is part of the character. Morgan Freeman used blinking for an effect in *The Shawshank Redemption* when he was first seen at his parole hearing. His character was constantly blinking to show how humble and reformed he had become; after that, he did not blink again.

### Using the Camera Eye

When staring at a fellow actor in a scene, the natural tendency is for the eyes to jump back and forth. On a screen, this is distracting and makes the character appear nervous or shifty. Pick one eye to stare at. If giving lines toward the camera, stare with the eye farthest from the lens; this will force the face inward for a stronger shot.

> There are five stages in the life of an actor: Who's Mary Astor? Get me Mary Astor. Get me a Mary Astor Type. Get me a young Mary Astor. Who's Mary Astor?
>
> —Mary Astor

### Advice to the Director about Actors

The first chance a director has to meet the cast probably will be at a table reading. At this opportunity, the director needs to be clear about what the goals are for the movie. Be brief and nail the concept in a few sentences. Rambling, Knute Rockne speeches will only cause confusion and can come back to haunt a director.

At the end of the read, the director should give some simple but insightful notes to the cast members, especially if an actor is trying too hard with emotions or beginning to effect a certain unwanted line delivery. Be diplomatic but firm. The first instructions are invaluable to an actor. At the beginning of a film, actors are thirsty to understand what the director wants from them.

Sometimes simple observations might pull the concept of the character together for an actor. Michael Caine remembers when he worked with the legendary director John Houston on *The Man Who Would Be King,* Caine was rattling his lines off rapidly. Houston stopped him and said, "You don't have to hurry, he's an honest man." Caine said that immediately he understood the nature of the character, and Houston never gave another note.

### Keeping Focus

The most important thing a director must do is remind an actor of the dramatic mood of a scene coming up. Because films are shot out of sequence, many times an actor will begin to peak early because it is the first few weeks of shooting and the creative juices are flowing. The director must know exactly what that character is feeling in each and every scene. If the director believes the actor is leaping emotionally too far ahead, a subtle comment should get things back on course. Most of the time an actor will have planned out the dramatic beats for a movie and no comments are necessary. But sometimes a group of actors can feed off of each other and spin out a scene in a new direction. It can be extremely confusing to shoot a scene early in the script and then turn around and do a scene toward the end. The director is the dramatic compass during a shoot.

### Actor Notes

Out of respect, a director might send an actor an e-mail or leave a phone message with a thought about an important scene the next day—not anything too specific, just a suggestion or idea. It can even be a question about how to make the actor feel more comfortable during the scene. Actors enjoy finding the soul of a character and eventually they will know the character better than anyone on the set once production begins. But a little communication from the director is always welcomed. It shows that the director is thinking about them and took time to reach out with a thought. If done with sincerity, this helps an actor to relax on the set and gives a sense of importance to an individual's work during a hurried schedule.

## Encouragement

Let an actor know if he or she is on target and gave a good performance in a certain scene. A simple compliment. It does not need to be hugs and fanfare. Silent star Blanhe Sweet said all she need from D. W. Griffith after a good scene was a nod and, "That's fine." Some things have not changed in a hundred years.

## Scheduling

Don't keep an actor waiting.

> The words "Kiss Kiss Bang Bang," which I saw on an Italian movie poster, are perhaps the briefest statement imaginable of the basic appeal of movies.
> —Pauline Kael

## A Closing Thought: Theater vs. Film

There has been an unfortunate rift between theater and film over the decades. In most fine arts colleges, film and theater are separate departments. A dean of a fine arts college at a major university was recently asked what the similarities between theater and film were. His blunt reply was that there are none. This is astonishing because stars like James Cagney, Spencer Tracy, James Stewart, Katharine Hepburn, Bette Davis, Marlon Brando, Al Pacino, and scores of others got their start in theatrical productions. And so did many film directors, including George Cukor, Elia Kazan, Arthur Penn, Francis Ford Coppola, and David Mamet and more recently Sam Mendes and Rob Marshall.

Theater is a great training ground for anyone interested in going into film or television. An actor working in front of a live audience is invaluable. For an aspiring director, there is no better way to learn how to work with actors, discuss ideas with designers, and to find the dramatic beats of a well-written script. There are components of theater so deeply ingrained in film that they are often overlooked, even by deans of colleges.

## The Directing Process

> If it's a good movie, the sound could go off and the audience would still have a perfectly clear idea of what was going on.
> —Alfred Hitchcock

The success of a film is predestined by the way a director runs a set. This is not a side-door definition of the auteur theory but a practical reality of making a motion picture. The crowning of an auteur is a critical crapshoot. The members of the French New Wave proclaimed Alfred Hitchcock an auteur, but in America he was considered for most of his career as a genre director, consistently losing his Oscar bids to Hollywood

## Actors Who Started in Theater

The names of a few of the actors who had notable theater careers and went on to receive Academy Award nominations or awards follow.

| | | |
|---|---|---|
| James Stewart | George Sanders | Anne Bancroft |
| Spencer Tracy | Marlon Brando | Geraldine Page |
| Katharine Hepburn | Karl Malden | Albert Finney |
| Humphrey Bogart | Peter Ustinov | Richard Harris |
| Laurence Olivier | Alex Guinness | Rex Harrison |
| Mickey Rooney | Richard Burton | Peter Sellers |
| Claude Rains | Jack Palance | Julie Andrews |
| Bette Davis | Audrey Hepburn | Martin Balsam |
| Vivien Leigh | Deborah Kerr | Maggie Smith |
| Olivia de Havilland | Grace Kelly | Alan Arkin |
| Henry Fonda | James Mason | Michael Caine |
| Cary Grant | Lee J. Cobb | Walter Matthau |
| Orson Welles | Rod Steiger | Robert Shaw |
| Barbara Stanwyck | Jack Lemmon | Vanessa Redgrave |
| James Cagney | Eva Marie Saint | Dustin Hoffman |
| Ronald Coleman | James Dean | John Cassavetes |
| Barry Fitzgerald | Yul Brynner | Gene Hackman |
| Hume Cronyn | Anthony Perkins | Alan Bates |
| Ethel Barrymore | Charles Laughton | Barbra Streisand |
| Gene Kelly | Joanne Woodward | James Earl Jones |
| Gregory Peck | Paul Newman | Glenda Jackson |
| John Garfield | David Niven | Peter Finch |
| Michael Redgrave | Sidney Poitier | Robert Duvall |
| Montgomery Clift | Shirley MacLaine | Robert Redford |
| José Ferrer | Charlton Heston | Al Pacino |
| Jean Simmons | George C. Scott | Robert De Niro |
| James Whitmore | Peter Falk | |
| Ralph Richardson | Peter O'Toole | |

icons like John Ford and Billy Wilder. On the other hand, Ford and Wilder were not embraced by the New Wave. The one common factor between these men and any other exceptional director, is how they conduct themselves on a set.

The old metaphor that making a movie is like going into battle is a fair comparison. The big difference is that to prepare for battle, officers and soldiers play military games. In film the director and crew step to the front lines without any advance exercise on how everyone will work together over several intense months. Sometimes the director and crew are green, making their first student film together, but most productions range from a few to an entire roster of veterans that have worked on productions in the past. The one recurring waterhole conversation with cast and crew revolves around stories about good directors and bad directors.

Most of the time, it makes no difference if the film turns out to be a bomb or a masterpiece; if a small army of diverse artistic personalities had a grueling, unorganized shoot, this becomes the indelible memory of the experience. The director is the center of the bull's-eye on a set. This is not to imply that a director must be a swell person who is always giving hugs and making light-hearted jokes. This can result in a happy set and a straight-to-video movie. The cast and crew might have pleasant memories of such a director but not an iota of respect.

No one steps on a sound stage with the intention of producing an awful movie. Even films that have been labeled one-star popcorn trash have evidence of a few individuals working tirelessly to make the costumes or props or makeup as professional as time and money will allow. Bad movies happen for a thousand reasons, even with a two-hundred-million-dollar budget. Ninety-five percent of the time, the reason for a bad movie can be traced back to a flawed or undeveloped screenplay.

With so many disappointing movies, it is a mystery why a star, line producer, or someone intimately involved in a production does not scream "Stop!" and bring everyone's attention to the fact that a substandard film is being made, then perhaps rally cast and crew to unite and repair the problems. There have been incidents in the past in which Bette Davis walked off a set, Marlon Brando had a director fired, and a star was replaced two weeks into a shoot. But the hard fact is that once a film goes into production it is almost too late to fix unresolved problems. Going into production with problems is like starting a car on an assembly line with only half a blueprint, hoping the workers will figure out what to add to make it wonderful as it passes by.

For every *Casablanca,* there are hundreds of movies that went before the camera with an unfinished screenplay and now are seen only on late-night cable channels. Even if the Hollywood myths are true about *Casablanca,* that the cast and

***300*** (2006) is a glimpse of the future of filmmaking that in many ways reflects a return to the Studio System when everything was shot on sound stages and the back lot; Zack Snyder made his CGI epic in a converted warehouse against a green screen.

crew believed they were in the midst of a stinker, there is not one moment in this classic in which the lighting is poor, the actors sleepwalk through lines, or the scenic construction looks haphazard. No one let down. This individual dedication to filmmaking goes back to the earliest days of motion pictures and is still obvious in a mega-budget era in which tent-pole films look incredible but often fail to satisfy audience expectations.

On the first day, a film production is a large group of highly talented people, each dedicated to excellence in his or her own department and all with the secret hope they are about to make something that will have a two-disc retrospective twenty years later. Most actors and crews are hired without seeing a script. They had no creative voice in the project they are about to work on, but all are willing to share their full creativity to make the film successful. This is a powerful force the director is greeted with, and it is up to the director to put this force to good use or squander it.

### The Screenplay

The single most important thing a director can do is to walk on the set for the first day of principal photography with a terrific screenplay. The bottom line is that movies are storytelling, and a well-crafted script generates excitement with everyone involved that literally no amount of money can buy. A sub-thought that is rarely spoken about nowadays is that a movie can live forever. Films with great screenplays like *Citizen Kane, Casablanca, Seven Samurai, Some Like It Hot, The Godfather, Annie Hall, The Shawshank Redemption,* and *The Usual Suspects* are still watched by millions of people around the world each year. Everyone making movies secretly wants to be part of classics like these. A director with a good script in hand will generate enthusiasm throughout every level of production.

## First Day of Shooting

The gathering of everyone on the first day of production, just before the first shot, can have an unsettling effect on a director. It is a moment of personal victory after months or years of intense meetings and setbacks to get a green light on the project. Now suddenly there are fifty to one hundred wide-eyed individuals awaiting instructions about the first camera setup.

The director has met with most of these people before, sometimes for hours, but to see them all assembled at once is quite a sight. This indicates that a mad race has begun to complete principal photography in a few busily scheduled weeks, at dozens of locations, with new people showing up each day, and a time clock to finish 2–5 pages or more per day. The unnerving feeling of "What have I gotten myself into?" is very common.

The cast and crew are expecting a traditional welcome from the director and perhaps a short ceremony to enlist the gods of good fortune. This is not a good time for a long oratory on triumph over adversary or a philosophical rambling about the screenplay's humanitarian theme.

This is the moment for that C. B. DeMille pep talk, perhaps flavored with a little humor, and a cleverly phrased request for everyone to give their best to make a great film. Most directors will have a good-luck ceremony after this. Some might read an inspirational passage or poem; others might have someone sing. Francis Ford Coppola has everyone join hands and say "poowabah" three times.

---

## Director's Checklist

### Things to do for a day's shoot . . .

Camera setup list for morning
Camera setup list for afternoon
Possible pickup scenes
Possible overtime to complete scenes
Revisions in screenplay
Coordinate with producer on the day's activities
Makeup review
Crowd scenes and/or stunt work with assistant director
Shooting list, script changes, actor notes, breaks, and so on with line producer
Green screen and other effects shots with special effects supervisor
Costume review
Notes on the day's shoot and script revisions with principal actors
Light check and camera setups with cinematographer
Sound check
Camera blocking rehearsal with actors/stand-ins
Begin day's shooting on time
Meet with assistant director, line producer, and crew heads on next day's shoot

The choice of what scene to shoot on the first day, if the director has any influence in the scheduling, can set the tone for the rest of principal photography. There are a lot of unspoken superstitions connected with filmmaking. Some directors like to immediately tackle the hardest scenes to get them out of the way, realizing that everyone's collective energy will sag toward the end of the schedule. Other directors like to pick scenes that should flow together easily and get usable footage on the first day. Each director will have a personal preference of where to begin; but many times, especially in television, this is predetermined by a meticulously worked out schedule and budget.

## Take 1, 2, 3 . . .

Perhaps the greatest demand on a director is to know exactly what to look for on each take. Within a few seconds, a director must recognize if all the elements have happened as envisioned. The primary concentration will be on the performances, because hours before will have been spent on lighting, practical components in the set, costumes, makeup, stunt rehearsals, and other technical matters.

Before calling the actors, a director should look through the viewfinder to be sure the shot is framed correctly, perhaps with stand-ins to make sure the pacing and camera movements are correct. This should not be done with a casual attitude of *playing* director but with a focused look at the dynamics within the shot. To halfheartedly putter around someone's area is an insult to the hard work that has been done and can quickly cause uncomfortable feelings.

During a take, twenty-four frames a second, the coordinated efforts of dozens of people have either fallen into place or something is not working correctly. To be satisfied with a take is a process of elimination. Each takes potentially means something is not right or that someone has failed to meet a requirement. After three or four takes, a director needs a certain amount of courage to continue. Unless the mistakes are obvious,

actors and crews become restless to advance to the next setup.

If a director is looking for something in particular, he or she should have no hesitation to keep shooting. There is a tidal wave of impatient body language on a set that a director needs to ignore or learn to deal with to get the perfect take. In an editing room, the most disheartening feeling a director can have is to wish for a couple more takes on a scene.

Once the cast and crew know that a director will do five, seven, or ten takes as an average, everyone will adjust to this pace, especially if they see the process is producing good results. The director's process is often a gut reaction, and each director will have a different approach, sometimes notoriously. Director William Wilder would have actors do twenty or thirty or more takes without giving a single note of direction on how to change the scene. He was literally looking for something different in a performance that transcended acting. Fourteen actors won Academy Awards under his direction, with a total of thirty-six nominations, so there was little to complain about.

Directors John Ford and Alfred Hitchcock liked as few takes as possible. Most directors want to nail that illusive "it" on the first take. There is an energy brought on by pure adrenaline that sometimes results in the fabled expression "a magic moment." Spielberg does not rehearse a shot with actors. He wants the camera rolling to hopefully capture this moment that borders between acting and raw nerves.

Peter Jackson on *The Lord of the Rings* trilogy had actors, especially in close-ups, do multiple takes. He encouraged actors to try different line deliveries, which gave him the opportunity in the editing room to shape the dramatic arc of performances. And to the extreme, Francis Ford Coppola had a million feet of film on *Apocalypse Now*. To edit the Vietnam epic took a year, with some key scenes being pulled from waste containers after originally being scrapped.

For decades, to discover if a take was good or bad would have to wait until the following morn-

Francis Ford Coppola was one of the shining stars of the New Hollywood movement, going from small independent films to *The Godfather* and *The Godfather: Part II,* seen here on the troubled production of ***Apocalypse Now*** (1979) with Marlon Brando; the making of this Vietnam epic is documented in *Hearts of Darkness: A Filmmaker's Apocalypse,* essential viewing for any aspiring director.

mental image of a take, no matter how short, the easier it is to spot something that is not working. This means studying the scenic and costume designs carefully and viewing films with the cinematographer for color, style, and composition.

If this previsionalization process is not done in advance, a director tends to hurry through takes from on-set pressures or shoot a lot of takes out of insincerity. One of the great pleasures of moviemaking is to instinctively recognize a take that had played in the mind months before. It is a small adrenaline rush brought on by planning and an increased familiarity with visual language.

ing during daily rushes. That meant that crews did not know if they could strike a set for half a day or if actors had to be called back. Now, with television monitors hooked into the cameras and digital replay, a take can be carefully examined right after "cut" is called. This allows everyone to look and make sure there are no problems in their individual areas and for the director to see if the shot meets expectations.

The problem with immediate replay is the pressure to go on to the next shot. With dailies, only select people were in the screening room. On a set, there are a hundred peeping eyes. The director has to look objectively and coolly without being hurried. But in this situation, with all due respect to Mr. Wyler, it is wise for the director to make comments about what is missing, what does not look right, or if a performance is off. Everyone is trying to achieve a level of perfection; and if they are told about perceived problems from the director, the impatience factor usually disappears.

Calling "action" on a take is a process that sometimes begins months before. The director ideally has thought through each take and has created storyboards. The more a director creates a

> "When my mechanical shark was being repaired and I had to shoot something, I had to make the water scary. I relied on the audience's imagination, aided by where I put the camera. Today, it would be a digital shark. It would cost a hell of a lot more, but never break down. As a result, I probably would have used it four times as much, which would have made the film four times less scary. *Jaws* is scary because of what you don't see,

> not because of what
> you do. We need to
> bring the audience
> back into partnership
> with storytelling.
> —Steven Spielberg

## Directing Styles

Deciding on the directing style for the movie is critical. In the past, directors often made many films over several decades in a single genre; and the visual language of their directing styles became permanently attached to these genres; Alfred Hitchcock with suspense, John Ford with Westerns, William Wellman with war dramas, Howard Hawks with screwball comedies, Michael Curtiz with action adventure, and Elia Kazan with social realism. Genres are still an essential part of marketing and mass audience identification with movies.

It can be argued that a modern director is an apprentice that continually learns from past directing styles; and the only original contribution by a new director for a contemporary take on these past genres is through technology, story updating, and the mixing of other genres. Examples of mixing genres include science fiction and film noir with *Blade Runner* or samurai warriors and Westerns with *The Magnificent Seven*. Story updating in gangster films ranges from *Little Caesar* to *The Godfather* to *The Departed*. And the use of technology to reinventing an old genre is clearly evident by watching *Captain Blood* and *Pirates of the Caribbean: Dead Man's Chest*.

The early directors created the visual language of motion pictures, and the generations of directors that have followed learn by watching movies and being attracted to certain styles and genres that appealed personally to them. This is inescapable. The words in the English language are made up of twenty-six letters in the alphabet. To deny this is denying there is an English language. Visual language has existed since the first cave paintings and with the rapid evolution of motion pictures has become incredibly complex.

One way to begin learning the many dimensions of visual language is through the study of genres, which, if carefully observed, have certain visual rules. Even the independent features of the French New Wave and America directors like John Cassavetes and Andy Warhol have a style that has become known as anti-Hollywood. Movie audiences are conditioned to these genre styles— and at the same time completely unaware of them. But they instinctively know when something is amiss. If Peter Jackson for *The Lord of the Rings* had directed the movies in the same style Oliver Stone used for *Natural Born Killers* then this billion-dollar franchise probably would have been DOA at the box office.

A director needs to be something of a chameleon. A master at this is Steven Spielberg who has a deep-rooted love for the old Studio System movies but was an important force in the New Hollywood Era. For *Raiders of the Lost Ark,* he borrowed from directors like Michael Curtiz and George Steven, who made *Gunga Din.* For *E.T. the Extra-Terrestrial,* he positioned the camera low, from the viewpoint of Elliott, the young boy, an approach he took from early Tom and Jerry cartoons. *Empire of the Sun* has a clean, beautifully photographed David Lean quality.

Spielberg then turns about and uses a documentary style in *Schindler's List,* shooting the film in black and white to heighten the connection with World War II. *Saving Private Ryan* is influenced by war footage. *A. I.: Artificial Intelligence* pays homage to his friend Stanley Kubrick. *Minority Report* is futuristic film noir. And *Munich* looks completely different from all his other films, which include *Jaws, The Color Purple, Jurassic Park,* and *War of the Worlds.* To Spielberg, finding the right visual style is important in capturing the traditional visual aspects of genres; but within this general framework, he brings his personal cinema touches.

## Green-Screen Directing

CGI is here and will probably never go away. But for an actor accustomed to real scenery, it can stretch the imagination. Working with actors against a green screen, the director needs to be clear about the specifics of the action. In the old Studio System movies, the actors were on large expansive sets built up around them and a few feet off the set were ladders and paint buckets. There was still that sense of reality. An actor in the middle of a green screen, staring up at a green dot as a focal point, can become confused and unintentionally let his or her performance wander in a different direction.

The more a director can give actors visual images to interact with or stare at off camera, the better anchored in reality the performances will be. If there is no sound recording for the scene, the director can talk the actors through the action, like in the silent movies. If there are storyboards, conceptual drawings, or simple animation, show these to the actors and, as well as possible, explain the ways these virtual people or creatures move and sound. For *King Kong,* Peter Jackson had Andy Serkis on a platform making eye contact with Naomi Watts. Acting is reacting. Whatever a director can do to create visuals for the actors to react to will undoubted, result in stronger, more convincing performances.

## The Film's POV

The viewpoint of a film and individual scenes are elements that the director must consider. Every film either focuses on the principal character or unfolds with multiple story lines. Alfred Hitchcock's *Rear Window* has the main character in every scene. David Lean's *Lawrence of Arabia* also concentrates on the title character, but *The Bridge on the River Kwai* intercuts between several story lines. John McClane in *Die Hard* is obviously the hero, but the story switches back and forth between him, his wife, the bad guys, the lone cop on the radio, and the obnoxious news reporter. In *The Shawshank Redemption,* Andy Dufresne is the main character but the entire movies is from the point-of-view of

The films of David Lean bridged the old Studio System with the New Hollywood, inspiring young directors like Steven Spielberg and George Lucas with massive epics like *Lawrence of Arabia* and *Doctor Zhivago,* which have a look and style unique from the movies of any other director; David Lean is seen on location for ***The Bridge on the River Kwai*** (1955) with Alec Guinness and Sessue Hayakawa.

Red, played by Morgan Freeman, who tells the story of an odd fish that comes to his prison.

Being conscious of a film's POV gives the director choices in the selection of camera angles and subtle changes in cinematography. In *The Bridge on the River Kwai,* when the British prisoners enter the Japanese camp, the weather is brutally hot with sudden tropical rainstorms. After Colonel Nicholson, played by Alec Guinness, stands up for the rights of his officers, effectively taking over control of the camp, the weather becomes balmy and cools off. This change of nature is a symbolic metaphor that stems from the actions of the main character and creates a color scheme for the film. Then with each scene that Guinness is in, Lean lets the camera favor his character's point of view. This allows audience members to warm up to a man that is rather self-righteous and cold, allowing them to share in his personal triumph and also experience his anguish when he becomes aware that he has unconsciously aided the enemy.

# On-Location Production Checklist

## Things to keep track of (in alphabetical order) . . .

Acting/speech coaches
Animal wrangler rehearsal for stunts
Early morning check on all equipment for the day's shoot
Edit points to the next sequence
Eye-line reaction to CGI effects by actors/crowd
Games, books, magazines, and so forth for actors, extras, and crew
Meals, snacks, special orders
Medical emergency plan
Montage action/chase sequences
Number of locations and repeat locations in area
Number of one-eighths for a day's shooting
Number of shot setups to cover a scene
On-location effects to measure for CGI effects
Online and phone/walkie-talkie communication with sets and locations
Permits and licenses cleared
Second stunt work rehearsals
Second unit crowd rehearsals for large scenes
Translator for mixed crews/cast
Union breaks, hours, lunch/dinner, and so on

Besides the film's POV, each scene will have a character's viewpoint, depending on who has control or the upper hand. In the opening scenes of *The Godfather*, Don Corleone is clearly in charge, and Francis Ford Coppola lets the camera favor his point of view. In the last scene with Don Corleone, his son Michael has now taken over the family business and the scene is from his viewpoint. Every scene in a film reflects the personality of a certain character. By studying this, the director can select the camera setups to reinforce these changing viewpoints and, by doing so, constantly manipulate the audience members' feelings about different characters.

## Developing a Mental Encyclopedia of Visual Language

On a set, the director is the sum total of the films that he or she has seen. Moments from movies that have been forgotten for years will suddenly surface to help a director in planning shots or mapping out a sequence. The human memory retains and stores visual images. The brain is constantly absorbing visual information, whether it is words on a page, an incident on the news, or a birthday celebration. People remember visually and are able to replay a particular moment in the mind.

It is part of the perpetual education of a director to see and study movies—all kinds of movies. How Martin Scorsese solved a problem finding the right angles in a scene becomes a visual textbook when a director runs into a similar problem. And Scorsese might have remembered something from a Sam Fuller that helped him. A director knowing that Scorsese was influenced by Fuller should spend a few nights watching Fuller's films.

To develop a mental encyclopedia, a director should approach a film like an artist studies the

The Hollywood misadventures of writer, director, producer, and actor Orson Welles is the stuff of movie lore; his first feature, made at the age of twenty-six, was *Citizen Kane,* which was a box office failure and disappeared from public view for over twenty-five years, only to be rediscovered and acclaimed by critics as one of the greatest films ever made; Welles is seen here in costume and makeup for ***Touch of Evil*** (1958), the last feature he made for a Hollywood studio.

old masters. Pick a director a month and view the early movies to the later ones to observe how the director's style and themes changed. This process allows a director to borrow from the past and stimulates creative ideas in purely visual terms. And it is the closest a director will get to taking an independent study with Hitchcock, Lean, or Orson Welles.

Spielberg talks about the influence of John Ford's movies on him, especially the continuing themes of duty and family. Ford's early films were shot quickly and have a traditional studio look about them. Then within a few years, from 1935 to 1941, the unmistakable Ford styled emerged with *The Informer, Young Abe Lincoln, Stagecoach,*

*The Grapes of Wrath, The Long Voyage Home,* and *How Green Was My Valley.* Following World War II were the classic Ford Westerns that include *Fort Apache, The Searchers,* and *The Man Who Shot Liberty Valance.* Just watching these movies is a master course in filmmaking, full of cinema tricks waiting to be used.

## Running a Set

To suddenly be in charge of a large group of creative people can bring the best and worst out of a director. Remember, no one liked working for Stalin. The main thing on a set is organization. The night before a shot, the director should spread out a ground plan of the set and with chess pieces or toy soldiers plan out the camera shots for the next day. "Arrested development" is one of the characteristics of a film director. If a director comes in prepared, with a realistic shot list in hand, the need for "control" vanishes. The line producer and department heads will do their jobs. Order is not achieved through yelling and creative fits but through maintaining a lively work pace.

As soon as a shot is finished, go on to the next one. Do not take time to chat with a cast member in between. Always stay in touch with what is happening. Do not interfere, but with body language make it clear that precious seconds are clicking past. To show a little impatience about setting up for the next shot is not a bad thing. However, to become dictatorial or ill-tempered about it will only drain energy from everyone on the set. Tension on a set eventually degenerates into gossip and small camps of dissension. This can spiral into a very unpleasant experience for the rest of the production.

Every film has a distinct personality, because the cast and crews are different. Some line producers are better than others, and some department heads demand more time with nonurgent problems. The director will need to decide how to handle the occasional thorny issues, and a one-on-one meeting behind closed doors is usually the best solution. Most people on a set follow the example of the director. If the director does not waste time, no one else will. And if for some unfortunate reason the director does not have a sense of humor, then one needs to be cultivated *immediately*. Well-timed laughter on a set is the great energizer.

## Setups

Spielberg completes thirty or more camera setups a day. Obviously, he has the best talents available that are ready to move in a split second from one set to the next. Spielberg likes to shoot fast because in his mind he sees the film coming together. Most directors average fifteen to twenty setups. The pacing of a director is something internal. The director needs to know what is comfortable to keep a clear head shot after shot. It is not about pacing but the quality of each shot.

Once a director knows his or her personal pace, the planning for a day's schedule becomes easier.

Sometimes a director plans too many shots and it becomes impossible to keep up with the schedule. For this reason, create a shot list in the order of importance. The most productive shooting time is in the morning or during the first hours of a shoot. Nail the critical shots first. If there is a long tracking shot that is essential, get it out of the way before the lunchbreak. Have an alternative plan if a shot is not working for a technical reason. And always shoot a master.

## Beware of the Urge to Make Changes

At some point in a production, there is the urge to make radical changes because all the pre-production planning seems dull or too safe. Resist

---

# A Little Practical Advice for Directors

Take acting lessons (you will find them useful every day).
Be (or become) someone fun to be around.
Learn entertainment law (you will find it useful every day).
Learn accounting (trust only your own math).
Learn which areas of film production you are weak in (then educate yourself).
Learn the art of writing business proposals (it is an art).
Pick a director (or cinematographer) each month to study (watch at least 8 films).
Think twice about going into business with friends (then think again).
Write angry letters or e-mails (then wait three days and read them again).
Never act like you know everything (even if you do).
Know what you are willing to give up (at least without a fight).
Prepare for the worst (then prepare more).
Hollywood loves success (Hollywood hates success).
Always create a backup plan (or two or three or. . .).
There is no such thing as a small credit (unless it is a naughty movie).
Know the territory (who's who and where they are at).
Know what is in development.
Know the recent movie grosses.
Know the latest news in the trades.
Know how to predict the next trend (if successful, then copyright how you did it).
No one stays up forever (remember the people that helped you).
Read, read, read (read . . .).

---

this temptation. The careful planning before going into a production usually has materialized a movie that is solid in its concept. One of the hazards of writing sitcoms is that the jokes on Monday do not seem funny on Tuesday. This happens on a film, usually brought on by fatigue and a sudden case of paranoia.

There is a sense of satisfaction on a set if a film is going in a good direction. No one will know for certain if it will be a great movie or a box office hit. But there is a united feeling that everything is pulling together and the story has lifted off the pages to the screen. A director walking in one morning and starting to make changes will throw off everyone's concept of the film. If this happens, department heads will be forced to do a turnabout and make changes; and these changes will beget more changes. Then in a couple of days these changes will seem dull. Trust the hard work done in pre-production. A film that gets out of control usually has an unhappy ending—commercially and critically.

## Cinematography and the Visual Language of Film

> There was once a language that everyone in the world understood—silent movies.
>
> —Lillian Gish

In the early years, at the beginning of the twentieth century, the terms "flickers" and "moving pictures" were commonly used. The silent films found in nickelodeons were projected at eighteen frames per section (fps) or less, instead of the twenty-four fps, that became the standard when sound was introduced. The flickering effect is created because at a slower speed the black frame between one photograph and the next is seen for a fraction of a second.

At a faster speed this effect disappears to the human eye because of persistence of vision. Actually, at twenty-four fps almost half of what the eye sees is blackness. Film is advanced through a camera one frame at a time, becoming a long series of individual photographs framed in black. When these images are projected, the eye ignores the black interruption between each photograph, thus creating the illusion of movement.

The fascination with movement began with mechanical optical toys that were hugely popular starting in the early nineteenth century, like the thaumatrope ("turning marvel") and the *zoetrope* ("wheel of life"). These toys, sort of the Game Boy of this era, usually consisted of a half dozen painted or photographic images in a state of movement, like a horse trotting. Thus the term *moving pictures* is a literal description of the process.

### The Roots of Visual Language

The basic alphabet of visual storytelling has not changed since D. W. Griffith's days. In its infant form, this alphabet consists of three elements: long shot, medium shot, and close shot. Cutting between these three camera setups can create tension, suspense, and humor and reveal how a character feels internally.

Immediately, other directors, like F. W. Murnau and Fritz Lang in Germany and Sergei Eisenstein in Russia, took Griffith's basic visual storytelling techniques and added revolutionary variations in camera placement, lighting, scenic design, and editing tempos. Each of these directors and all directors after them had a slightly different definition of a close shot or medium two-shot. The placement and movement of the camera became associated with the defining style of the director. Murnau is identified with long takes, often done with a handheld or mobile camera; Lang used master shots so that the sets and lighting created a

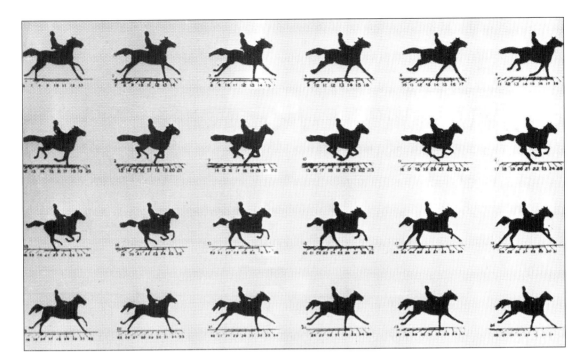

Eadweard Muybridge's landmark photographs (shown here in the popular silhouette version) made with a series of cameras in 1878 to prove that all legs of a running horse left the ground captured the public's attention, promoting sales of the zoetrope, with which people would watch the same image for hours with complete fascination.

tense dramatic mood around his actors; and Eisenstein shot a scene from every imaginable angle so he could then edit all the images into a fast-paced montage.

Alfred Hitchcock, who studied in Berlin during the expressionist movement, was heavily influenced by Murnau. One of the techniques he learned was the point-of-view (POV) shot, which allows the audience to "see through the eyes" of a screen character. This technique causes every individual watching the film to feel like he or she is singularly part of the action. The process of creating a POV sequence begins with a close-up of an actor staring off center of the camera. The next shot is in the opposite direction, a 180-degree turn from the close-up, with the camera positioned in the place and height of the actor. When these two shots are edited together, audiences believe they are seeing what the screen character is looking at. In

*Psycho,* when Norman Bates stares through the peek hole in his parlor, the next shot is of Marion Crane undressing in her motel room. For these few seconds, every audience member has become a voyeuristic serial killer.

Using this same process, Steven Spielberg in *Saving Private Ryan* puts the audience in the eyes of Captain John Miller, played by Tom Hanks, watching the bloody chaos around him during the first assault of the D-Day invasion. There is a moment when Hanks's character goes into a state of shock after a shell explodes behind him. He gazes around in confusion, seeing a living hell on Earth of soldiers catching fire and one GI looking for his missing arm. The same POV technique that Hitchcock used throughout his career to create suspense is now used by Spielberg to place the audience in the nightmare of battle.

Each great director has contributed new images to the visual language of film. Now one minute of film can have over a hundred different elements at work. A single shot that might take hours to set up and is only seen for seconds on screen, is influenced by lighting, set design, editing tempos, music, sound effects, casting choices, and camera placement. The three basics of film (long shot, medium shot, and close-up) now have thousands of variations that reflect the combined efforts of a small army of exceptionally talented individuals. Look at close-ups of a favorite actor from three films by three directors. Each one will have a different look, depending on the dynamics.

Great films become visual memories in the human mind, and because real-life experiences create memories, these moving images become the collective whole of each individual that sees them. The exceptional aspect of visual language is that it is universal. In the silent era, Charlie Chaplin's *The Kid* could be shown anywhere in the world and people would laugh and cry at the antics and compassion of The Little Tramp. There were no words to get in the way. Today, blockbusters like *The Lord of the Rings: The Return of the King* and *The Pirates of the Caribbean: At World's End* are popular worldwide because they are mostly visual adventures told through montage, music, and sound effects.

Visual language has evolved from a single master shot of Fred Ott sneezing to a thousand different elements of light influencing the senses every minute. Each director, cinematographer, scenic artist, costume designer, sound engineer, composer, and actor has forged a slight variation on visual language. The problem is that after a mere hundred years, these variations have become overwhelming because there is no definitive study of the ABCs of visual language. Steven Spielberg talks about how he uses master shots like those of John Ford, and George Lucas tips his director's hat to the influence of Saturday morning serials such as *Buck Rogers* and *Flash Gordon*.

Many filmmakers starting out today will find watching these old movies like learning Latin because they are in black and white and the edit-

ing pace is slow. But instinctively these filmmakers will use the same camera setups or storytelling techniques, because the basics of visual language have been passed on and refined by each generation of filmmakers. The shadowy film noir undertones of *The Maltese Falcon* can be found in *Chinatown* and in *L.A. Confidential.* And touches of Metropolis can be found in *Dr. Strangelove, Blade Runner,* and *The Matrix.*

The problem of filmmaking is not a conquest over technology but the potential loss of a complex visual heritage out of a lack of interest. For example, *Gone with the Wind,* the jewel in the crown of the Studio System, was shot with Technicolor cameras that weighed over 150 pounds and had lenses and film stock that required hundreds of foot-candles, creating almost unbearable temperatures on the sound stage to light a simple close-up. Over the decades, this motion picture has been watched by ten times the number of people who have seen James Cameron's special effects spectacular *Titanic.* What is essential to understand is that *Gone with the Wind* added lasting moments to the visual language of filmmaking. And because of this, without *Gone with the Wind,* there might not have been a *Titanic.* Certain movies endure because they continue to influence new filmmakers.

> " I think when sound came in it was a great catastrophe. "
> —Vilmos Zsigmond

## Elements of Cinematography

Ever since D. W. Griffith experimented with Billy Bitzer on over four hundred short films, the relationship between director and cinematographer has become the most intimate on a film production. The director has a vision. The cinematographer brings that vision to life on the

## Visual Language Mathematics

A film has an average of 12 edits per minute
Or 12 separate bits of visual information.

At 12 edits per minute, in 120 minutes there are 1,440 edits
Or 1,440 separate bits of visual information.

However, a modern action movie can average 24 edits per minutes,
Which is a rate of 2.5 seconds, equaling 2,880 edits per two-hour movie
Or 2,880 separate bits of visual information.

Using the old proverb, if one picture is truly worth 1,000 words,
Then one action movie equals 2,880,000 words.

At a reading pace of 400 words per minute,
One movie equals 7,200 hours of reading
Or 330 days to absorb as much written information as watching one movie.

If a person watches 4.5 hours of movies, television, Internet searching, and games per day
Using 12 edits per minute, this equals 3,240 edits per day
Or 3,240 separate bits of visual information daily.

screen. This is not subtracting from the contributions of other departments; but ultimately, it is through the eyes of the camera that all visual components are brought together into one complex image. The choice of color and angles will affect sets, costumes, makeup, the way an audience responds to an actor, and even a composer's selection of musical themes.

Cinematography is capturing light bouncing off an object. People are influenced by the changes in light, just like a camera. On a cloudy day, the iris opens up to let in more light, like the shutter on a camera. On a sunny day, the iris grows smaller, letting less light hit the retina. When the wind blows, dust filters the air. In a heavy rain storm, objects in the distance become blurred.

Vision allows people to be living cameras. Walking up to an object is in cinema terms a tracking shot. Kissing someone creates an extreme close-up. Watching a live performance from the first row is a very different experience than watching from the last row of the balcony.

Through evolution, people see a steady image when walking or running, instead of a rocking image like from a handheld camera. Walking around listening to music on an iPod is underscoring. How people selectively recall images is editing.

The cinematographer's job is to capture what the mind envisions in a creative state and bring it to life on the screen. The human *imagination* is still one of the great mysteries. How each person pulls from the almost unlimited store of visual information stored in the brain to create stories, drawings, diagrams, dance movements, or recipes is a daily miracle that goes unappreciated. Because each person is singularly affected by his or her experiences, which are recorded in the brain visually, each individual can imagine an unlimited number of uniquely original ideas. And ideas are, in effect, short movies in the mind.

Remembering the highpoints of a vacation is a homemade movie. Recalling scenes from a violent experience is a documentary. These are remarkable, because these would be huge computer files; but to the human brain, recall is an elementary function. What is truly amazing is the spontaneous creation of new images. Someone who watches the news about an air disaster suddenly imagines he or she is in the airplane. For a brief moment, the person is creating a story, from a personal point of view that involves the other senses and feels as real as the Star Tours ride at Disneyland.

An examination of this story takes some of the mystery out of it. The plane in the person's mind is probably an image of one they have flown in. Some of the people on the plane might be friends or family members. The area the plane is flying over might also be pulled from personal memory. These are all personal images being borrowed for this short mental movie. What happens next is the incredible part. The person then imagines the plane breaking apart a few rows away. He or she also sees strangers rushing away or trying to help others.

Without living this experience, how does the person realistically imagine a plane breaking apart? Perhaps from sheer imagination. Or from nightmares. Or from scenes out of movies. Most likely, a combination of all of these. But what about the strangers in this split-second movie? How does a person imagine a realistic human being he or she has never seen? The answer might be that none of them are strangers but real people seen in airports, grocery stories, restaurants, and other places the mind has taken a mental mug shot of. There is no way to know for sure without being able to process the short mental movie onto a tangible matter for closer inspection.

This is what writers, artists, architects, and others who work in a visual profession have done since the beginning of recorded time—a recording process that began with pictures on a wall. These talented individuals try to get the pictures out of their minds onto paper, canvas, fresco ceilings, or a stage. Arguably, writers have always seen visual images and attempted to convert them into words. Homer certainly witnessed a Cyclops in his imagination. Dante had a very clear picture of Hell.

And William Blake not only wrote "Tiger, tiger burning bright" but also drew a picture of the beast.

However, the images in the minds of those that excelled in the various avenues of the visual arts *saw movement*—not descriptive words or a still picture on a canvas or actors reciting lines on a stage but the realistic, three-dimensional moving images in the mind that sparked the imaginative process. Great paintings are a frozen moment of motion— the hand of God giving life to Adam found in Michelangelo's Sistine Chapel ceiling, the sensation of flickering light in Rembrandt's *The Night Watch,* or the frenzy of flight in van Gogh's *Wheat Field with Crows.* When film arrived during the height of the movements for impressionism, expressionism, and surrealism, a new and different artist was born—the cinematographer.

## The Cinematographer

The visual knowledge of a cinematographer is far more intricate than that of most directors. There is no other guild in the motion picture industry that requires more experience and preparation to qualify for membership. A cinematographer, as Vittorio Storaro states, is the sum total of everything he or she sees. A dedicated cinematographer will have studied the classic films for style and technique and is an admirer of the great black-and-white cinematographers from the Studio System. A cinematographer is a perpetual student that studies the behavior of light reflecting from a surface and wonders how to get that same effect on film. A cinematographer will spend endless hours in museums or going through art and photography books.

What is astounding is how quickly the art of photography developed after the first cameras were manufactured. Many of the early photographers had grown up with studying the art masters. They were perhaps struggling artists themselves before they ventured into this new trade of being able to click a shutter and capture an image in a second. They quickly cultivated an understanding of the nature of light and experimented endlessly with lenses and emulsions. During the Civil War, over a million photographs were taken.

When motion pictures arrived, these pioneer photographers applied their knowledge of single-frame composition and light variation to moving images. Because many of these early cinematographers had rapidly advanced the philosophy of the photographic image, motion pictures became a wonderful new toy to experiment with. In an explosion of enthusiasm, these experiments happened around the world. And because it was film and mass produced, *The Cabinet of Dr. Caligari* could open in Berlin and be shown in New York two weeks later.

Cinematographers in the Studio System would spend hours lighting a star for a close-up, using filters, back lighting, and reflectors to get the right look. Greta Garbo demanded that William Daniels be the cinematographer on her movies. This effort for perfection became known as painting with light. But it was also a science that required a practical knowledge of lenses, chemicals, and engineering. Because of the high quality in cinematography that started in the Silent Era and has continued ever since, audiences tend not to fully appreciate the gorgeous images that constantly fill the screen. It is a shame, because many of the legendary cinematographers—like Daniels, Gregg Toland, John Alton, Jack Cardiff, Freddie Young, Boris Kaufman, Vittorio Storaro, Vilmos Zsigmond, and Conrad Hall—are also the great artists of the twentieth century.

Many cinematographers are associated with certain directors. Joseph Walker worked with Frank Capra during the 1930s. Greg Toland worked with John Ford and William Wyler; and for Toland's contributions on *Citizen Kane,* Orson Wells shared the final credit of the movie with him. Robert Burks was Alfred Hitchcock's cinematographer during what is considered the Master of Suspense's golden era in the late 1940s and 1950s. Gordon Willis shot the *Godfather* movies with Frances Ford Coppola. Bernardo Bertolucci has had a career-long collaboration with Vittorio Storaro. Roger Deakins makes movies with Joel and Ethan Coen. Douglas Slocombe shot the *Indiana Jones* movies with Steven Spielberg. Since *Schindler's List,* Janusz Kaminski has collaborated with Steven Spielberg.

> All of the great films are a resolution of a conflict between darkness and light. There is no single way to express yourself. There are infinite possibilities for the use of light with shadows and colors. The decisions you make about composition, movement, and the countless combinations of other variables is what makes it an art.
> —Vittorio Storaro

## Selecting a Cinematographer

To find the right cinematographer, it is best to watch the work the person has done on other projects. There may be a style the cinematographer prefers that is repeated in all the films. This could mean there is not the willingness to explore different visual ways to tell a story. It could also mean, as is very common in this profession, that the cinematographer has been hired because other directors have liked this particular look and consequently the cinematographer has not been given the freedom to explore variations. In either case, this is a starting point for a discussion, and the

An establishing shot in John Ford's ***The Searchers*** (1957), filmed in Monument Valley. The image is broken horizontally into 1/3s with the clouded sky taking 2/3s, giving the desert landscape below a sense of vastness. Ford once told a young Steven Spielberg that to be a good director he had to know where to aim the camera on an establishing shot. If he had shown 2/3s of the desert, then the characters would have looked consumed by the land and the romance of the image would have been lost.

The action is moving from left to right, the most forceful direction in visual language. The eye naturally goes to the left of the screen and then follows the men on horses. Because ***The Searchers*** is about a long journey, Ford decided that the trip away from home would go left to right, and the return trip would be shot right to left, so the audience would have a visual sense of direction.

The eyes of the audience are forced toward the men by framing the shot between two mesas and then waiting for clouds to fill the top of the screen. For a shot this perfect, Ford probably had extras ready and in position for days until the right cloud formation rolled in.

In **Unforgiven** (1992) director Clint Eastwood uses a long shot (which can also be described as an establishing shot) to achieve a different effect than in Ford's *The Searchers.* Here the earth drops below 1/3 letting the gray sky dominate, creating a somber mood; the leafless tree fills the center left of the screen, where the eye naturally looks first, and because the tree is barren, this reinforces a sensation of despair. The branches of the tree force the viewer to look down at the solitary, lone figure of a man standing before a grave. There is no movement, so the attention stays on the man with a feeling of sadness.

This silhouetted tableau, framed by the tree and gravestone, becomes a small picture inside a large one. The man is as tall as the trunk of the tree, and his hat almost touches the 1/3 division of the screen, suggesting a powerful man. The giant tree, apparently dead, symbolically underscores the theme of the film, that no matter how old and powerful someone is—death always wins.

This full shot (also referred to as a full-figured shot or medium long shot) is from ***The Road to Perdition*** (2002), the last film by the great cinematographer Conrad Hall. Here Hall plays with classic composition, underexposing to give a film noir look. This is the moment when Paul Newman, as crime boss John Rooney, is murdered. A heavy rain is falling, and Rooney has three bodyguards holding umbrellas for him, establishing a man of power; but he and his men are on the right side, the weakest position on a screen.

On the left, completely removed from the others, in the most powerful position, is a lone man without an umbrella and in full silhouette—like a medieval depiction of death. Rooney and his men are backlit, allowing for a touch of bounce light to faintly highlight his face; they walk without expression, with the shadows darkly stretching out before them, reinforcing the death theme. If Rooney had been on the left, there would have been a sense of hope for the character; by placing him and his bodyguards on the right, Hall subconsciously removed that hope in the mind of the viewer.

In this medium tracking shot in **Blood Diamond** (2006), Leonardo DiCaprio is running on the left side of the screen, which is the first thing the eye sees in this rapidly edited sequence and implies that he is in control of his destiny—for the moment. On the right side is a burning car, heightening the moment of danger. Cinematographer Eduardo Serra has used a short lens on DiCaprio, keeping him in focus; but everything behind him is slightly blurred, aiming up at a slightly low angle, once again giving a visual sense that he will get out of this situation.

In this two-shoot (the most commonly used camera setup) from **Schindler's List** (1993), Steven Spielberg and cinematographer Janusz Kaminski are showing that Itzhak Stern (Ben Kingsley) is in complete control of the conversation with Oskar Schindler (Liam Neeson). Stern is seated and Schindler is standing. Normally, the person standing is perceived as being the dominant party, but Schindler is on the right side of the screen and Stern is in the power position on the left.

Though Stern is sitting, Schindler is slightly bent over, further weakening his stature. Behind Schindler are three windows at sharp angles, taking the attention from him, but Stern is seated in front of dark cabinets, so the eye has no reason to stray. Stern has his arms folded and stares directly left to right, while Schindler is compromised by looking down and right to left. And from the desk lamp to Schindler to Stern is a triangle, with the tip pointing directly at Stern.

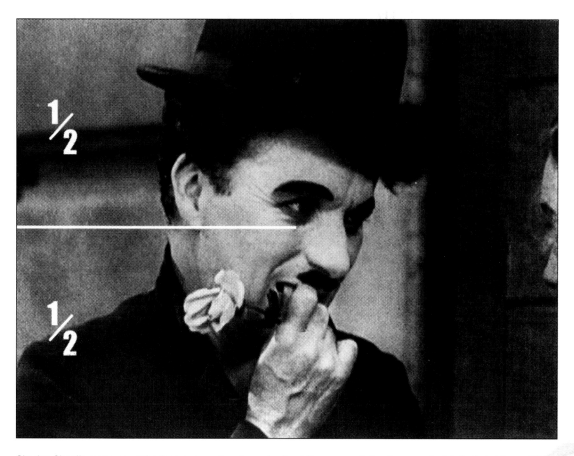

Charles Chaplin was one of the first screen stars to understand the power of the close-up. In this last shot from **City Lights** (1931), The Little Tramp meets the flower girl (Virginia Cherrill) who was blind but because of his self-sacrifice she can now see. However, she has never seen the man that helped her, believing him to be a millionaire. By touching his hands, she recognizes that The Little Tramp is her true benefactor.

Chaplin places the camera over Cherrill's shoulder, creating a reverse-angle shot, and frames his head and shoulders to the left of center. His eyes, which are important to the success of this final scene, are aligned slightly above horizontal center. He stares down left to right, making eye contact with her. The camera is angled upward, giving him a strong presence. Without a single word, Chaplin is able by the expression in his eyes to show his love and happiness for her—which anybody anywhere in the world understands.

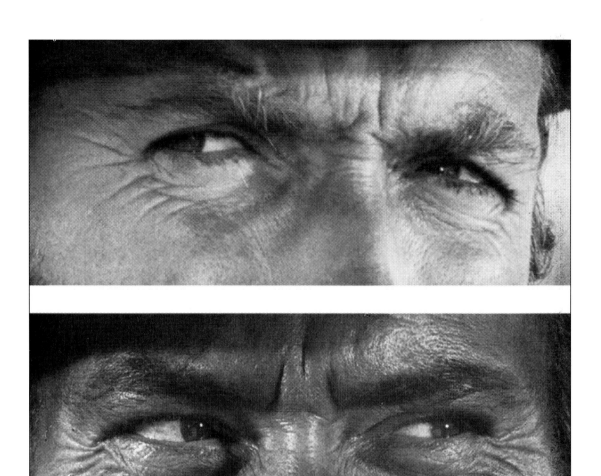

In the epic spaghetti Western, ***The Good, the Bad, and the Ugly*** (1966), Sergio Leone uses extreme close-ups to heighten the suspense during the final showdown. Extreme close-ups are used sparingly to evoke certain emotions from the audience. Suddenly an actor's eyes can be ten feet high on the screen, which if timed correctly can make people jump in their seats. In this case, Leone uses extreme close-ups to show how cool and calm Clint Eastwood is and the nervousness in Lee Van Clef's eyes.

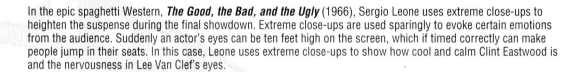

Throughout the ingenious thriller *The Third Man* (1949), director Carol Reed uses Dutch-angle shots (the term comes from *Deutsch*—meaning German—angle, which was experimented with during the expressionism movement). This tilted camera angle creates a psychological uneasiness about a character, alerting the audience to something abnormal or nightmarish. Hitchcock, who was trained in German cinema, used Dutch angles in many films. Here Orson Welles, as the notorious Harry Lime, enters a café to meet an old friend—clearly with murder on his mind.

cinematographer will be impressed that the director took the time to do some research.

If the cinematographer is married to one style or a certain method of shooting, this could be a disastrous collaboration for the director because his or her vision will not be fulfilled. If the cinematographer favors natural over artificial light to achieve a look, this could possibly affect the screenplay. Story changes might become necessary to change the times of day of scenes. This would mean that the conversations about the screenplay would always come back to a predetermined look the cinematographer is comfortable with.

It is very unlikely this scenario will happen, because most cinematographers are eager to explore new styles and methods. When director William Friedkin had a similar talk with Owen Roizman about the documentary look he wanted for *The French Connection,* Roizman replied he was a cinematographer and should be able to do anything. The next step, if the cinematographer is willing, is to do a start-and-stop through movies and ask how certain scenes were shot. These can be films made by the cinematographer or films that have a look the director is attracted to. Have a long discussion. Everybody likes to talk about their own work, and cinematographers do not always get that opportunity.

The other important topic to talk about is what the cinematographer's requirements are. There may be certain crew people the cinematographer wants to use on a project, or certain equipment rentals that are expected. Because crews should not be hired before a cinematographer or any department head comes on board, these conditions should not be a problem. But always ask.

> ## It's not what you light—it's what you DON'T light.
> —John Alton

## Working with a Cinematographer

The characters are the director's responsibility to bring to life through the writing process and casting. The mood that surrounds and defines those characters is the job of the cinematographer. The conversations between director and cinematographer have everything to do with the essential art of the movies. Working with the screenwriter is dealing with refining the plot, getting the right dialogue, and finding the pace of the story.

But this work can go through changes once a cinematographer goes through a screenplay. These are not story or dialogue rewrites but ways to tell the story visually. Scenes that seem so obvious throughout the long hours of story discussions might need visual reinforcement as far as a character's loyalty or the despair someone is experiencing. And, of course, a lengthy, meaningful monologue might disappear entirely and be replaced by an emotional close-up on the eyes of the actor playing the character.

Cinematographers look at the screenplay as being the source to draw ideas from. When reading a script, a cinematographer is thinking about the best way to tell the story visually through light, camera movement, colors, lenses, and post-production effects to correct the final image. Characters are defined by their relationship with light, and the theme of the story is reinforced with a carefully planned color scheme. With digital technology and DVD releases, a cinematographer's involvement with a movie can extend over several years.

The planning process between a director and cinematographer is often the most satisfying on a production. This is an opportunity to discuss the basic fundamentals of filmmaking—creating moving pictures to tell a story:

- If this opportunity was not possible before, then this is the time to watch and discuss movies that might have a visual influence on the current project.
- Go through the screenplay and talk about each scene in terms of POV, the source of light, and

camera movement versus character movement. Design a visual concept for each scene.

- Lay out the storyboards and examine each shot, always being open to change. Talk about the opening shot of a scene and decide the first thing the audience should look at.
- Listen to music and attempt to predict how each scene will be affected by music, sound effects, or a voiceover. Music is a heavy influence on the way people see visual images, and sometimes the cinematography can go deliberately counterpoint to the mood of the music to build suspense or foreshadow upcoming events.
- Make decisions about using cranes, tracks, Steadicams, and other filmmaking toys, along with the use of handheld cameras. Each of these create different visual sensations and can distract from a scene if not used as a clearly designed effect.
- Every lens will create a different mood and perception in the mind of the audience. The choices of lenses play with the psychology of the viewer; and though the person is not aware of these constantly changing dynamics, the cumulative effect can be powerful.
- Bring in art and photography books to bounce around ideas regarding composition and camera setups. This is a chance to pull out the dusty college art history book and discuss light and color in the paintings of Johannes Verneer or Edward Hopper.
- Decide on an overall color scheme. Talk about characters and color like musical themes and how a character might dominate a scene by a certain color motif.

## Influence of Color

Every color evokes a different response from an audience. Vibrant reds raise a viewer's temperature a fraction of a degree, and cold blues lower the temperature. The study of how color evokes emotional reactions from people became a subject of study during the Renaissance and is used by cinematographers to subtly manipulate audience feeling. Certain colors have a symbolic reference. Bright green is associated with learning and education. A rich yellow is used to depict pleasant memories or to promote the idea of heroism. A pure blue represents the feeling of freedom or a spiritual purity.

Roger Deakins in *The Shawshank Redemption* avoided using these three colors except in pivotal story moments. In the scene in which the prisoners are tarring the roof, bright green is seen in the distant fields. In this scene, Andy Dufresne tells the prison guard that he can help him keep all of his inheritance if he "trusts his wife," thus educating the tough guard about an income tax loophole. For his assistance, Andy asks for a few cold beers for his friends. The next scene is filtered in yellow, as the prisoners drink their beers and look at Andy with admiration. At the end of the film, the rich blue of the Pacific Ocean fills the screen.

> In feature films the director is God; in documentary films God is the director.
> —Alfred Hitchcock

> You're looking at a character whose head is enveloped in flames, and then in slow-motion helicopter blades slicing through his body, superimposed upon a whirling ceiling fan, and strange sounds and music intermingling from different sources;

> you're probably aware you're watching a film, not an imitation of real life. Even dreams, despite their odd surreality, don't look quite like that. Inevitably, the super-imposed images in *Apocalypse Now* betray a self-consciousness because they come at the very beginning and are intended to expose and explore Willard's inner state of mind. If there had been no resonance between that scene and the film as a whole, the opening would have been a meaningless exercise, empty virtuosity.
>
> —Walter Murch about the opening of *Apocalypse Now*

## On Set with the Cinematographer

The on-set association between director and cinematographer is sometimes baffling even to people with film knowledge. George Cukor, the great director from the Studio System of MGM, said that he never looked through the viewfinder of the camera and left the setups to the cinematographer. George Roy Hill, who usually called his own shots, gave Conrad Hall total control during *Butch Cassidy and the Sundance Kid.* And Stanley Kubrick was involved in every detail of lighting and camera setup.

To work out a relationship with the cinematographer in advance is extraordinarily important. During production, the cinematography is under huge time constraints finishing up one shot and going to the next. Because of advanced discussions and finalized storyboards, the cinematographer should know what is expected for each setup. But a cinematographer is always finding "happy accidents" and will bring these to the attention of the director.

If a film goes into production without a lot of prep time nor a stack of storyboards, the working relationship can become precarious. The potential difficulties arise from how much the director knows about the complex art of cinematography. The assumption is that the director always calls the setups and the cinematographer runs around making them happen. This is not *and should not be* the reality. The relationship between director and cinematographer should be a mutual admiration society. Because of training and professional intuition, the cinematographer will probably have a better visual instinct during production.

Once production begins, there is no time to change concepts and try new ideas. If there are no storyboards to lead the way, then the director needs to bring in a shot list and calmly discuss them with the cinematographer. Afterward, give the cinematographer the freedom to match the shots as closely as possible. Always listen to advice from the cinematographer; and, without dramatics, usually take the advice.

Have a monitor set up so the director can see what is happening through the lens. When the cinematographer says the lights and camera are ready, study the shot, and perhaps do a run through with the actors. Trust the cinematographer to catch any shadows or hot spots during the rehearsal. If there are creative differences, try to resolve them quietly and away from the cinematographer's crew. But the best way to avoid friction on set is to have long conversations in advance, share ideas, come to an agreement on the look of the film, and take the time to plan shots and draw storyboards. With the costs of filmmaking rising, shooting wildly, like the good old days of Godard and Cassavetes, is not an economically wise approach if a long, productive career is desired.

## Editing

### The Editor as Writer

> " Never make a cut without a positive reason. "
>
> —Edward Dmytryk

An editor is probably as close to a time traveler as anyone will come. Every scene in a movie cheats real time. The most common example is someone getting out of a car, and then in the next cut the person enters a room. In actually, two minutes might have passed from the car to the walk to the room, but on film it is presented as continuous action. This is an obvious altering of the perception of time. What is unnoticed by moviegoers is the small cuts. During a scene with a long conversation, an editor actually plays with time. An actor's pause is cut out, a sentence is transposed or eliminated, an awkward facial expression is cut away from, or three frames are added to reinforce a dramatic stare.

Editing is the skillful manipulation of years, weeks, and minutes to create a two-hour film without the audience becoming disoriented. The editor's job might begin with enough exposed film to stretch from Los Angeles to Las Vegas and ends deciding if a moment works better with six frames or four frames. With twenty-four frames per second (fps), even 1/24 of a second can make a notable difference.

In an effort to reduce the running length of *Terminator 2: Judgment Day*, director James Cameron had the idea of cutting one frame out of every twenty-four frames. Since film is projected at twenty-four fps the assumption was that the missing frame would slip by invisibly. With this theory, every twenty-four seconds would total one saved second, or almost six minutes out of the entire film. Instead of being unnoticeable as expected, the resulting footage had distinct jumps every second, destroying the continuity of each scene.

This illustrates the effect a single frame has on a moment of action. Steven Spielberg talks about working with Verna ("Mother Scissors") Fields on *Jaws*. His discovery was that the difference between seeing a terrifying open-mouthed shark and a big, silly rubber fish was just two frames. The old rule of thumb in special effects was to hold no longer than three seconds on a cut to a rocket model or monster makeup. Any longer and the audience would spot the artificiality of the effect. Today, it would be only a couple of frames. Fortunately with CGI, rapid cutting to camouflage an effect is not necessary.

### A Quick History

Editing began gradually in films. The first movies were continuous shots with no editing at all, usually a twenty-second peek at a real event. With George Méliès *A Trip to the Moon* (1902) scenes were edited together that looked like theatrical presentations. There was no internal editing of two-shots or close-ups. A year later, Edwin S. Porter began to use editing to heighten the drama with fast cutting in *Life of an American Fireman, The Great Train Robbery,* and scores of others.

From 1908 to 1915, D. W. Griffith experimented with internal scene editing for dramatic effect. Griffith also perfected cross-cutting, editing back and forth between simultaneous actions to heighten suspense, especially with a dramatic chase to rescue. Then 1925, Sergei Eisenstein made *Battleship Protemkin* and introduced in the modern editing concept known as Soviet montage.

In the sequence *The Odessa Steps Massacre*, he used over a hundred shots, letting images of soldiers and innocent citizens collide together, drawing audiences into the horror and panic of the moment.

Two years later, just when silent movies were perfecting a pure visual language, sound came roaring in and movies returned a theatrical look with limited editing because of sound engineering difficulties. Ironically, the only silent film to win the Best Picture Academy Award was William Wellman's *Wing* with incredible aerial dog fights, shot with multiple cameras over several months.

During the Studio System in the 1930s and 1940s, the moguls did not want the camera to be the star, as it was in Germany and Russia in the years before. The "invisible edit" became the preferred method of cutting movies. With this approach, it was believed that audiences were not distracted from the story by the mechanics of filmmaking. The simplest description of the technique is that the edit happens during movement. For example, a man is seen in a medium shot as he starts to turn. If the next shot is a close-up of the man completing the turn, taken from the same vantage point, the viewer is unaware of the editing process.

Director Edward Dmytryk's seven rules, from his book *On Film Editing*, are examples of classical Hollywood cutting:

*Rule 1: Never make a cut without a positive reason.*

*Rule 2: When undecided about the exact frame to cut on, cut long rather than short.*

*Rule 3: Whenever possible cut 'in movement.'*

*Rule 4: The 'fresh' is preferable to the 'stale.'*

*Rule 5: All scenes should begin and end with continuing action.*

*Rule 6: Cut for proper values rather than proper 'matches.'*

*Rule 7: Substance first—then form.*

The mobility of movement found in the last years of the silent era disappeared from the screen after sound arrived, partly because of the Hollywood studio's philosophy of seamless filmmaking; but the technical reason was that the motorized cameras were extremely heavy. The Arriflex 35 and other lightweight cameras were introduced in the 1960s and changed filmmaking. What would become known as the action montage returned with movies like *Bullitt* and *The French Connection*. In 1986, the supersonic aerial montages in *Top Gun*, edited to surround-sound rock 'n' roll music, finally picked up where *Wing* left off sixty years before.

## Frame-by-Frame Storytellers

Alfred Hitchcock, who was trained in Germany during the height of the expressionism movement, is the only major director during the Studio System that continually let the camera be the star. He described movies as being little bits of film edited together to tell a story. His detailed storyboards gave a visual concept of a movie; but, more important, they showed the psychological interconnection between multiple images. He knew that audience members believed what they saw, like a nice "harmless" young man taking care of his invalid mother. With this simple knowledge, he could play with the instinctive reactions of moviegoers and take them on a funhouse ride. To Hitchcock, the editing was the real storytelling element that was unique only to motion pictures.

Editors tend to be exceptional storytellers who never receive true credit for their dramatic contributions in movies. An editor is one of the last people to be associated with a film, usually in a room with a nervous director or overwrought producer trying to meet a deadline. Most of the old theatrical traditions associated with editing are now gone: the long strips of film hanging on lines or around the editor's neck, the sweet smell of glue, the editing guillotines with sticky blades, and the flatbed editor. Only Steven Spielberg and his longtime editor Michael Kahn still cut film on a Moviola. Everybody else in the industry is now editing electronically.

Alfred Hitchcock uses **Rear Window** (1954) as his favorite example of the visual influence of editing. The two shots are from James Stewart's point of view (POV), where the camera is placed in a close-up with Stewart looking slightly off left. To create a POV, the next shot edited in is what Stewart is looking at. By using this simple technique, Hitchcock lets the audience see through the eyes of the character. Almost every shot in **Rear Window** is a POV, which he also uses in *Notorious, Vertigo,* and *Psycho.*

In this example, Hitchcock does not change the shot of Stewart; it is the same in both edits, with no alteration of expression. However, the audience sees two different reactions from Stewart because of the POV that is edited in. The first is of Miss Torso doing her early morning dance exercises. When Hitchcock edits back to Stewart, audiences see his expression as that of an older man with dirty thoughts on his mind.

In the next POV, Raymond Burr is acting very suspicious after his wife has disappeared late at night. This time when Hitchcock edits back, audiences see his expression as one of deep concern, with the suspicion that a murderer is living across from him. The same shot of Stewart is used each time, but two different audience reactions are generated from what is edited in between.

However, the process remains unchanged: to find the pace and dramatic heart of a story. Films are stories. An editor must take thousands of feet of film and trim them down into one self-contained, coherent, involving story. The editing choices are not between which shots look prettier or are artistically satisfying but between which shots tell the story the best. To do this, an editor must understand acting, the language of camera angles, the influence of sound and music, and especially the structural dynamics of writing.

There are hundreds of books, magazines, and seminars about screenwriting that tell how to establish conflict by page 30 and build to an exciting climax. But this flood of film storytelling advice did not start until the 1980s. So why did the movies of the Golden Age of Hollywood hit these plot points so perfectly without the structural advice found in these books? The truth is that a completed screenplay might have the right plot points on the right pages, but in reality the one-minute-per-page theory is an estimate. Some scenes go longer because of the nature of the dialogue. Other scenes are quicker because of action. And a chase described in two lines on paper might be ten minutes when shot. Yet on screen, most films hit the thirty-minute setup point and unfold in the three-act paradigm structure.

The involvement of the editor is one of the biggest and most overlooked reasons that movies have hit these structural signposts over the decades. The editor methodically cuts down scenes, picks the strongest visual takes, and tosses out unnecessary lines of dialogue. With these trims and changes, most movies time out to the plot points endlessly written about in screenwriting books.

Unquestionably, the director is sitting next to the editor during most of the process, and this association is the very definition of collaboration. But no one knows a movie in the final stage as well as the editor. By this point, the editor is familiar with every frame of film and knows the best takes to advance the story. A writer can describe a man in a scary Halloween mask; a director can shoot a man in a scary Halloween mask; but the editor is the one who makes the audience collectively jump when the man in the mask is seen.

## Time in the Movies

### The Six Realms of Movie Time

Linear—Real Time
Linear—Traditional Storytelling
Simultaneous or Overlapping
Flashback
Flash Forward
Altered Realty

## Movie Time

Time in a film begins with the screenplay and a writer's decision on how to structure the story. The vast majority of movies are linear, following a continuous time line. Unfolding a story from the beginning to end is the simplest method for an audience to comprehend the events. Tragedies going back to Ancient Greece, epic poems, the novel, and short stories used the linear structure. In education, textbooks give information by starting at the beginning of a subject in history, mathematics, or science and advancing with new facts in increasing amounts. This is the universal learning process. The mind assimilates knowledge by gathering new information one step at a time.

Until the late nineteenth century, writers followed the age-old traditional format of starting a tale at the beginning. Authors like Herman Melville and Charles Dickens occasionally used the first-person narrative. This allowed stories to have a major character present the events of a great adventure. The first chapter of *David Copperfield* simply states, "I am born." *Moby Dick* opens with, "Call me Ishmael." This served as a wrap-around device that broke up the third-person linear narrative.

Then Marcel Proust, William James, James Joyce, William Faulkner, and other writers began to explore the mysterious inner workings of the mind with stream-of-consciousness narration. This was an attempt to capture the free flow of thoughts or dreams people experience every hour of the day. In large part, this was a response to the writings of Sigmund Freud and Carl Jung. On stage, this movement evolved into German expressionism.

The mind learns progressively by building on facts but then recalls these facts in a random fashion without an apparent relationship to time. A single thought could be comprised of recently acquired information and old knowledge, resulting in the projection of an original idea. In an instant, the mind jumps from the present to the past, back to the present, and then to the future. The mind does this with images, not words.

After Steven Spielberg's *Jurassic Park* (1983), the term CGI (computer-generated imagery) was on everyone's lips. The final giant step in the art of movie wizardry had been achieved by George Lucas's Industrial Light and Magic. With this evolving technology, a new field of editing opened up. Frames were edited together as usual, but now images within the frames could also be edited and rearranged, a technique that Lucas has referred to as cyber or three-dimensional editing.

## Dinosaur Sound Effects from
# *Jurassic Park*

### Tyrannosaurus Rex

The T-Rex's roar was made up of a baby elephant mixed with a tiger and an alligator. The sound of its breath was a whale's blowhole. A dog attacking a ball was used for the sounds of it tearing a Gallimimus apart.

### Velociraptor

A mix of hissing geese, dolphin screams, walrus bellows, human rasps, and an African crane's mating call were used to create the various raptor sounds.

### Dilophosaurus

The sounds this hissing, venom spitting dinosaur made were produced by combining a hawk, a swan, and a rattlesnake together.

Special-effects pioneer Linwood Dunn observed that an effect was only as good as someone's reaction to it. The importance of music and sound effects in bringing a visual effect alive is profound, to the point that Spielberg and Lucas credit the marriage of sound to sight as being 50 percent of the success of an effect. Sometimes what audience members think they are hearing is the manipulation of some very unexpected sounds.

The great writers of twentieth century modernist literature took the novel to new heights with stream-of-consciousness narration, but the average reader has to approach these books with the utmost concentration. These are words creating complex visual thoughts, like "Molly Boom's Soliloquy" in Joyce's *Ulysses*. Music was more successful in mixing themes and time, allowing the audience to imagine individual images. The philosophy of Soviet montage grew out of the experience of music exciting the imagination process.

Like the mind, movies could manipulate time by moving forward or backwards, overlapping images, or altering the order of events. Each movement of time could be clearly visible or barely noticeable because of the elimination of a few frames. Playing with time is the primary job of an editor.

## Linear—Real Time

People live in real time, minute by minute, one day at a time. To depict a full day would be excruciatingly dull. But occasionally there are two-hour stretches that can be highly dramatic. Theater has always used the concept of long, continuous action spaced between intermissions. Commonly, the action in a play takes place during a single day or part of a day. The acts are in real time, but intermissions can bridge the passage of a few hours, like in *The Philadelphia Story, Long Day's Journey into Night* or *Who's Afraid of Virginia Woolf?* This allows for a drama to develop at a realistic pace, and, on the practical side, limit the number of sets.

*On the Town, Rebel Without a Cause, The High and the Mighty,* and *American Graffiti* are movies that take place in one day or less. The editor intercuts the events as they happen. The cinematography tells the audience of time passages as each sequence progresses from day to night or night to day. Blackout or dissolves are avoided because in cinema language these techniques imply that long stretches of time have passed.

*The Set-Up, High Noon, 12 Angry Men* (based on a television drama), *The Usual Suspects,* and *24*

take place in real linear time. This means that the story events happen during a two-hour period. *The Set-Up* is a tense film noir by director Robert Wise about a washed-up boxer who makes a comeback, not knowing gangsters have bet against him. *High Noon* by Fred Zinnemann is the groundbreaking Western about a lone sheriff waiting for the noon train with outlaws sworn to kill him. Zinnemann cuts to clocks shot in close-ups at extreme angles.

*12 Angry Men* is about a lone juror in white that holds out for justice. Director Sidney Lumet uses the transition from day to night and changes in the weather to keep the audience informed about the passage of time. Bryan Singer in *The Usual Suspects* cheats real time by having Verbal Kint tell about an ill-fated operation in flashbacks, as he spends two hours being interrogated by a U.S. Custom officer. And the hit television suspense series *24* covers one hour in real time each week.

In actuality, none of these movies is in real time. *12 Angry Men* comes closest since it is one location except for a couple of minutes at the beginning and end. Lumet uses several traditional techniques to alter time:

- The actors are rehearsed to make them familiar and comfortable with the lines. By doing this, the actors work at a lively pace but their performances do not seem rushed. Internal pacing in a movie is as much the editing process as cutting scenes together. Pacing establishes the rhythm of a film, something that cannot be achieved by editing alone. A movie in which actors are delivering lines leisurely and without different inflections can never be changed in the editing room.
- Long scenes are blocked in the camera, meaning the actors moved around within the focus range, hitting marks, and trading positions for close-ups, two-shots, or long shots. By blocking in the camera, there were fewer edits, giving the sensation that long periods of time have passed.
- In the early scenes, when the jurors appear to be in deadlock, there are fewer edits, with cut

points extended a few frames beyond the audience's anticipation, giving the feeling that time is moving slower. The typical audience member has seen so many films that there is a built-in sense of cutting continuity. If an edit point is suddenly extended a few extra frames over a sequence, it can create a feeling that time has slowed down.

- A reason to establish rapid line delivery is to create time for reactions and moments that need a few extra seconds for dramatic effect. Such a moment is usually covered with a series of "frozen seconds." At a key point in the action, something occurs that calls for actors to react in astonishment or disbelief at what has just happens. This is covered by the director with individual close-ups or tight two-shots. When edited, what might in real time be a two-second pause before action resumes becomes two or three times longer. Though in actuality this has been a collective pause by the group, audiences accept these frozen second, because they are seen so frequently in movies and television.

The other films in this real-time category use many of these techniques, but because the action transpires over multiple locations the editing of time becomes easier. The audience does not expect to see an actor's full, unexciting journey to various locations. For each person Gary Cooper visits as sheriff in *High Noon,* seconds and probably minutes are not shot of him walking to these locations. Once a location is established, less screen time is necessary for travel time.

## Linear—Traditional Storytelling

Linear time over many days, months, or years is the traditional time in film, as it is in literature. Storytelling begins with the introduction of a central character and the current events of the world that character is living in. Then events sweep up the character and take control of his of her life. To follow the character trying to regain control over these adverse circumstances creates suspense and hopeful expectations. Stories build to a carefully calculated climax or showdown, and to flip-flop scenes around in a linear structure would destroy the emotional values of the story.

In *Casablanca,* if the movie opened with Rick saying good-bye to Ilsa at the airport, then flashed back to the beginning, this would drain the mystery and intrigue out of every scene. The editor's mission in a linear film is to find the takes that have the actors' best moments in terms of the dramatic content of the story and to create highs and lows—or, as Hitchcock would say, an emotional rollercoaster—to hold the audience's short attention for a two-hour movie. An editor cannot build tension and excitement in sequences if the director does not provide coverage that provides strong images that tell the story visually.

## Simultaneous or Overlapping

Intercutting stories in a movie was a discovery waiting to happen. D. W. Griffith perfected this technique in *The Birth of a Nation* in 1915, and it has been a part of almost every motion picture since. Showing multiple tales in action is the defining characteristic of film. Overlapping or simultaneous events create different clocks for different characters. If separate events overlap, this is a series of linear stories that are headed in a common direction. Time is shared back and forth, with each story advancing from the last point of action. *Schindler's List* unfolds in this matter, intercutting between different events that are closely interconnected.

Simultaneous action means that two or more stories are happening at the same time. This is common in movies about a big heist or an impossible mission. Most of *Lord of the Rings* involves simultaneous action. To show this as it really happens would involve multiple images on the screen, each showing what was occurring in real time. This has been done in movies like *The Thomas Crown Affair* (1968) and is used on *24.* Traditionally, time is cheated and the stories are told separately. For an action sequence, stories are often intercut quickly, giving the illusion of events happening at the same time.

## Flashback

Flashbacks appeared early in world cinema. It is a method of revealing information about one or more characters that then becomes vital information in the story. A flashback is from the viewpoint of a single character, though different characters can have flashbacks during a film or television series like *Lost.* To create a flashback, the editor needs a shot of the actor playing the character to cut away from. Many of the older movies will have an actor blow smoke toward the lens of the camera or create a haze effect to let the audience know what follows is something from the past. Music and sometimes a sound effect reinforce the transition. At the end of the flashback, the edit needs to return to a shot of the actor to indicate the conclusion of the sequence.

Flashbacks are the truth about an incident, because during a flashback the audience is in the mind of the character. In *Stage Fright,* Alfred Hitchcock had a false flashback to deceive moviegoers about who the killer was and was greeted with piles of letters complaining about the dirty trick. A flashback can be a few frames, like in Sidney Lumet's *The Pawnbroker* about a man struggling with memories of the Holocaust, or an entire movie, such as Billy Wilder's *Double Indemnity* in which Walter Neff dictates a sordid tale of passion and murder. Flashbacks are almost a requirement in film noir, with such classics as *Out of the Past* and *Detour.*

Dreams are not flashbacks. A dream is technically set up the same way, with establishing shots of the actor to transition in and out from. A flashback is a character recalling an incident. A dream is typically in the mind of a sleeping or unconscious character, like Dorothy in *The Wizard of Oz.* Thus, dreams are usually false information or projections of fear. They take place as the character sleeps, so the moment is immediate, not in the past. Daydreams or fantasies follow the same rules, because they are often false or wishful information and occur as the character thinks, such as Ratso Rizzo in *Midnight Cowboy.*

## Flash Forward

A true flash forward is rarely used in films. There is a brief moment in *Easy Rider* in which an image of a burning motorcycle is seen before the accident occurs. To jump forward in time is usually an extension of a linear story, and to imagine the future is part of a daydream. The flash forward is associated with the French New Wave and is often intended to confuse or disorient, like in *Last Year at Marienbad.*

## Altered Reality

Altered reality is when events are presented out of order. This technique, which usually begins with the writer, is becoming increasingly common in films. The best-known examples are *Pulp Fiction* and *Memento,* in which events are told out of sequence or backward. Any film that breaks the linear structure could fit in this realm.

*Citizen Kane* has five people recalling their memories of Charles Foster Kane, each with a personal twist and often conflicting details. *Rashomon* is about a rape and murder told from four completely different points of view, one of them from a dead man. In *Annie Hall,* Woody Allen talks directly to the camera and skips around in time as he tells his bittersweet love story.

A rough cut of a film is full of giant holes. This edited version is the foundation for the final elements that include audio-dialogue replacement (ADR) or dubbing, sound effects editing, music, and special effects. Each of these elements changes the dynamics of the film enormously. George Lucas recalls a special screening of the rough cut of *Star Wars* for his friends. There was no John William's score, World War II dog-fight footage filled in for the special effects, and none of the sound effects had been added yet. With the exception of Steven Spielberg, everyone else predicted that the film would be a box office disaster.

With the quantum leaps in motion picture technology, the duties of an editor have increased. With digital editing programs, the editing process often begins on the first day of shooting, and the director is involved throughout the production.

Three steps are involved in creating a highly suspenseful moment from Peter Jackson's fantasy masterpiece *The Lord of the Rings: The Fellowship of the Ring* (2001).

During the Studio System, the film would be given to the editor after shooting and the director would not be asked to participate. But the biggest changes for an editor are in the areas of special effects and music.

With computer-generated imagery (CGI), the impossible has become commonplace. The old three-second rule involving artificial-looking special effects is gone. Now a cut to a dinosaur can be held as long as production money will allow. Despite the fact that the editor will not see the completed effect until months later, there is the ability to treat a Tyrannosaurus like another actor. The editor must judge by the reactions of actors against a green screen how long to hold the reverse angle-shot, which is being created hundreds of miles away.

The other significant changes are the length and incredible complexity of action montages. The final encounter in *The Pirates of the Caribbean: At World's End* lasted over thirty minutes with occasional lines of dialogue. This means that hundreds of images must be assembled without music or sound effects. The rough cut will be used by the composer and sound effects wizards to create the final phase of production. Sound and music are essentially mathematics. A line of music or the blast of a cannon shot must fit the edited scene perfectly, or the work will have to be done over again.

Turn the volume down completely and watch ten minutes from a favorite film. This is approximately what the editor has assembled without benefit of sound and music. Spielberg, Lucas, or any director will agree that after all the months or years of putting a film together 50 percent of the entertainment value comes from the sound and music. Watch *Jaws* or *Star Wars* without John Williams' incredible scores, and this will become immediately apparent.

Charles Chaplin as "The Little Tramp" walks into the sunset with Paulette Goddard in **Modern Times** (1936); with all the movie technology, sometimes a simple picture can last forever.

The editor must be able to cut together scenes with dialogue to hit the right dramatic tempo, and then take thousands of feet of film with no dialogue and find the right tempo for an extended montage without the final music or sound. To understand the almost insurmountable feats of an editor will give an appreciation of the editor as a visual storyteller.

## The Perfect Picture

A good movie can entertain, excite the emotions, and plant the seeds of intellectual thought.

A film can add to the collective memory of anyone that sees it and, at the right time and place, be a lasting influence on a person's life. A film is one picture at a time, twenty-four per second, 172,800 over two hours. But the influence of a single picture can be eternal; The Little Tramp strolling into the sunset with his sweetheart; Dorothy, the Tin Woodsman, the Scarecrow, and the Cowardly Lion dancing down the Yellow Brick Road; or Don Corleone making an offer no one can refuse. The essence of great filmmaking starts by realizing the power of a single shot.

# 125 Films That Changed the World

## An Evolution of Visual Language and Directing Styles Every Filmmaker Should Know

1. *Horse Running* [Muybridge]
2. *The Arrival of a Train* [Lumiere]
3. *The Kiss* [Edison]
4. *Trip to the Moon*
5. *Rescued by Rover*
6. *The Great Train Robbery*
7. *Birth of a Nation*
8. *The Cabinet of Dr. Caligari*
9. *Metropolis*
10. *Nosferatu*
11. *Potemkin*
12. *Tillie's Punctured Romance*
13. *Way Down East*
14. *The Four Horsemen of the Apocalypse* [Valentino]
15. *The Gold Rush*
16. *Sherlock Jr.*
17. *Safety Last*
18. *Poor Little Rich Girl*
19. *Napoleon*
20. *Un Chien Andalou*
21. *Pandora's Box*
22. *Greed*
23. *Flesh and the Devil* [Garbo]
24. *The Thief of Bagdad* [Fairbanks]
25. *M*
26. *The Blue Angel*
27. *Sunrise*
28. *The Jazz Singer*
29. *All Quiet on the Western Front*
30. *Steamboat Willie*
31. *Dracula*
32. *Frankenstein*
33. *City Lights*
34. *42nd Street*
35. *Red-Headed Woman*
36. *Gold Diggers of 1933*
37. *Top Hat* [Fred Astaire and Ginger Rogers]
38. *King Kong*
39. *Public Enemy*
40. *It Happened One Night*
41. *The 39 Steps*
42. *Night at the Opera* [or *Duck Soup*]
43. *Snow White and the Seven Dwarfs*
44. *Triumph of the Will*
45. *Gone with the Wind*
46. *The Wizard of Oz*
47. *Stagecoach*
48. *The Grapes of Wrath*
49. *Citizen Kane*
50. *Maltese Falcon*
51. *Casablanca*
52. *Notorious*
53. *The Best Years of Our Lives*
54. *Sunset Boulevard*
55. *Marty*
56. *The Day the Earth Stood Still*
57. *On the Waterfront*
58. *Rebel Without a Cause*

59. *Shane*

60. *High Noon*

61. *The Searchers*

62. *The Ten Commandments*

63. *Rashomon*

64. *The Bicycle Thief*

65. *Psycho*

66. *Breathless*

67. *Seven Samurai*

68. *The Seventh Seal*

69. *La Strada*

70. *La Dolce Vita*

71. *The Bridge on the River Kwai*

72. *North by Northwest*

73. *The Defiant Ones*

74. *Anatomy of a Murder*

75. *From Here to Eternity*

76. *Ben-Hur*

77. *West Side Story*

78. *Tom Jones*

79. *A Hard Day's Night*

80. *Goldfinger*

81. *A Fistful of Dollars*

82. *Lawrence of Arabia*

83. *Dr. Strangelove*

84. *Zapruder Tape* [Kennedy Assassination]

85. *2001: A Space Odyssey*

86. *In the Heat of the Night*

87. *Bonnie and Clyde*

88. *The Graduate*

89. *Easy Rider*

90. *Butch Cassidy and the Sundance Kid*

91. *The Wild Bunch*

92. *The French Connection*

93. *Clockwork Orange*

94. *The Godfather*

95. *Chinatown*

96. *Dirty Harry*

97. *M*A*S*H*

98. *Taxi Driver*

99. *Annie Hall*

100. *Enter the Dragon* [Hong Kong cinema]

101. *Animal House*

102. *Rocky*

103. *The Exorcist*

104. *Alien*

105. *Jaws*

106. *Star Wars*

107. *Raiders of the Lost Ark*

108. *E.T. the Extra-Terrestrial*

109. *China Syndrome*

110. *Road Warrior*

111. *Jane Fonda's Workout*

112. *Top Gun*

113. *Jurassic Park*

114. *Silence of the Lambs*

115. *GoodFellas*

116. *Das Boot*

117. *Pulp Fiction*

118. *The Unforgiven*

119. *Saving Private Ryan*

120. *Toy Story*

121. *The Blair Witch Project* [web site]

122. *There's Something About Mary*

123. *The Crying Game*

124. *Titanic*

125. *Lord of the Rings* [the trilogy]

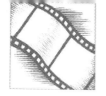

# Film Development Project

**Format:** The projects should be presented in a three-hole report cover (ideally, clear front)—*please, not in a 3-ring binder*—with dividers between each section.

**Title Page:** With the name of your project, for example, **Production Book for (name of screenplay),** one-third of the way down, followed by your name and an e-mail address.

**Screenplay:** The first ten-page draft of your screenplay (this applies to adapted and original work) written in the correct format. These ten pages can be an entire story or the very beginning of a feature-length movie.

**Revision Notes:** These notes are about how to rework your first draft so it captures the audience attention more quickly, establishes "the mood" of the story, introduces the major characters, and gets the plot rolling. These notes can also suggest a change of time period or location for the story— anything to make it feel like an involving movie that you would want to sit through!

**Revised Screenplay:** This is the revised screenplay or "shooting script" that will be the foundation for all the production information. This may be very close to the first draft or completely revised—it is your call.

**Treatment:** A one-page—as short and tight as you can get it—"pitch" description of your story.

**Breakdowns:** There must be breakdown sheets listed separately for

1. **Actors:** List by character name or visual identification, for example, First Policeman, the actors in *each* scene even if they are walk-ons and without lines.

2. **Scene Locations:** List in script order the place, interior/exterior, and general time, for example, Day, Night, Dawn, and seasonal look, Winter, Spring.

3. **Major Properties:** List for each scene objects like cars, boats, anything too big to carry.

4. **Hand Properties:** List for each scene important props the actors need for their characters.

5. **Set Dressing:** List for each scene all the dozens (or hundreds) of things that make a house seem like a home and an office a personal reflection of the character, such as, photos, souvenirs, books.

**Production Design:** Sketch or find paintings/photographs to demonstrate the look for your locations, most particularly the buildings and rooms that comprise the dramatic trappings of the story. Beside the visuals should be notes on lighting, climate (clouds, bright and sunny), and alteration to the structures (giant windows, looming trees).

**Costume Design:** Sketch or find paintings/photographs to demonstrate the costumes for the actors, especially the perfect attire to put a "visual label" on your leading players, plus, at the same time, something that will give character clues (dark business suit pulled right off the rack, short pink dress a little too snug). Include notes on personal touches.

**Locations:** Realizing the real locations might not be available or too costly; suggest places you can shoot that "cheat" the look of your story. You do not want to take crews and a large cast globe hopping, so look for locations that can double for vastly different looks.

**Casting:** Put together your dream cast, but include possible backups just in case Julia Roberts is not available. Try to find head shots to give an impression of how everyone will look together, plus notes on why a certain actor is perfect for a part.

**Shooting Schedule, Part 1:** Using the breakdowns for actors and locations, put the scenes together

1. Shot in a single interior location, such as, bedroom, office.

2. Shot in a specific exterior location, such as, street in front of house, park.

3. Shot in traveling locations, such as, freeways, river.

4. Organize in general locations, such as, New York, Paris, *or* the location being used to cheat a look.

**Shooting Schedule, Part 2:** Now look at your schedule breakdown and see if there are gaps when you are not using your leading actors. Because you are now paying for expensive people *not* to work, study the schedule breakdown and move around the location blocks to create the tightest time frame for the principal actors.

**Storyboards:** As a director, picture where the camera is for each line of dialogue or montage sequence. Using the storyboard miniatures, write in the camera direction (i.e., close-up, tracking shot) and the first words of the dialogue as a reference point. This process is directing *and* editing, so feel free to cut to someone listening or overhearing the conversation. This could mean one page of your screenplay has only four storyboard pictures, or you could end up with twenty or more pictures. Once you list all your shots, draw stick figures (or be very nice to a friend with artistic gifts) for each shot to represent the angle and location of the camera. (Only George Lucas has his drawings published, so go for a blueprint, not a museum piece.)

**Music and Sound Effects:** Put together a breakdown on music (suggestion of "established" songs and tunes to use until John Williams arrives) and the *nature* of the sound effects, for example, enemy spaceship has the roar of an angry mechanical tiger.

**Marketing:** Put together a press release for your film, highlighting the actors and the must-see story. Then draw—or verbally describe—a poster with a "hot" logo and a one-line teaser. Also, do a little research and suggest which studio would do the best job distributing your film—which has taken three years to make!

# Glossary

> **Motion pictures are an illusion.**
>
> —George Lucas

**$100,000,000 Club**   A term used for any motion picture that reaches $100 million in domestic box office sales. *Jaws* was the first movie to break this mark, though in today's dollars, *Gone with the Wind* would have had this distinction.

**above-the-line costs**   The expenses negotiated separately by high-profile movie stars and certain directors and producers, which are considerably higher than the normal rates given to most actors in a production. Under special circumstances, story rights, screenwriters, and cinematographers can also be part of these arrangements.

**art director**   See **production designer**.

**ASC**   Stands for American Society of Cinematographers. These letters often follow the name of the guild member in the screen credits. In England, a member would be identified with the letters **BSC** for British Society of Cinematographers.

**associate producer**   The individual that performs a limited number of functions as delegated by the producer; often in charge of the daily operations of a production.

**auteur theory**   A term that is associated with the rise of the French New Wave, which declares that the director is the "author" of a production, meaning that certain directors leave a recognizable mark on the films they make. *Notorious* by Alfred Hitchcock is a notable example of the auteur theory.

**below-the-line costs**   The general expenses for a production which include set construction, camera supplies, equipment rental, travel, meals, film processing, and crew members and most performers that work under salaries established by different guilds or unions. Certain individuals can negotiate for salaries greater than the fixed minimum but not in terms of the millions of dollars received by those in the **above-the-live costs.**

**best boy**   A term that goes back to the early days of film production given to first assistant to the key electrician or gaffer. The term is all inclusive; there are no "best girls."

**blockbuster**   A movie that is a runaway hit. The term originates from the nickname given to large bombs used by the Royal Air Force and the United States Air Force that could demolish extensive areas, like a city block.

**blocking a scene**   This is the process of arranging all the key elements in a given shot, from the camera movement to the choreography (or blocking) of the performers.

**bomb**   The complete opposite of a blockbuster; this is a movie that fails to generate expected box office revenue.

**box office**   The revenue generated by a movie. The term originates from the small, often glass-enclosed structure located in front of older theaters where patrons purchased tickets for a show.

**breakeven**   The point at which the box office revenue on a movie equals the production costs. The marketing budget and studio overhead expenses are generally not figured into the breakeven amount; thus, the actual expense of a movie could be much greater. This gets into an area that is sarcastically referred to as "creative accounting."

**casting director**   The individual responsible for locating the best performers to appear in a movie or television production. This individual works closely with the director and producer during the audition process to find the right personalities to fit each role. Other duties include checking for schedule conflicts and the guild status of each performer.

**cinema verité**   A term associated with the film-making style of the French New Wave, for which the "truth" of a moment was the primary objective. This artistic process attempts to capture the rough, unadorned look of documentaries; often, the actors improvise the dialogue and the camera is handheld to create this in-the-moment effect.

**cinematographer**   Also known as the director of photography or DP, evolving from the early cinema term *cinema photographer*. The individual oversees the use of the camera, lighting equipment, and electrical and grip work on a production. The cinematographer coordinates with the director the use of filters and film stock and is involved in all steps of film development. Cinematographers, like the great artists, have defined the look and mood of the twentieth century through the process of "painting with light."

**composer**   The individual responsible for creating the musical underscore of a movie. A composer will work closely with one or more arrangers on the full orchestration.

**co-stars**   The performers that share top billing with the movie star; their names often appear immediately under the title.

**costume designer**   The individual responsible for the design and construction (or rental) of the costumes for the principal players and the supporting cast. The costume designer works closely with the production designer on the use of color, texture, embodiment, and hand props for each costume or group of costumes.

**development**   The process of taking a story or concept from the germ of an idea to a fully realized project ready to be green-lighted for production. A development package often includes a completed screenplay (for the moment), a director, producer(s), one or more stars, and potentially a production designer. The term "production hell" is given to a project that is stuck in the development process because of endless changes to the screenplay or other key elements, often imposed by studio heads.

**DGA**   The Directors Guild of America, the union that represents directors, assistant directors, and production managers.

**digital revolution**   The catchphrase given to the widespread use of inexpensive cameras, computers, and software for editing and CGI effects. It also relates to the rapid changes in technology and the impact they have on society.

**director's cut**   The edited version of a movie prepared by the director. As the history of motion pictures shows, this is not always the same as the *release print*, which is controlled by the producers. Directors who have seen their cut version taken away from them and drastically altered include Erich von Stroheim, Orson Welles, and Sam Peckinpah.

**distribution**   The process of rental, shipping, marketing, and selling the properties of a completed film for the theatrical market.

**documentary**   A process of capturing life as it happens and editing the footage down to a short or feature-length presentation. This process is also known a nonfiction film. Robert J. Flaherty is considered the father of the modern documentary.

**domestic box office**   The revenue made by a motion picture in North America on its original release.

**executive producer**   The credit given the person (or persons) that has been influential in arranging of production funds and, sometimes, above-the-line talent for a movie. In motion pictures, the executive producer normally does not have a hands-on role in the production; however, in television, he or she can be very involved in the day-to-day activities.

**expressionism or German expressionism**
Derived from the early twentieth-century art movement that quickly found its way into early silent films. This cinematic style attempts to depict the inner psychology of a character through exaggerated mood lighting, scenic design, and unusual or subjective camera placement and movement. *The Cabinet of Doctor Caligari* is the most famous film of the expressionism movement, but directors like Fritz Lang and Alfred Hitchcock use the basic principles of expressionism in their films.

**extras**   Actors that have brief appearances in movies, usually with little or no dialogue, that are used in scenes ranging from background people in an elevator to large crowd sequences.

**film noir**   Literally translated as "black film," this genre is associated with urban crime thrillers of hard-edged realism that often take place in the dead of night. Film noir was highly popular during the mid-1940s and 1950s and is identified by low-key, high-contrast lighting. Classic noir films include *Double Indemnity, Out of the Past,* and *The Asphalt Jungle;* post-noir films including *Chinatown, The Usual Suspects,* and *L.A. Confidential.*

**gaffer**   The chief electrician on a movie or television set, also known as key electrician; a "best boy" is the assistant to this position.

**genre**   Early motion picture studios quickly began to put movies into groups, identified by subject matter or a common cinematic look, like Westerns, crime, adventure, musicals, film noir, and other shorthand definitions.  Putting movies into categories is useful in the film industry because it is an easy way to market new releases, allowing audiences to know what to expect when the lights go down; plus, genres gives the studios a way to track the popularity of certain kinds of movies around the world.

**grip**   A stagehand that is assigned to several different tasks on a set, often demanding physical strength.

**gross**   The total revenue generated by a movie before production and distribution expenses are deducted.

**Home Box Office or HBO**   It is also a general term used for movies and special events that generate money from pay-per-view television.

**international box office**   The realm outside of the domestic box office, that is, the rest of the world.

**line producer**   The man or woman that is responsible for the day-to-day demands of the production during the weeks of shooting; among many duties, this invaluable individual is the direct link between the director and the producers.

**location scout**   A person who travels to different states or countries to seek out ideal locations that are right for the visual demands of a motion picture.

**marketing**   The process of creating favorable "hype" or publicity for the release of a new motion picture. An effective marketing campaign can begin a year in advance of a premiere with sneak previews in theaters and well-placed articles in magazines and newspapers. Today, marketing includes the use of Web sites, advertising tie-ins, television spots, print ads, press junkets, exclusive interviews, and the coordination of hundreds of local advertising agencies around the world.

**merchandising**   Closely tied in with marketing campaigns, merchandising is the licensing of a movie's visual and story elements to corporations to create special products, which can include special permissions for the likeness of stars and character actors. The first successful merchandising sales are associated with the Western character Hopalong Cassidy, but *Star Wars* set the standard for modern widespread merchandising that includes computer games, toys, food items, clothing, jewelry, CDs, books, and numerous other items.

*Mise en scène*   A French term borrowed from the theater for "placing into a scene"; in film, this refers to the artistic arrangement and physical staging of actors, set pieces, and props within the frame.

**narrative film**   A motion picture that tells a story in a traditional three-act structure, usually in a linear format; this is the style of storytelling that is associated with the vast majority of Hollywood features, from *The Birth of a Nation* to Steven Spielberg's *War of the Worlds.*

**neorealism or Italian neorealism**   A movement that broke from the escapist Hollywood motion pictures to show slices of unvarnished human drama, usually involving the personal tragedies of common people. The directors of this movement shot on real locations, often using available light, with nonprofessional actors, to create an immediate sense of realism associated with documentary filmmaking. This movement lasted roughly from 1945 to 1960 or from the productions of *Open City* to *Two Women.*

**New Wave or French New Wave**   A movement that paralleled the final years of neorealism. The New Wave is associated with a group of French film critics turned directors who set out to deliberately break the Hollywood traditions of the "invisible camera" and linear storytelling. The movies had a freedom of camera movement that had not been seen in cinema since the final years of silent films, and the stories unfolded naturally, with dialogue often improvised by the actors, avoiding the melodramatic structure of studio pictures. The French New Wave exploded on the scene with *The 400 Blows* and *Breathless,* ushering in an era of what became known as "personal filmmaking."

**persistence of vision**   This is the human phenomenon that gives the illusion of continuous motion when people are watching movies. When a single frame is brightly projected on a movie screen, a split second image is retained by the eye, thus creating a natural progression from one image to the next, twenty-four times a second.

**postproduction**   The steps after principal photography to complete a motion picture for release, including editing, music scoring, sound effects editing, sound mixing, and special effects.

**preproduction**   The process of preparing a motion picture for production, which involves a working screenplay, scenic and costume designs, storyboards, location scouting, and casting.

**producer**   The person or group in charge of a film production from development to final release. The prime duty of a producer is to obtain funding and hire the small army of individuals to create the motion picture. A good producer is familiar with all the elements of filmmaking and is involved in each step of a production.

**production**   The process of shooting a motion picture, from location work to sound stages to green- or blue-screen special effects photography.

**production designer**   Also referred to as **art director** during the Studio Era; the person, along with the director and producer(s), who creates the physical look of a motion picture through extensive drawings, sketches, and models. This individual oversees the coordination of color design, costumes, and other visual elements. William Cameron Menzies is often credited as being the first production designer.

**property**   A term given to a book, short story, article, comic book, or original screenplay that is optioned or bought with the intention of making a motion picture.

**scene**   A piece of action shot in one location. A scene can consist of one camera shot, but normally is a series of shots that advances the dramatic tension of a motion picture.

**sequence**   Usually comprised of several scenes, a sequence is like a short story within a motion picture, unifying similar elements of action. Examples of sequences are the chase in *The French Connection,* the attack on the Death Star in *Star Wars,* and Gandalf's arrival at the beginning of *Lord of the Rings: The Fellowship of the Ring.*

**Set dressing**   Objects that are placed on a set to give it the flavor of location and/or personality. This can range from chairs, curtains, and pictures on a wall in a living room to garbage cans and trash in an alley. The trick of good set dressing is to have the audience believe that a character actually lives or works in a certain house or office.

**shooting permits**   Contractual permissions granting the right to shoot in certain locations. This can range from closing off a street for an action scene to filming inside a public building to using a famous landmark in a sequence. With these permits, release forms are often required from people that serve as background extras in a shot.

**shooting script**   This is the final screenplay used for production, often with detailed shot descriptions and numbers corresponding to panels on a storyboard. A shooting script will invariably go through many writing changes during the course of a production.

**sneak preview**   The showing of a new motion picture to invited audiences to get reactions before the scheduled opening date. Producers will "test" a film at previews to see if it needs additional cutting or if the ending works as anticipated.

**social realism**   A spin-off of the Neorealism movement closely associated with American films shot on locations using a documentary approach. Many of these films became associated with strong social themes like anti-Semitism, racial prejudice, and the need for reform. Though elements of this movement continue to appear in films like *The Gangs of New York* and *Mystic River,* the height of

social realism was from 1947 to 1959 or from *Gentleman's Agreement* to *The Defiant Ones.*

**sound design**   The comprehensive and integrated steps taken to create a complete environment of sound for a motion picture, including dialogue, music, and sound effects.

**special effects (SPFX or SFX)**   An all-inclusive term given to mechanical, optical, or digital effects that have to be created during postproduction to seamlessly blend in with footage shot during the production phase.

**stars**   The popular term given to actors that have achieved an enduring affection or admiration from audiences. Starting in the 1980s, being a star was not enough for certain celebrities and the term "superstar" was given to performers like Arnold Schwarzenegger, Tom Cruise, Julia Roberts, and Tom Hanks.

**stop-motion animation or stop-action animation**   The frame-by-frame process of adjusting an object in almost imperceptible degrees and photographing it to create the illusion of motion once the scene or sequence is completed. The most famous early use of this time-consuming technique is the 1933 version of *King Kong.* Though modern movies use computer-generated imagery (CGI) instead of small-scale models, the actual process remains the same.

**storyboard**   The process of envisioning a motion picture by drawing the camera setup or "what the camera sees" for each individual shot. In a modern motion picture, this could amount to over two thousand separate sketches. Alfred Hitchcock is the first director associated with the storyboard process.

**supporting players**   Actors that have secondary leads in a motion picture, usually with dialogue and multiple scenes, a status that separates them from extras. These performers have also been referred to as "character actors" and "sidekicks" in Westerns.

**visual language or visual grammar**  The ability to express complex dramatic actions visually without the reinforcement of words or dialogue. Visual language can be as simple as a still photograph or as complex as a complicated sequence edited together with long shots, medium shots, and close-ups. Each frame conveys information resulting from the interaction or deliberate contrasting of costumes, sets, color design, cinematography, and the blocking of actors. Once all these elements are put into motion, they pass on hundreds of bits of information each second. Though the basic building blocks of visual language are comprised of a limited number of camera setups, each director puts a personal imprint on this universal art form through a multitude of creative selections he or she makes.

# Web Site Address

http://filmproductionthecreativeprocess.com

## On the Web Site

Agencies

Contracts for talent

Equipment rentals

Guild listings

Insurance

Interviews

Release forms

Resource materials

Sample business proposal

Shot-by-shot breakdowns

Storyboard art

Extended glossary

# Author's Bio

**Ron Newcomer** has been involved with more than 1,700 stage, television, or film productions in his professional career. As producer, he created the Scottsdale Culinary Festival, Great Women of Jazz, the International Magic Festival, Paperback Theatre, the Classic Cinema, the annual Scottsdale Arts Festival, Shakespeare & Co., Dynamics of Filmmaking, and the Scottsdale Film Festival.

As associate or co-producer, he has worked with the San Diego Old Globe Theater, John Houseman's The Acting Company, The Royal Shakespeare Company, The Arizona Theater Company, the Ashland Shakespeare Festival, The Nederlander Organization, The American Film Institute, The Academy of Motion Picture Arts and Sciences, The Sundance Institute, Boss Films, and Walt Disney Productions.

As a reporter, he covered the Vietnam Peace Movement; the Robert Kennedy presidential campaign; and conflicts in Northern Ireland, Belgrade, and Athens. His experiences in Belfast with the Irish Republic Army (IRA) were written as a special series titled *In the Land of Lucifer*. He also has served as a special feature writer for *The Hollywood Reporter*.

His books include *The Films of Glenn Close* (Carol Publishing) and *Moments in Film: An Essential Understanding* and *Film Production: The Creative Process* (both for Kendall/Hunt Publishing); and he is working on *Dear Mr. Spielberg, Drop Dead* about film education, *Teaching Film: The Complete Curriculum* with Gus Edwards, and a mystery novel *The Alfred Affair*.

As a screenwriter and development director, he has been associated with Robert Wise Productions, Bungalow 78 Productions, Max Youngstein Productions, Dark Horse Productions, Bungalow 78 Productions, and New World Pictures. His screenplays *Full Moon Lover* and *New West* won top honors in the Arizona Screenwriting Competition.

Twelve of his plays and musicals have been produced, including the Playwright's Award winner *Vladimir's Waterloo; The Return of Mata Hari; The Incredible Adventures of Doktor Thrill*, based on the paintings of Earl Linderman; and the adaptation of the Howard Koch and Orson Welles radio drama *The War of the Worlds* as a live virtual reality show.

In 2004, he created The Movie Magic Foundation for visual technology education and is currently working with the Alfred Hitchcock estate on an interactive educational program. At Arizona State University, he has been honored with the Distinguished Teacher of the Year Award from the Herberger College of Arts and given Special Honors by the ASU Student Affairs for his contributions to the quality of student life at Arizona State University.